Chuck and Blanche Johnson's

Savor Michigan Cookbook

Michigan's Finest Restaurants
Their Recipes & Their Histories
with Matt Sutherland

Wilderness Adventures Press, Inc.™
Belgrade, Montana

Published by Wilderness Adventures Press, Inc.™
45 Buckskin Road
Belgrade, MT 59714
1-866-400-2012
Web site: www.wildadvpress.com
E-mail: books@wildadvpress.com
First Edition

Printed in Singapore

ISBN 978-1-932098-45-7 (1-932098-45-3)

OTHER TITLES AVAILABLE IN THIS SERIES:

Savor Arizona
Savor Colorado Mountains and Western Slope
Savor Denver and the Front Range
Savor Idaho
Savor Montana II
Savor Oregon
Savor Greater Seattle
Savor Wild Game

TABLE OF CONTENTS

INTRODUCTION XI
MAP OF FEATURED RESTAURANTS XIII
MICHIGAN FACTS XIV

— Detroit —

COACH INSIGNIA 1
Lobster Corn Dog 3
Coach Crab Cake 4
Coconut Curry Ahi Tuna 5

THE WINE SPECTATOR AWARD 6

GIOVANNI'S 7
Giovanni's Risotto 9
Manzo Di Braciole 10
Olindo's Special 11
RATTLESNAKE CLUB 13
Roast Yellow and Red Beet Salad 15
Pastrami Scented Wild Alaskan Salmon 16
Cocoa and Coffee Crusted
Filet of Prime Cab Beef 18
Spice Crusted Pineapple Steak 20

TRAVERSE CITY: A FOOD & WINE MECCA 22

SELDOM BLUES 23
Blue-B-Que Bass 25
Pan Seared Veal Medallions 26
AZ Bronzed Salmon 28

— West Bloomfield —

THE LARK 29
Gulf Shrimp with Lime Tequila Glaze 31
Sweet Fennel Flan 32
Roast Goose with Cranberry Sauce 33
Frozen Grand Marnier Soufflé 35

— Farmington Hills —

TRIBUTE 37
Foie Gras and Monkfish Liver Torchon 39
Watermelon Soup 41
Scallop, Fluke and Tuna Sashimi 42
Lobster Barigoule 43

— Southfield —

BACCO RISTORANTE	45
Zuppa di Farro	47
Melanzane alla Parmigiana	48
Spaghetti al Salmone	49
Costoletta di Vitello Valdostana	50
Buttermilk Panna Cotta	51

— Birmingham —

RUGBY GRILLE	53
Citrus Roasted Black Cod	55
Sauté of Dover Sole A La Meunière	57
Braised Wagyu Beef Short Rib	59
BIG ROCK CHOPHOUSE	61
Cajun Steak Bites	63
Seared Salmon with Mushroom Ragout	64
Big Rock Chili	65
Beef Short Ribs	66

— Novi —

CHERRY BLOSSOM	67
Enoki Bacon	69
Shiitake Hakata	69
Sakura Roll	70
Sunomono Combination	71
Kamo Nabe	72

— Milford —

FIVE LAKES GRILL	73
Grilled Vegetable Terrine	75
Cherrywood Smoked Trout	76
Grilled Yellow Fin Tuna	77
Chocolate Pâté with Praline and Raspberries	78

— Okemos —

RESTAURANT VILLEGAS	79
Michigan Wild Ramp Quiche	81
Baked Michigan Navy Beans	83
Great Lakes Whitefish Meatballs	84
My Paella of Aspen Hills Rabbit and Michigan White Shrimp	86

— Port Austin —

THE FARM	87
Roasted Artichoke with Brie	89
Vegetable Strudel	90
Lake Michigan Salmon En Croute	91
Pan Seared Whitefish	92
Fiery Grilled Beef Salad	93

— Ann Arbor —

EVE	95
Moroccan Scallops	97
Michigan Corn Pudding	99
Michigan Rabbit Braised in Cèpe Cream	100
Sugared Mint Leaves	103
THE EARLE UPTOWN	105
Broiled Artichoke Stuffed	107
Seared Sea Scallops	108
Broiled Loup de Mer	109
Duck Breast	110

— St. Joseph —

BISTRO ON THE BOULEVARD	111
Quick Tomato Bisque	113
Barley Risotto	114
Roasted Loin of Lamb	115
Osso Bucco	116

— Holland —

BUTCH'S DRY DOCK	117
Shrimp Fondue with Pistou Gruyère Alfredo	119
Java Chili Rubbed Salmon	120
Grilled Beef Tenderloin	121
Flourless Chocolate Cake	122

— Saugatuck —

THE DINING ROOM AT CLEARBROOK	123
Figs, Bleu Cheese, and Walnuts in Phyllo Canapés	125
Blueberry, Peach, and Watercress Salad	126
Thai Chicken Salad on Crostini	127
Warm Tomato Torte, Wilted Spinach, & Apple Salad	128
Pan-seared Sea Scallops	130
Peppered Flank Steak over Sweet Potato Gratin	132

— Grand Rapids —

THE 1913 ROOM 133
Celeriac Cream with Maple Popcorn 135
Salad of Frisée and Belgian Endive 136
Roasted Breast of Pheasant 137
SAN CHEZ BISTRO 139
Baba Ghanoush 141
Mezze Café Hummus 142
Fire Roasted Mussels with Harissa Sauce 143
Paella 144

— Muskegon —

THE SARDINE ROOM 145
Mixed Greens with Apples, Pecans,
and Gorgonzola 147
Brandy Buttered Sea Scallops 148
Turkey Melt Sandwich with Roasted Shallot Aioli 149
Brandy Dijon Filet Mignon 150
Macadamia Nut Crusted Florida Grouper 151

— Traverse City —

AMICAL 153
Thai Crab Cakes 155
Chicken Pot Pie 156
Raspberry Crème Brûlée 157
TRATTORIA STELLA 159
AgnelloCrudo con Pomodoro(Due Preparazione) 161
Zuppa di Porcini 162
Costoletta de Maiale con Mela e Maple Sciroppa 163
Tonno alla Liguriana 164
Panna Cotta con Fragola e Vaniglia 166

— Maple City —

NORTH 167
Roasted Potato & Shiitake Mushroom Soup 169
Chicken Strudel with Mustard Sauce 170
Pheasant Wellington 171
Crème Brûlée 172

— Leland —

THE RIVERSIDE INN 173
Potato Gnocchi 175
Ostrich Fillet with Morel Mushroom Sauce 177
Rustic Yukon Gold Mashed Potatoes 178
Caramel Apple Spice Cake 179

— Bellaire —

LULU'S BISTRO	181
Aged Goat Cheese, Roasted Beet and Hydro Watercress Salad	183
Baked Jumbo Lump Crab	184
Seared Sea Scallops	185

— Ellsworth —

TAPAWINGO	187
Chestnut Soup	189
Cheese Beignets	190
Yukon Gold Potato Soup	191
Roasted Cervena Venison Loin	192
Caramel Apple with Cream Cheese Ice Cream	194
Chewy Salted Caramels	195
ROWE INN	197
Morel Mushroom and Wild Rice Bisque	199
Pork, Duck, Dried Cherry and Mixed Nut Terrine	200
Apricot Ginger Sauce	201
Morel and Leek Pierogi	202

— Bay Harbor —

LATITUDE° RESTAURANT	203
Warm Asparagus Salad	205
Morel Mushroom Burgers	206
Morels Stuffed with Ham Duxelle	207
Morels Stuffed with Pheasant Mousse	208

— Petoskey —

CHANDLER'S	209
Grilled Romaine Salad	211
Lemon Parmesan Gnocchi	212
Honey Manchego Potato Croquette	213
Classic Steak Tartare	214

— Harbor Springs —

THE NEW YORK RESTAURANT	215
World Famous, Award Winning White Bean and Lobster Chili with Ancho Chile Cream	217
Chicken Breast with Crab Stuffing, Roasted Pepper Aioli, and Corn and Potato Risotto	218
Roast Pork or Veal Loin	219

— Mackinac Island —

GRAND HOTEL	221
Roquefort and Brie Cheese Praline	223
Roasted Vegetable Salad	224
Tartare of Buffalo Tenderloin	225
Buffalo Tenderloin	226
Green Olive and Cucumber Granita	227
Mackinac Whitefish Bisque	228

— Drummond Island —

BAYSIDE DINING	229
Wild Mushroom Crostini with Leek Hay	231
Halibut Bayside	232
Spinach Salad with Maple Sherry Vinaigrette	234

— Marquette —

CAPERS RESTAURANT	235
Brie In Pastry with Dried Cherries	237
Polenta with Ratatouille	238
Prosciutto Wrapped Salmon with Caper Sauce	239
Seared Tuna with Spicy Mango Purée	240

— Hancock —

NORTH SHORE PUB 'N GRILL	241
Venison Medallions	243
Seared Ahi Tuna	244
Rubbed Ribeye	245
Wild Boar Scaloppini	246

GLOSSARY	247
CULINARY SOURCES	248
PHOTO COPYRIGHTS/CREDITS	250
ABOUT THE PUBLISHERS	251
INDEX	252

Mackinac Bridge Construction, 1958.

Detroit Harbor, Detroit, Date Unknown.

Photograph of workers inspecting cherries as they pass along the sorting belts, before going to the pitters; marked or blemished cherries are removed, August 1, 1958.

INTRODUCTION

Like certain rare friends in our lives, we are attracted to authenticity in the restaurants we frequent—places that are completely devoid of phoniness. As the premier tourist destination for much of the upper Midwest, Michigan is blessed with physical beauty, true Midwestern graciousness, and extremely high-caliber restaurants spread over the length and width of the state. In fact, the choices are so plentiful, diners in Michigan expect a bit more than usual; namely, extra measures of warmth and friendliness coupled with authentic, beautifully presented food. The book in your hands is a celebration of the best Michigan has to offer featuring thirty-five restaurants on par with some of the best in the nation. Unfortunately, space limitations necessitated that we leave out several very worthy dining establishments. We apologize to them, and encourage readers to let us know their favorites for possible inclusion in future editions of *Savor Michigan Cookbook*.

— *Matt Sutherland*

Our growing collection of *Savor Cookbooks* has featured fine restaurants in many areas of the West. With this new addition to our series, we are expanding into the rich culinary bounty of the Midwest. We have spent many pleasant times in Michigan with friends, and have personally enjoyed meals at some of the fine restaurants in this book. We were also lucky enough to have Matt Sutherland agree to take on this project. As co-founder of the Traverse Epicurean Classic, Matt's knowledge of the Michigan culinary scene is vast indeed.

It is important to note that all of the featured restaurants were by invitation. None of the restaurants were charged for appearing in this book. Matt selected them based on the excellence and uniqueness of their food, as well as their ambience. Many have interesting histories. Matt also looked for places that feature comprehensive wine lists. We, along with Matt, want to thank the owners, managers, chefs, and all the restaurant staff members who participated in getting this project to fruition.

The reader can use this book in several ways. As a travel guide, the reader can learn something about a restaurant's history, philosophy, and ambience, as well as the type of cuisine that it features. The map in the front gives the reader a perspective of the state and approximately where each restaurant is located.

Reading the recipes is a fun way to get a "taste" of each restaurant, and trying them out at home can be fun for the home chef as well as his or her guests.

— *Blanche and Chuck Johnson*

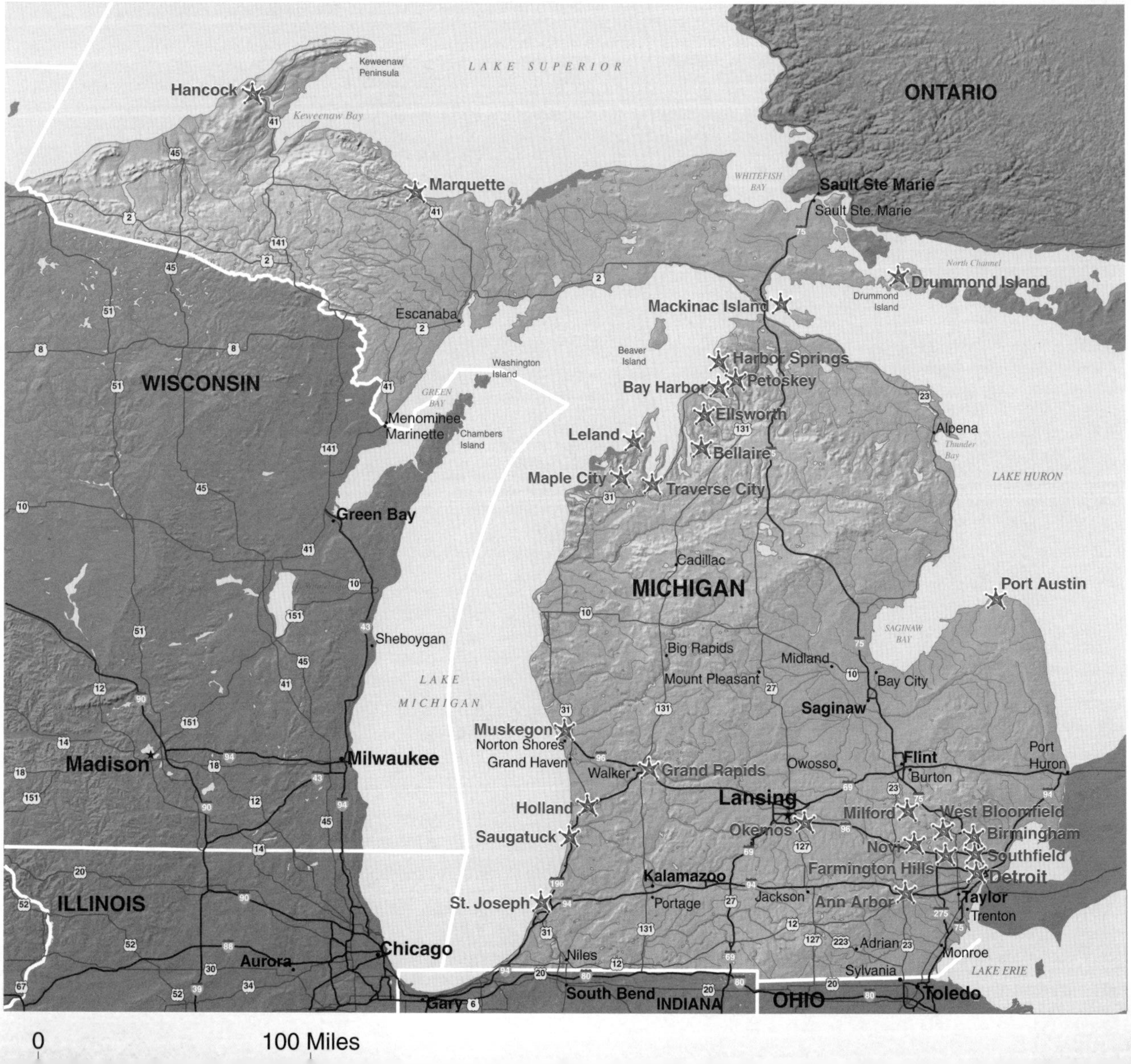
LAKE SUPERIOR
ONTARIO
Keweenaw Peninsula
Hancock
Keweenaw Bay
Marquette
WHITEFISH BAY
Sault Ste Marie
Sault Ste. Marie
North Channel
Drummond Island
Drummond Island
Mackinac Island
Escanaba
WISCONSIN
Washington Island
Beaver Island
Harbor Springs
Petoskey
Bay Harbor
Ellsworth
Bellaire
Leland
Maple City
Traverse City
GREEN BAY
Menominee
Marinette
Chambers Island
Alpena
Thunder Bay
LAKE HURON
Green Bay
Cadillac
MICHIGAN
Port Austin
SAGINAW BAY
Sheboygan
Big Rapids
Midland
Bay City
Mount Pleasant
LAKE MICHIGAN
Saginaw
Muskegon
Norton Shores
Grand Haven
Walker
Grand Rapids
Owosso
Flint
Burton
Port Huron
Madison
Milwaukee
Lansing
Holland
Saugatuck
Okemos
Milford
West Bloomfield
Birmingham
Novi
Southfield
Farmington Hills
Detroit
Kalamazoo
ILLINOIS
St. Joseph
Portage
Jackson
Ann Arbor
Taylor
Trenton
Chicago
Aurora
Niles
Adrian
Monroe
Sylvania
LAKE ERIE
South Bend
INDIANA
OHIO
Toledo
Gary
0
100 Miles

Savor Michigan Cookbook
Restaurants Featured

DETROIT
Coach Insignia
Giovanni's
Rattlesnake Club
Seldom Blues

WEST BLOOMFIELD
The Lark

FARMINGTON HILLS
Tribute

SOUTHFIELD
Bacco Ristorante

BIRMINGHAM
Rugby Grille
Big Rock Chophouse

NOVI
Cherry Blossom

MILFORD
Five Lakes Grill

OKEMOS
Restaurant Villegas

PORT AUSTIN
The Farm

ANN ARBOR
eve
The Earle Uptown

ST. JOSEPH
Bistro on the Boulevard

HOLLAND
Butch's Dry Dock

SAUGATUCK
The Dining Room

GRAND RAPIDS
The 1913 Room
San Chez Bistro

MUSKEGON
The Sardine Room

TRAVERSE CITY
Amical
Trattoria Stella

MAPLE CITY
North

LELAND
The Riverside Inn

BELLAIRE
Lulu's Bistro

ELLSWORTH
Tapawingo
Rowe Inn

PETOSKEY
Chandler's

HARBOR SPRINGS
The New York Restaurant

MACKINAC ISLAND
Grand Hotel

DRUMMOND ISLAND
Bayside Dining

MARQUETTE
Capers Restaurant

HANCOCK
North Shore Pub 'n Grill

Michigan Facts

Michigan fishmonger, 1940.

Admission to Statehood:
   January 26, 1837 (26th)
Eleventh largest state in the union
   96,810 square miles
   240 miles east to west
   490 miles north to south
Elevations – 572 feet to 1,979 feet
Counties – 83
Population (2000) – 9,938,444
11 Indian Reservations
78 State Parks
72 State Forests
19 State Recreation Areas
1 National Historic Park
1 National Scenic Trail
2 National Lakeshores
1 National Park
3 National Forests
1 National Memorial
Nicknames:
   Wolverine State / Great Lakes State

Primary Industries:
   Car Manufacturing
   Farming
   Tourism
   Timber
   Fishing
Capital – Lansing
Bird – Robin
   (Turdus migratorius)
Flower – Apple Blossom
   (Pyrus coronaria)
Tree – White Pine
   (Pinus strobus)
Mammal – White-tailed Deer
   (Odocoileus virginianus)

Photograph of men in automobiles in front of the State Capital building, Olds and Reo, c. 1905.

Coach Insignia

COACH INSIGNIA

Renaissance Center
Detroit, MI 48243
313–567–2622
www.mattprenticerg.com/urc/
coach.asp

Monday – Thursday 5:00pm – 10:00pm
Friday – Saturday 5:00pm – 11:00pm
Closed Sunday

Coach Insignia

Executive Chef David Hubbard

Of all the fixed conversations between men and women none quite compares to the marriage proposal. No other comes loaded with equal doses of intimacy, excitement, and gut-churning importance. In the best of circumstances, it may happen only once a lifetime, a fact that adds immensely to the experience. For our purposes, it's interesting to remember where these milestone moments take place: extremely elegant restaurants. And, just maybe we can go a step further and call these blessed dining spots our most romantic, impressive restaurants, absolutely fitting for the presentation of a ring. In Michigan, *proposal central* is Coach Insignia, on the 72nd floor of Detroit's Renaissance Center. From an 820-foot perch offering stunning views of Canada, the St. Mary's river, and this still proud, beautiful city, it's not hard to understand why giddy-eyed men make this "the place".

Coach Insignia is one of Michigan's premier *classic* steakhouses offering the best cuts of Stockyard Angus beef in portion sizes ranging from seven-ounce Center Cut Filet Mignons to twenty-four-ounce Porterhouses. (With marriage on the mind, it's interesting to note that in moments rife with nervous energy men tend to eat with rare gusto while women pick at their food a bit, and actually eat less.) And, like any good steakhouse, Coach also offers their "ultimate" version of Surf & Turf: Grilled Filet, Porcini & Morel Ragout, Maine Lobster Thermidor, Roasted Fingerling Potatoes & Asparagus, no doubt a bestseller amongst the soon-to-be betrothed.

Executive Chef David Hubbard is boisterous and adventuresome, pushing Coach in eclectic directions. A recent menu offered eight appetizers including several Asian-influenced seafood dishes such as Seared Day Boat Tuna Sashimi (Citrus Ponzu, Seaweed Slaw, Wasabi Caviar & Fresh Ginger), Orange Ginger Glazed Prawns (Asian Slaw & Sesame Vinaigrette), and the delightfully daffy Maine Lobster Corn Dogs (Olive Oil and Vinegar Slaw, Whole Grain Mustard Hollandaise). Additional apps include Short Rib Martini (Horseradish Whipped Potatoes, Root Vegetables & Short Rib Jus), as well as Dueling Foie Gras, a decadent presentation of foie gras cooked two ways featuring banana brûlée, apple demi, brioche, and chipotle cherry jam.

Aside from the Angus and Surf & Turf, other notable entrées are Lamb T-Bones (Goat Cheese & Eggplant Croquette, Traditional Ratatouille, Fingerling Potatoes, Red Wine Demi Glaze), Calves Liver & Onions (Cipollini Onions, Trumpet Royal Mushrooms, Bacon, Veal Demi), and lastly, Tasmanian Salmon (Sweet Potato, Leek, Bacon & Corn Hash, Tomato Beurre Blanc).

Coach Insignia's wine cellar is overseen by Master Sommelier Madeline Triffon, and boasts over 800 selections. The onsite, day-to-day sommelier duty of helping couples decide on exactly the right bottle of bubbly to seal the deal falls upon the able shoulders of Patrick Peterson and Michelle DeHayes.

 Best of Award of Excellence

LOBSTER CORN DOG

The Lobster Corn Dog was put on the menu as a playful play on words. Something very elegant as lobster in a very Midwest homey food application. Not only was it fun, but the Lobster Corn Dog has become our signature appetizer. Well, who doesn't love fried lobster?

Ingredients

2 4-5 ounce lobster tails, shell removed
   and split lengthwise
2¾ cups flour
1 cup corn meal
1 teaspoon baking powder
1 tablespoon sugar
   pinch salt

6 cups soda water
½ cup flour seasoned with salt, pepper,
   and paprika
2 6-inch bamboo skewers
4 cups blend of olive oil and vegetable
   oil for frying

Preparation

TO CREATE batter, mix flour, corn meal, baking powder, and sugar. Add soda water slowly while mixing with whisk. Mixture should look like pancake batter.

HEAT oil in deep saucepan to 350 degrees. Stick skewers all the way through each tail long ways to make a kabob. Dredge the lobster in a small amount of seasoned flour and dip them into the evenly mixed batter. Carefully deep fry lobster tails until golden brown, approximately 6 – 10 minutes. Serve with a hollandaise infused with stone-ground mustard. (Note: recipe for batter will make about 12 - 16 corn dogs.)

Serves 4

Wine Suggestion: Pierre Gimmonet Brut Champagne

COACH CRAB CAKE

Although many versions of crab cakes can be made and every crab lover has their own favorite way to make crab cakes or a favorite restaurant in which to eat them, I would love you to try our recipe and enjoy this staple in our dining room. With jumbo lump crab and a basic, not overly done sauce, this recipe might just surprise even the pickiest crab cake

critic. Enjoy!

Ingredients

1 pound jumbo lump crab
2 tablespoons mayonnaise
2 tablespoons panko breadcrumbs

1 tablespoon olive oil
   salt & pepper

1 teaspoon Old Bay Seasoning
1 teaspoon Tabasco
1 tablespoon celery, minced
1 tablespoon white onion, minced

Preparation

IN LARGE mixing bowl, fold ingredients together without breaking up jumbo lump crab. In small sauté pan on medium high heat, sear crab cakes with olive oil, caramelizing both sides of the cake. Serve with favorite spicy tartar sauce, or substitute drawn butter or cocktail sauce.

Serves 2

Coconut Curry Ahi Tuna

My motto in the kitchen is: Buy fresh ingredients, keep the food simple, and let the true flavors of the dish do the work. Often, chefs get caught up over-working food. This recipe is a classic example of using the highest quality seafood and homemade gnocchi and letting the true flavor (with a touch of flair) of coconut and curry do the work for you! This is a true favorite of mine.

Ingredients

2 cups coconut milk
2 tablespoons curry powder
¼ cup heavy cream
2 8-ounce pieces of Ahi or day-boat tuna

sesame seeds
1 tablespoon olive oil
2 cups frozen or homemade gnocchi
salt & pepper

Preparation

IN A saucepan, reduce coconut milk and curry powder by half. Add cream and season with salt and pepper. Sauce should coat the back of the spoon.

Press small amount of sesame seeds into both sides of tuna. In hot pan with the olive oil, sear tuna on high heat until golden brown. It is recommended that tuna is served at rare or med-rare.

BLANCH gnocchi in salted boiling water. Heat up coconut broth and add blanched gnocchi to the broth. Slice tuna and set atop gnocchi shingled. Garnish with fresh vegetables or fried sweet potatoes.

Serves 2

Wine Suggestion: Cuilleron Condrieu "La Petite Cote" Rhone

THE WINE SPECTATOR AWARD

Many of the restaurants included in this cookbook have been recognized by *Wine Spectator*, the world's most popular wine magazine. It reviews more than 10,000 wines each year and covers travel, fine dining and the lifestyle of wine for novices and connoisseurs alike. Through its Restaurant Awards program, the magazine recognizes restaurants around the world that offer distinguished wine lists. Restaurants are responsible for submitting their own lists.

Awards are given in three tiers. In 2006, 3,772 restaurants earned wine list awards. To qualify, wine lists must provide vintages and appellations for all selections. The overall presentation and appearance of the list are also important. Once past these initial requirements, lists are then judged for one of three awards: the Award of Excellence, the Best of Award of Excellence, and the Grand Award.

- Award of Excellence—The basic Award of Excellence recognizes restaurants with lists that offer a well-chosen selection of quality producers, along with a thematic match to the menu in both price and style.
- Best of Award of Excellence—The second-tier Best of Award of Excellence was created to give special recognition to those restaurants that exceed the requirements of the basic category. These lists must display vintage depth, including vertical offerings of several top wines, as well as excellent breadth from major wine growing regions.
- Grand Award—The highest award, the Grand Award, is given to those restaurants that show an uncompromising, passionate devotion to quality. These lists show serious depth of mature vintages, outstanding breadth in their vertical offerings, excellent harmony with the menu, and superior organization and presentation. In 2006, only 77 restaurants held Wine Spectator Grand Awards.

 Award of Excellence    Best of Award of Excellence

 Grand Award

Giovanni's

Giovanni's Ristorante

330 S. Oakwood Blvd.
Detroit, MI 48217
313-841-0122
www.giovannisristorante.com

Tuesday – Thursday 11:00am – 9:00pm
Friday 11:00am – 10:00pm
Saturday 4:00pm – 11:00pm

Giovanni's Ristorante

Executive Chef Paul Tootikian,
Fran & Randy Truant, Owners

On a lonely stretch of West Oakwood on Detroit's southwest side there's a humble one-story building bearing a sign with the name Giovanni's Ristorante. Walk a few steps through the front door into a dining room filled with black-and-white family photographs and modest antiques of the type found in many American-immigrant homes. Note the crisp linen and smart table service but glance around at the other diners; keeping in mind that Frank Sinatra, Tony Bennett, Red Skeleton all reserved these same tables not long ago and others, like Joe Torre and Larry King, continue to do so whenever in Detroit. Let that serve as a reminder to those restaurateurs writing big checks to interior decorators, management teams, etc.

Giovanni's Ristorante is run by the mother-son team of Fran and Randy Truant. Fran's mother Rosa—Giovanni was her father's name—established the restaurant in 1967 as a delivery-only pizza parlor only a few yards from the family home. In the early 1970s they converted to full service and over the years, added three dining rooms and an ornate oak bar, all while maintaining Rosa's original "family home" ambiance.

During service hours, Randy is an ever-present face in the dining room, but he's also actively involved in menu planning and other back of the house operations. Executive Chef Paul Tootikian, 82-year-old pasta maker Irma Morri, and other talented hands in the kitchen work seamlessly to produce an array of traditional dishes as well as more contemporary Italian fare from all regions of the old country. They utilize a brick oven to bake Pizza Bianco and Pizza Margherita, two favorites on the Antipasta menu along with Bistecca Calamari Fritta, Peperoni E Salsiccia, and the simple, elegant Shrimp Giovanni.

Morri's experienced hands are kept busy readying fresh pasta for Giovanni's extensive selection of angel hair, linguine, tagliatelle, or fettuccine served with a choice of four classic sauces. In addition, various preparations of lasagne, gnocchi, and ravioli compete for attention. Finally, the Piati Della Casa offerings prioritize several preparations of veal. Two of special note: Veal di Granchio (medallions of Provimi veal sautéed with asparagus and crab in a delicate brandy glaze), and Saltimbocca alla Romano (medallions of Provimi veal topped with a thin slice of prosciutto di Parma, sage and fontina cheese sautéed in a white wine sauce). The beef choices include Giovanni's signature Manzo di Braciole (thinly sliced beef tenderloin, rolled around prosciutto di Parma, garlic and parsley braised in a Chianti tomato mushroom sauce.)

Giovanni's has long been recognized for their stellar collection of Italian wines. A heartbreaking fire just two years ago destroyed over 3,000 bottles but, through Randy's diligence and expertise, the list is undeniably one of Detroit's best.

 Award of Excellence

Giovanni's Risotto

This is a very versatile dish. You can make it as a side with the braciole, or eat it by itself. We also pair this with our Shrimp Giovanni down at the restaurant for an appetizer. Chef Paul's favorite tip, "Add spinach and Boursin cheese when finishing the dish and let it simmer for a few minutes. This makes it extra special and decadent."

Ingredients

1 cup Arborio rice
2 cups chicken broth
1 cup onion, finely diced
½ cup heavy cream

½ cup grated Parmesan cheese,
    preferably Reggiano Parmigiano
⅓ stick of butter

Preparation

IN HEAVY saucepan, sauté onion and butter over medium heat, until onions are transparent. Add Arborio rice and chicken broth. Lower the heat to a simmer and cover rice. Stir occasionally so rice does not stick to bottom of pan. Continue to add more chicken broth if needed to keep rice moist. When risotto starts to thicken, add heavy cream and Parmesan cheese. Take off heat and let rest for 10 – 15 minutes.

Serves 4

Wine Suggestion: Bracco Pinot Grigio

Pasta maker Irma Morri

MANZO DI BRACIOLE

This was a favorite recipe of Grandpa Giovanni who is the namesake of the restaurant. Randy's grandmother Rosie would cook this on Sundays for the family down at the restaurant. Randy states, "What makes our braciole different from others..., we actually use filet mignon that is not typical for the dish, but it makes it really tender."

Ingredients

4 4-ounce filet mignon
  salt & pepper
  Pesto (recipe follows)
4 thin slices of prosciutto
  olive oil

  flour
2 cups sliced mushrooms of your choice: button, crimini, portobello
1 cup rich red wine
1 cup tomato sauce

Preparation

GENTLY pound out each 4-ounce filet as thin as possible without tearing the meat. Lightly salt and pepper the pounded meat. Brush the filet with Pesto and lay a thin slice of prosciutto on top of each filet. Fold each side into the center without overlapping the meat. Then from the bottom roll up tight. Cover the bottom of a heavy non-stick skillet with olive oil. Heat the oil for a few minutes. Lightly cover the braciole with flour. Brown both sides of the braciole in the olive oil pan. Add mushrooms and simmer until wilted. Gently stir in red wine and tomato sauce. Add one teaspoon of pesto and simmer for 5 to 10 minutes, depending on desired temperature of meat. While simmering, try to keep the braciole covered in the sauce. Serve with Giovanni's Risotto.

Serves 4

Wine Suggestion: Castello di Corbara Cabernet Sauvignon

For the Pesto

½ cup basil, rough chopped
½ cup parsley, rough chopped
1 cup extra virgin olive oil
¼ cup pine nuts, toasted

3 large garlic cloves
  salt & pepper
¼ cup Reggiano Parmigiano cheese

ADD all ingredients except cheese to food processor and blend to a fine purée. After blending ingredients, stir in cheese. For best results, serve ASAP. The pesto can be frozen and used as needed, but avoid keeping in refrigerator for long periods of time.

Yield: 1½ cups.

Olindo's Special

This dish is named after Fran's husband Olindo. He was a lover of seafood because his family's roots stem from Udine on the Adriatic Sea. At the restaurant we make this dish with our homemade pasta, but you can use the pasta of your choice to make it easier. We recommend linguine. For all of you who are wondering, yes, Fran does have a dish named after her, but you will have to come to the restaurant to find out what it is!

Ingredients

6 large shrimp
6 large sea scallops
3 tablespoons olive oil
2 roma tomatoes diced
6 artichoke hearts cut in half

2 cups tomato sauce
½ cup Pesto (See recipe under Manzo Di Braciole)
   salt & pepper

Preparation

IN HEAVY sauté pan cover bottom with olive oil. Sauté shrimp and scallops until lightly browned. Drain excess oil and add diced tomatoes, artichokes, tomato sauce and Pesto. Simmer for 5 minutes and salt and pepper to taste. Serve over your choice of pasta.
Buon Appetito! Remember in Italia, no cheese with seafood.

Serves 2

Wine Suggestion: Tramin Sauvignon Blanc

Men working at a cherry canning machine, 1958.

Rattlesnake Club

RATTLE/NAKE

300 River Place
Detroit, MI 48207
313-567-4400
www.rattlesnakeclub.com

Tuesday – Thursday 11:30am–10:00pm
Friday 11:30am–11:00pm
Saturday 5:30pm–11:00pm
Closed Sunday & Monday

Rattlesnake Club

Chef / owner Jimmy Schmidt

From Henry Ford to Ty Cobb, Jimmy Hoffa, Berry Gordy and the many great Motown Records musicians, Detroit's contributions to culture, and first-tier standing among America's cities, is undisputed. Similarly, we can't forget iconic culinary families like Stroh (beer), Vernor (ginger ale), Sanders (hot fudge sauce), and more recently, Schmidt, as in Jimmy Schmidt, owner of Detroit's Rattlesnake Club, and Michigan's most recognized, award-winning chef. Foremost, among those honors is the James Beard Foundation naming him Best Chef of the Midwest in 1993. In addition, he has authored or co-authored several books including the acclaimed *Cooking for All Seasons*.

Schmidt's insistence on fresh, seasonal ingredients prepared as nutritiously and creatively as possible had a profound affect on Detroit's culinary scene in 1988 when the Rattlesnake Club debuted. He was one of the first to work with local farmers, asking them to provide him with heirloom varieties of fruit and vegetables and to adapt their farms to more sustainable practices. All of this came naturally to him at a time when few other chefs seemed to care. In the main, Schmidt completely embraces the full bounty of what Michigan has to offer. It is not lost on him that his state is the nation's second most diverse agriculturally.

The Rattlesnake Club explores so many culinary traditions and ethnic flavor profiles that it is difficult to place any particular cooking style designation on it. New American or Contemporary, yes, but they don't encompass the innovation at work. On a recent menu under Starters, for instance, the dishes were separated as Cool or Warmed and included Ahi Tuna Study: Silky Tartar in Black Sesame Cone, Spice Seared Cube with Foie and Smokey Bacon, Crisp Flash Fry with Ginger & Chile Aioli. Another Cool offering: Pastrami Scented Roasted Duck Foie Gras, framed with Black Bread Crisps, Pomegranate & Cippolini Marmalade. Performance artists would appreciate the warmed app, Roasted Porta Bella & Wild Mushroom Cylinder: Mâche, Crispy Shallots, Roast Squash, Syrah Essence & Truffle Oil.

On to a few entrées leading with Atlantic Swordfish & Vanilla Infused Pineapple Kabob: Seared Cube Topped with Caramelized Pineapple, Vanilla Bean Skewer, Crispy Ginger & Froth, Asian Basil Oil. Also of note, Roasted Rack of Michigan Baby Lamb: Pistachio & Pomegranate Crust, Ragout of Chanterelles, Pearl Beets, Cippolini Ravioli & Silky Pistachio Beans, Crunchy Sage. Every dish served at the Rattlesnake Club is beautiful. Museum-quality presentation is a hallmark of Schmidt.

The Rattlesnake offers an Artisan Cheese Course Tasting of six artisan cheeses listed with several complementary wines by the glass. As expected, the wine list is honored every year by *Wine Spectator*. Predominantly American, it offers many of California's most sought after wines.

Award of Excellence

ROAST YELLOW AND RED BEET SALAD

I hated beets as a child with their sharp, angular almost bitter flavor. I later discovered the technique of deep roasting beets in a foil pouch, which captures their sweet, silky and rich personality.

Ingredients

2 medium yellow beets
2 medium red beets
4 tablespoons extra virgin olive oil,
    divided
    sea salt
1 teaspoon freshly ground black pepper,
    divided
2 tablespoons cabernet vinegar
2 tablespoons prepared horseradish

¼ cup yogurt
4 tablespoons fresh-snipped chives,
    divided
2 Belgium endives, cut into ¼-inch
    slices
2 cups red oak or red bibb lettuce,
    cleaned as necessary and torn into
    bite-size pieces

Preparation

PREHEAT oven to 400 degrees. Lay a piece of aluminum foil on your counter and place the beets in the center. Drizzle with 2 tablespoons of olive oil. Generously season with salt and half of the pepper. Fold the foil over, crimping the edges to seal the beets into a pouch. Place on a baking sheet and onto the lower rack of the oven. Cook until tender, about 45 to 60 minutes as tested by inserting a skewer into the beets without resistance. Remove from the oven and allow to cool in the foil. Clean by rubbing the skin off the beets with paper toweling. Slice paper thin with a mandoline or very sharp slicing knife.

IN A blender, combine the vinegar, horseradish, and yogurt. While blending slowly, pour in the remaining olive oil. Add in half of the chives. Season generously with salt (to balance the tart acid) and the remaining black pepper. Reserve.

SELECT four 8- to 10-ounce ramekins or metal pyramid molds. Line each with plastic wrap. Take the beets and line the inside of the mold, slightly overlapping and creatively alternating the yellow and red colors of the beets. In a medium bowl combine the endive and lettuce, then add the horseradish dressing and toss to combine. Compact the salad in your hands and press firmly into the molds. Invert the molds onto the center of the chilled serving plates. Gently pull on the edges of the plastic wrap to release from the molds. Remove and discard the plastic wrap. Sprinkle the edges of the plate with the remaining chives and a little black pepper.

Serves 4

Wine Suggestion: J Pinot Gris, Sonoma Valley

Pastrami Scented Wild Alaskan Salmon

with Pinot Noir Sauce, Roasted Onion Ragout with Raviolini and Parsley Oil

The pastrami spices are perfect to frame the flavor of wild salmon; for me, more of a natural combination than heavy beef.

Ingredients

4 *fillets of wild Alaskan salmon, about 6 ounces each*
Pastrami Spice Blend (recipe follows)
24 *raviolini made of spinach, roasted cipollini onion and Parmesan and honey pepper bacon (can substitute complimentary ravioli flavors such as spinach and cheese.)*

Carotino® oil (can substitute olive oil)
Roasted Cipollini Onions (recipe follows)
½ *bunch flat leaf parsley, leaves picked*
Pinot Noir Sauce (recipe follows)
Parsley Oil (recipe follows)
¼ *cup snipped fresh chives*

Preparation

PREHEAT oven to 400 degrees. In a medium non-stick skillet heat a drizzle of Carotino® oil over high heat. Dust the surfaces of the salmon with the Pastrami Spice Blend and add to the skillet to sear, about 3 minutes. Turn the fillets over and transfer the entire pan to the oven to finish cooking, about 5 to 6 minutes depending on the thickness of your fish. Carefully remove the skillet (remember the handle is very hot).

ADD the raviolini to a pot of boiling water cooking until tender, about 4 minutes. While they are cooking, in a medium non-stick skillet heat a 1 tablespoon of Carotino® oil over high heat. Add the Roasted Cipollini Onions, cooking until slightly browned—about 4 minutes. Drain the raviolini and add to the onions, tossing to combine. Season generously with salt and black pepper. Remove the pan from the heat. Add the ½ bunch of parsley, tossing to wilt.

TO SERVE, divide and mound the raviolini in the center of each warm serving plate. Position the salmon atop the raviolini. Drizzle the Pinot Noir Sauce over the salmon. Drizzle the Parsley Oil around the plate. Sprinkle with the chives. Serve immediately.

Serves 4

Wine Suggestion: Patton Valley Pinot Noir, Willamette Valley

For the Pastrami Spice Blend

1 tablespoon ground coriander
1 tablespoon sea salt
1 tablespoon freshly ground black
   Tellicherry pepper

1 teaspoon red pepper flakes
¼ teaspoon ground allspice
⅛ teaspoon ground cinnamon
⅛ teaspoon ground cloves

IN A small bowl combine the seasoning spices. Reserve.

For the Pinot Noir Sauce

1 bottle Pinot Noir
2 tablespoons honey

IN A medium saucepan combine the red wine and the honey, bringing to a boil over high heat. Cook until reduced and thickened to coat the back of a spoon, about 15 minutes. Reserve at room temperature.

For the Parsley Oil

½ bunch flat leaf parsley, leaves picked
¼ cup snipped fresh chives

¼ cup white wine
½ cup olive oil

IN A blender, combine the parsley and chives with the white wine. Purée until smooth and bright green. Season with salt and black pepper. While the blender is running, drizzle in the olive oil. Reserve at room temperature, or refrigerate if not using immediately. Parsley Oil may be kept for up to one week.

For the Roasted Cipollini Onions

2 cups cipollini onions, peeled
   Carotino® oil (can substitute olive oil)
   salt & pepper to taste

PREHEAT oven to 400 degrees. Lay a large piece of aluminum foil on your counter top. Position the cipollini onions in the center of the lower half. Drizzle with a little Carotino® oil and season. Fold the top half of the foil over the onions, folding the edges to seal to form a pouch. Place the foil on a cookie sheet for safe handling. Place on the lower rack of the oven cooking until tender, about 45 minutes. Remove from the oven and allow to cool enough to handle. Cut the onions into quarter sections and reserve.

COCOA AND COFFEE CRUSTED FILET OF PRIME CAB BEEF
with Five Onion Tart

The combination of the cocoa and coffee shadow the beef with deep, eerie, smoky flavors. The beef tastes smoky but doesn't have the bitterness of traditional smoke. The umami flavors from the cocoa add a savory sweetness without sugar. The chiles hide in the background and gently warm your palate. Once you taste this combination you too will be addicted to these incredible flavors.

Ingredients

4 *filets of prime tenderloin of beef, about 8 ounces each*
Cocoa-Coffee Spice Blend (recipe follows)
Carotino® oil (can substitute olive oil)
1 *cup diced winter squash*

8 *sprigs of broccolini*
4 *potato crisps (optional)*
2 *tablespoons rosemary oil*
Cabernet Sauce (recipe follows)
Five Onion Tart (recipe follows)

Preparation

RUB the surfaces of the steaks with a little oil. Place the steaks on the grill cooking until well seared, about 6 minutes. Turn over and continue cooking to your desired degree of doneness, usually around 6 minutes for medium rare, depending on the heat of your grill and thickness of your steak. Remove the steaks from the grill.

IF you did not tumble the steaks (see Cocoa-Coffee Spice Blend) proceed as follows: Brush the steaks with the Cabernet Sauce and roll all surfaces with the Cocoa-Coffee Spice Blend. Return the steaks to the grill to toast the spices for 1 or 2 minutes.

WHILE the steaks are cooking, in a medium non-stick pan sauté the squash and broccolini in a few drops of Carotino® oil until al dente—tender but still slightly firm to the bite. Season with salt and pepper. Keep warm.

TO SERVE, position the Five Onion Tart in the center of your plate. Position a sprig of broccolini and squash on each side of the tart. Place the steak atop the tart. Drizzle the steak with the Cabernet Sauce and top with the potato crisp. Drizzle the rosemary oil around the plate and serve.

Serves 4

Wine Suggestion: Trefethen "Halo" Cabernet Sauvignon

For the Cocoa-Coffee Spice Blend

3 tablespoons natural cocoa powder
2 tablespoons ground espresso coffee
1 tablespoon ground New Mexican
   chiles
1 tablespoon sea salt
1 tablespoon freshly ground black
   Tellicherry pepper

1 cup brewed coffee (if using vacuum
   marinator)
2 tablespoons Carotino® oil (if using
   vacuum marinator)

IN A small bowl combine the seasoning spices. If using a vacuum chamber marinator, add the brewed coffee and the oil to the spices. Place the spices and steaks in the chamber and proceed by manufacturer's directions.

For the Cabernet Sauce

1 bottle full bodied red wine, preferably
   Cabernet Sauvignon or Syrah
2 tablespoons honey

IN A medium saucepan combine the red wine and the honey, bringing to a boil over high heat. Cook until reduced to a thickness that coats the back of a spoon, about 15 minutes. Reserve at room temperature.

For the Five Onion Tart

2 large cloves garlic sliced paper-thin
½ cup shallots, peeled and julienne
2 tablespoons Carotino® oil (can
   substitute olive oil)
2 tablespoons olive oil

1 Vidalia onion, peeled and julienne
1 leek, white part only, cut in half and
   rinsed
½ cup snipped fresh chives
½ cup finely grated Parmesan cheese

PREHEAT your grill or broiler. Meanwhile, in a non-stick skillet over medium heat combine the oil with the garlic and shallots, cooking until they are opaque and tender, about 8 minutes. Remove to a bowl and keep warm. Return the skillet to the fire and increase the heat to medium high. Add the 2 tablespoons of olive oil, the onion and the leek, cooking until tender and browned, about 10 minutes. Transfer to join the garlic and shallots and add the chives and Parmesan. Season generously with salt and pepper. Form into 4 round tarts and keep warm.

SPICE CRUSTED PINEAPPLE STEAK
with Ginger White Chocolate Ice Cream

This dessert takes sweetness to the savory and umami side of the taste buds. The total flavor combination activates the traditional senses of sweet, sour, bitter and salty as well as umami. I love the sake umami flavor background and frontal ginger ice cream over the spicy, caramelized and slightly salty pineapple.

Ingredients

*1 tablespoon whole black Tellicherry
  peppercorns*
1 teaspoon white peppercorns
1 teaspoon whole allspice
2 teaspoons coarse sea salt
pinch red chile flakes
1 teaspoon granulated garlic
1 teaspoon granulated onion
1 teaspoon dried orange rind
*4 pineapple steaks, formed by first
  trimming the pineapple of its outer
  skin and eyes, then cutting the
  pineapple in 4 even sections from the
  top to the base of about 4 inches long*

2 tablespoons unsalted butter
1 tablespoon minced fresh ginger
4 tablespoons palm or turbinado sugar
1 cup sake
*1 vanilla bean, cut lengthwise, seeds
  scraped*
*4 servings of Ginger White Chocolate
  Ice Cream (recipe follows)*

Preparation

ON A cutting board or butcher black combine the black and white peppercorns with the allspice. With the edge of a heavy skillet coarsely crush the spices. Transfer to a fine sieve to sift off the fine spice powder (save as a pepper blend for other dishes). Transfer the coarse peppercorns to a small bowl and mix in the coarse sea salt, chile flakes, onion, garlic and orange rind. Firmly press the pineapple steaks into the peppercorn mix to affix to the surface. In a large heavy non-stick skillet, heat the butter over medium high heat. Add the ginger cooking until tender, about 2 minutes. Add the pineapple cooking until it begins to soften slightly, about 3 minutes. Add the sugar cooking until well caramelized and very tender, about 8 minutes. Add the sake and vanilla seeds cooking until the liquids are reduced to make a tight syrup. Remove from heat.

TO SERVE, place the pineapple steaks, flat side up, in the center of each serving plate. Using a round pastry cutter, cut and remove a piece of ice cream to match the center of the pineapple. Drizzle the caramelized pan sauce over the ice cream and around the plate.

Serves 4

Wine Suggestion: Sake, or Chateau Roumieu-Lacoste Sauterne

For the Ginger White Chocolate Ice Cream

4 cups sake	10 pasteurized egg yolks
½ cup fine diced preserved ginger	8 ounces white chocolate
12 ounces half-and-half	1 tablespoon pure vanilla extract
½ cup turbinado sugar	pinch salt

IN A small saucepan, combine the sake with the ginger over medium heat, cooking until reduced to ¾ cup. Add the half-and-half and bring to a scald. Remove from heat. In a medium saucepan combine sugar and yolks. Whisk in the warm cream mixture. Place on medium heat cooking, while constantly stirring, until thickened to coat the back of a spoon. Immediately pour over the white chocolate in a large bowl, stirring to dissolve the chocolate and stop the cooking. Stir in vanilla and salt. Stir until very smooth. Following the manufacturer's instructions, process in an ice cream maker until just about solid. Pour and smooth into a plastic-wrap lined, small square metal baking pan so that the ice cream makes a depth of 2 inches. Cover well and freeze until solid overnight.

NOTE:
The Pineapple Steak plays a sweet and savory twist on the palate while the rich white chocolate ice cream seasoned with sake and ginger cleanse the palate of the spicy bite. Umami is the fifth taste sense along with sweet, bitter, salty, and sour. Although it has been referred to for centuries, the actual taste receptors were scientifically identified for the first time in 2002. These umami taste receptors are stimulated by certain specific amino acids that are the core building blocks of proteins. Hence the umami taste receptors are often called the "protein tooth".

Cocoa and Coffee Crusted Filet of Prime Cab Beef

TRAVERSE CITY: A FOOD & WINE MECCA

Are you interested in hanging out with a fun-loving bunch of celebrity chefs on a beautiful autumn weekend in Traverse City? Well, here's your chance. The Traverse Epicurean Classic, recognized as one of the nation's top food, wine, and cookbook events featuring an incredible number of top chefs, cookbook authors, and wine experts takes place annually in mid-September at the Great Lakes Culinary Institute in Traverse City. Several thousand people attend from around the Midwest. Over the years, stars like Marcus Samuelsson, Mario Batali, David Rosengarten, Terrance Brennan, Cheryl Alters Jamison, Molly Stevens, Marcel Biro, as well as Michiganders' Brian Polcyn, Eric Villegas, and Pete Peterson have all participated in cooking demonstrations, gala dinners, wine receptions, and more. Typically, more than sixty cooking and wine classes are scheduled, allowing cooks and wine lovers of any skill level to learn from the best.

Receptions and the incredibly popular Wine Pavilion are supported by top international wine importers such as Frederick Wildman, Pernod-Ricard, Winebow, Wilson-Daniels, Dreyfus Ashby, Vineyard Brands, Fosters, E & J Gallo, Kobrand, Torres, Banfi, and Chateau Ste. Michelle. Hundreds of wines are available for sampling. In addition, several top Traverse City restaurants host celebrity chefs for a series of Great Chefs Dinners featuring a collaborative menu between the local and incoming chef. Top wineries and winemakers provide the wine pairings. To be sure, the Great Chefs Dinners sell out quickly.

The absolute "must" event is the closing Grand Reception, where each guest chef prepares and serves a small dish from dozens of tasting tables. Of course, all participating wine importers are on hand to pour their most prestigious vintages, and northern Michigan's most acclaimed wineries are represented, as well. It's truly a night to remember.

All Epicurean Classic events are priced individually.
The Epicurean Classic is typically scheduled the second weekend after Labor Day.
Proceeds benefit The Greater Lakes Culinary Institute.
www.epicureanclassic.com - information and registration online.
Phone: 231-933-9688

Seldom Blues

400 Renaissance Center
Detroit, MI 48243
313-567-7301
www.seldomblues.com

Monday – Thursday 11:00am–10:00pm
Friday 11:00am–12:00am
Saturday 5:00pm–12:00am
Sunday 11:30am–4:00pm

Seldom Blues

Executive Chef Jerry Nottage

Jerry Nottage
EXECUTIVE CONCEPT CHEF

When music is the topic, no city in the United States – or the world for that matter – matches Detroit. Whether blues, rock, jazz, or hip-hop, the Motor City's cast of locally produced talent over the past hundred or so years is a mind-boggling list of superstars.

It's a wonder then, why more Detroit restaurants don't model themselves on the supper-club theme. What better way to showcase both the music and vibrant culinary scene? Especially, when we have such a prominent example in Seldom Blues, named by the Detroit Free Press as *Michigan's Best Restaurant* in 2006. From its 15,000 square-foot, 300-seat setting at the base of the Renaissance Center, offering panoramic views of the river, and almost-nightly music, Seldom Blues lays claim to Detroit's only premier fine dining and jazz supper club. The short list of legendary musicians who have played there include Earl Klugh, Angela Bofill, Patty Austin, Bob James, and yes, even Stevie Wonder.

Frank Taylor, a 20-year veteran of the hospitality and restaurant industry, is the visionary behind the restaurant. In 2004, he brought together a strategic group of partners including Robert Porcher, then-defensive end for the Detroit Lions, Alexander Zonjic, an internationally acclaimed jazz musician, and renowned chef, Jerry Nottage.

Nottage's dinner menu opens with an array of starters including Jumbo Lump Crab Cake, Applewood Smoked Bacon Wrapped Colossal Shrimp, Popsicle Lamb Chops, Sautéed Escargot, Ahi Tuna Carpaccio, Crab and Brie Gratin, and Raw Oyster Martini.

The list of entrées feature a range of creative dishes leading with Lobster Pontchartrain, a duet of lobster tails lightly dusted and baked, finished with a shrimp, jumbo lump crabmeat, mushroom and champagne butter sauce; Steak Porcher, a marinated beef rib chop, grilled and topped with roasted-garlic butter; Chateaubriand Classic For Two, served with wild mushroom ragout, duchess potatoes, and béarnaise sauce; or Herb Crusted Rack of Lamb accompanied by rosemary and Port demi glace, to name just a few. Nottage and his talented staff also offer several combination platters for the indecisive.

The dessert menu entices with Rhythm and Blues Chocolate Cake, and Southern-inspired favorites like Fresh Banana Pudding Parfait, Toasted Coconut Crème Brûlée, and Key Lime Pistachio Mousse Cake.

Seldom Blues features both a lobby bar and main bar to enjoy any of eighteen wines by the glass or a favorite cocktail. The wine list will appeal to oenophiles from novice to expert served by knowledgeable sommeliers and waitstaff.

 Award of Excellence

BLUE-B-QUE BASS
with Roasted Redskin Hash and Chive Oil

A colorful dish that tantalizes the taste buds. – Chef Carl Miller

Ingredients

2   sea bass fillets, approximately 8
    ounces each
4   ounces Drake's Batter Mix
    olive oil
1   tablespoon olive oil

Roasted Redskin Hash (recipe follows)
Blue-B-Que Sauce (recipe follows)
Chive Oil (recipe follows)
5-6 fresh blueberries
½   ounce micro greens

Preparation

PREHEAT oven to 350 degrees. Dredge sea bass in Drake's Batter Mix. Sear dredged fillets on a flat top or a skillet with the olive oil over medium-high heat, turning over as each side becomes golden brown. Finish the sea bass in a 350-degree oven.

Arrange Roasted Redskin Hash in the middle of the plate. Place finished sea bass on top of the hash and then top with 2 ounces of Blue-B-Que Sauce. Squirt the Chive Oil around the edge of the plate. Place the blueberries on top of the sea bass and finish by placing the micro greens on top of the blueberries.

Serves 2

Wine Selection: Sauvignon Blanc- Hanna Russian River

For the Roasted Red Skin Hash

1   pound red skin potatoes, diced
¼   cup roasted red bell peppers, diced
¼   cup Vidalia onions, diced
3   teaspoons Cajun seasoning

1   teaspoon salt
3   ounces white wine
3   ounces olive oil

COMBINE red skin potatoes, red peppers and onions in a large braising pan. Season with Cajun blend and salt. Toss with equal parts white wine and olive oil until ¼-inch of liquid is present on bottom of pan. Roast in high heat. Stir occasionally until potatoes are soft in the middle and crisp on outside. Keep warm.

For the Blue-B-Que Sauce

1   lemon
1⅓ cups Baby Rays BBQ Sauce
⅓   cup ketchup

⅓   cup honey
½   cup brown sugar
½   cup dried blueberries

HALVE the lemon and squeeze out the juice in a medium saucepan. Add the rest of the ingredients and bring to a boil on a low flame. Remove from the heat and allow it to cool to room temp before using.

For the Chive Oil

1   *bunch fresh chives*
½   *cup extra virgin olive oil*
¼   *teaspoon sea salt*

BLANCH the chives in boiling water for 10 – 15 seconds. Drain and instantly place chives in an ice bath. Dry thoroughly by patting dry with paper towels. Chop the chives roughly and place in blender or food processor. With machine running, add oil and salt and process until smooth. Store overnight in refrigerator, then strain through a mesh strainer. Place oil in a plastic squirt bottle.

Pan Seared Veal Medallions
with Prosciutto Crème Sauce, Tomato Risotto, Crispy Fried Red Onions

This is a delicate dish with a lot of rustic flavor. – Chef Carl Miller

Ingredients

4   *3-ounce veal medallions*
    olive oil
8   *spears of asparagus*
    Tomato Risotto (recipe follows)
    Prosciutto Crème Sauce
    (recipe follows)

Crispy Fried Red Onions
(recipe follows)
pinch of chopped chives
salt & pepper

Preparation

PREHEAT oven to 350 degrees. Season veal medallions with salt and pepper and sear on both sides until golden brown in an oven-friendly sauté pan with a small amount of olive oil. Finish the veal in the oven to your desired temperature. Season asparagus spears with salt and pepper and grill until al dente.

TO SERVE, using warmed plates, place the asparagus so the tips are at the upper right and the stems are at the lower left. Pile Tomato Risotto in a tight oval on the bottom of the plate, covering the asparagus stems. Set two veal medallions against the bottom of the risotto and add the Prosciutto Crème Sauce along the bottom of the meat. Garnish with the Crispy Fried Red Onions on the left edge of the plate. Finish by sprinkling chives on the sauce.

Serves 2

Wine Suggestion: Jacob's Creek Cabernet Shiraz

For the Tomato Risotto

2 tablespoons garlic, minced	2 ounces tomato, chopped
2 tablespoons olive oil	2 tablespoons basil, chiffonade
¾ cup risotto rice	2 ounces butter
½ cup white wine	3 ounces Asiago cheese
4 cups chicken stock	salt & pepper

IN A small saucepan heated over medium flame, sauté garlic in olive oil for 30 – 40 seconds though do not brown. Add rice and stir another minute until rice is almost translucent. Stir in white wine. When wine is absorbed, begin adding stock, ⅓ cup at a time, until half the liquid is gone. Stir in tomato. Continue adding stock until the rice has absorbed a majority of the liquid. Stir in basil. Finish by stirring in the butter and Asiago cheese. Add salt and pepper to your liking.

For the Prosciutto Crème Sauce

½ cup shallots, minced	8 ounces prosciutto, finely chopped
2 cups white wine	32 ounces heavy whipping cream
2 cups white wine vinegar	cornstarch and water slurry
2 tablespoons black pepper	salt & pepper

IN A medium saucepan, heat shallots, white wine, vinegar, and black pepper over medium heat and let reduced by one-third. Add the prosciutto and heavy whipping crème and continue simmering for 5 minutes. Thicken with cornstarch and water slurry. Season with salt and pepper. This sauce recipe can be cut in half if necessary.

For the Crispy Fried Red Onions

2 red onions, thinly sliced	salt, pepper, and paprika
½ cup all purpose flour seasoned with	1 cup vegetable oil

HEAT oil in heavy-bottomed sauté pan over medium high heat. Toss onion slices in seasoned flour and fry until golden brown. Transfer to a towel or a paper linen to remove excess grease.

AZ Bronzed Salmon

A signature dish for the owner, which is also very popular with our guests. -Chef Carl Miller

Ingredients

6-8 shiitake mushrooms
  salt & pepper
  olive oil
2 6-ounce fillets of salmon

AZ Vegetables (recipe follows)
AZ Sauce (recipe follows)
½ ounce pea shoots

Preparation

PREHEAT oven to 375 degrees. Remove the stems from the mushrooms and toss in oil, salt and pepper. Arrange on a sheet tray and roast in the oven for 15 minutes. Cool and set aside for service. Oil, salt and pepper salmon fillets and sear on a flat top or in a skillet. Place in an ovenproof pan and finish in the oven (approximately 5 – 6 minutes), bringing the salmon to the desired temp.

PLACE AZ Vegetables in the center of a hot serving plate. Place the roasted shiitake mushrooms at the corners of the plate, leaving one corner free. The salmon goes on top of the vegetables. Using the AZ Sauce, design the plate in a pattern that fits the chef's taste. Finish by placing pea shoots atop the entire dish.

Serves 2

Wine Suggestion: Saintsbury Brown Ranch Pinot Noir

For the AZ Vegetables

4 ounces bok choy cabbage
4 ounces nappa cabbage
2 ounces red onion, julienne
2 ounces red and yellow pepper, julienne

1 ounce sesame oil
2 teaspoons black sesame seeds
  olive oil
  salt & pepper

JULIENNE all vegetables and cook in a hot skillet with a small amount of olive oil. Season with salt and pepper. Once cabbage is wilted add sesame oil and black sesame seeds.

For the AZ Sauce

1 cup teriyaki sauce
1 cup hoisin sauce
  salt & pepper

IN A bowl, whisk together the ingredients, and season. Set aside for service.

The Lark

the Lark

6430 Farmington Road
West Bloomfield, MI 48322
248-661-4466
www.thelark.com

Dinner Only
Tuesday – Saturday 5:30 – 9:00pm

The Lark

Executive Chef John Somerville
James & Mary Lark, Owners

O nly the most courageous new world restaurants claim the moniker "European-style country inn." You just don't tempt fate like that, unless of course, you are very, very good at what you do. For twenty-five-plus years, Jim and Mary Lark have emphatically proven their otherworldly restaurant skills to virtually every food, wine, and travel magazine in the United States. The list of awards bestowed upon The Lark is epic in length.

It's a common experience for Lark patrons to recline into their high-backed leather chairs and gaze at the terra cotta walls, Portuguese tile murals, and fountain built into a walled garden behind the dining room's ornately framed windows, and question their whereabouts. "Can I really be in West Bloomfield Township just north of Detroit?" they must surely ask themselves. No doubt, The Lark is Michigan's favorite country inn - sophisticated but not fussy, impeccably proper including tuxedoed waitstaff, but not intimidating. The friendliness of Jim, Mary, and Carl Gerych, their bartender for all of twenty-five years is all part of the legend.

Executive Chef John Somerville's impressive background includes work with Gary Danko at The Lord Fox in Ann Arbor. When he joined The Lark in 1994, the kitchen was under the direction of famed Marcus Haight. Gangly, professorial, and intuitively creative, Somerville is perfectly suited to prepare the demanding French/Continental fare offered prix fixe, in five courses. Meals begin with a carte blanche selection of cold appetizers served from an hors d'oeuvre trolley, followed by Somerville's ever changing preparations of soup, pasta, or hot appetizers, and a palate-cleansing serving of granita, before the main course.

And, what a list of main courses it is. Sautéed Mediterranean Sea Bass (with sweet fennel, artichokes & mandarin orange glaze), Pan Roasted Maine Lobster (with vanilla flan, fall vegetables, & late-harvest Riesling sauce), Portuguese Copper Cataplana (large white gulf shrimp, clams, mussels and Chorizo sausage with San Marzano-shellfish broth), and Truffled Lasagna (pumpkin & squash filling and Parmesan-Reggiano sauce), to name only a few. Elaborate preparations of duck, beef, veal, lamb, and rabbit also call for attention. No doubt, savvy diners are in the habit of reserving a table for ten close friends so that every dish on the menu can be seen and sampled.

The Lark wine cellar is similarly difficult to put into words. A legendary collector, Jim Lark has compiled over 1,200 selections of predominantly European labels, including the most sought after Bordeaux and Burgundy. Ladies and gentlemen, you can scarcely find better anywhere in the old country.

 Best of Award of Excellence

GULF SHRIMP
with Tapioca Pudding and Lime Tequila Glaze

Ingredients

1 pound extra large shrimp, peeled, de-veined	salt & pepper
3 cups seafood stock	Tapioca Pudding (recipe follows)
4 tablespoons butter	Lime Tequila Glaze (recipe follows)
	watercress sprigs (optional garnish)

Preparation

IN A sauté pan add stock and butter over medium heat. Simmer to create poaching liquid then add shrimp seasoned with salt and pepper. Cook until just done.
TO SERVE, place a large dollop of Tapioca Pudding in middle of plate. Add shrimp around pudding and spoon Lime Tequila Glaze over shrimp. Garnish with a sprig of watercress.

Serves 4

Wine Suggestion: A full bodied, opulent dry Riesling pairs well with this modern classic. Try the JJ Prum Wehlener Sonnenuhr Kabinett

For the Tapioca Pudding

½ pound large tapioca pearls, soaked in cold water overnight	1 tablespoon vanilla extract
½ pound small tapioca pearls, soaked in cold water overnight	1 vanilla bean, split in half, seeds removed
2 quarts heavy cream	2 cups sugar (more or less if desired)

DRAIN tapioca pearls. Ideally, the pearls should remain whole as opposed to falling apart or becoming crushed. Add pearls along with all other ingredients to a large saucepot over medium heat. Bring to a simmer stirring regularly to prevent sticking to the bottom of the pan. Cook till large tapioca pearls are al dente, approximately 20 – 30 minutes. If pudding becomes too thick, add a little heavy cream to loosen.

For the Lime Tequila Glaze

4 egg yolks	½ lime tequila vinegar (preferably Cuisine Perel brand)
1 egg	
1 cup sugar	

BRING a large pot of water filled half way to a boil. In a stainless steel bowl that fits into the top of the pot of water, place all ingredients. Using a balloon whisk, mix constantly till light and fluffy, being careful not to let the eggs scramble by letting the mixture become too hot.

SWEET FENNEL FLAN
with Lemon Verbena Beurre Blanc

Ingredients

2 *bulbs fennel, trimmed and chopped*
1 *onion, peeled, chopped*
1 *teaspoon olive oil*
1 *quart heavy cream*
½ *cup sugar*
1 *tablespoon fennel pollen*

4 *eggs (approximately)*
8 *egg yolks (approximately)*
  Verbena Beurre Blanc (recipe follows)
  Pearl Vegetables for garnish (recipe follows)
  sweet sabayon (optional)

Preparation

PREHEAT oven to 350 degrees. Heat oil in a large saucepot and begin to sweat fennel and onions over medium heat until tender being careful not to brown the vegetables. Add cream, sugar and pollen. Bring to a boil then simmer till slightly reduced. Adjust seasonings. Purée in a bar blender or food processor. Strain through a chinois. Cool.

DETERMINE the number of eggs you need by taking an 8-ounce ladle and counting the number of cups of fennel purée you have. The ratio is 1 egg plus 2 egg yolks per cup of strained fennel purée. Beat eggs in a bowl. Add to cool fennel purée. Adjust seasonings. Heavily spray individual stainless steel ramekins. Fill ¾ full with fennel mixture. Place in a water bath. Tightly seal with plastic wrap and aluminum foil. Cook at 350 degrees for 20 minutes.

TO SERVE, remove flans from their molds. Place on a plate. Spoon Lemon Verbena Beurre Blanc around. Scatter pearl vegetables around and top with a sweet sabayon (optional).

Serves 4

Wine Suggestion: A rich, creamy, fruit-driven Chardonnay pairs well with this flan. Our suggestion: Staglin Rutherford Chardonnay

For the Lemon Verbena Beurre Blanc

1 *pint fresh lemon juice*
½ *cup sugar*
1 *cup lemon verbena*

1 *cup heavy cream*
1 *pound butter, cubed*

IN A saucepan over medium heat reduce lemon juice, sugar, and lemon verbena by three-quarters. Add cream and reduce by half. Remove from heat and whisk in the butter. When completely dissolved strain through a chinois and keep warm.

For the Pearl Vegetables

Mini Parisienne scoop: cusa and yellow squash, peeled carrot and new (purple) potato. Blanch separately in lightly salted boiling water until just done.

ROAST GOOSE
with Stuffing, Glazed Chestnuts & Cranberry Sauce

For the Goose

1   *10 – 12 pound goose, wings and fat*
    trimmed, rubbed with garlic, salt and
    pepper
    Stuffing (recipe follows)

Glazed Carrots (recipe follows)
Glazed Chestnuts (recipe follows)
Cranberry Sauce (recipe follows)

Preparation

PREHEAT oven to 325 degrees. Roast goose in oven (preferably, Chinese oven) until skin is crisp and breast is cooked all the way through. Cool. Carefully remove breast meat keeping skin in tact. Carefully pull thigh meat away from the carcass. Reserve carcass of bird for another use such as stock. Keep meat warm until ready for service.

TO SERVE, slice the breast meat and chop the thigh meat. Attractively arrange sliced goose breast on top of chopped thigh meat. Place warmed Stuffing and Glazed Carrots around. Sprinkle Glazed Chestnuts with their syrup on top of stuffing. Ladle Cranberry Sauce over goose meat and around plate.

Serves 4

Wine Suggestion: A California Cabernet that's neither too fruity nor too intense, with smooth tannins, pairs well with this dish. Our suggestion: Shafer Napa Valley Cabernet Sauvignon

For the Stuffing

1   *onion, diced*
2   *stalks celery, diced*
3   *carrots, diced*
2   *pounds whole hog ground sausage*

¼   *pound sage, chopped fine*
    light chicken stock
    bread crumbs, diced

IN sauté pan, brown all vegetables and sage with sausage until all fat is rendered out. Drain fat. Add stock and simmer until root vegetables are soft, about 20 minutes. Add breadcrumbs until liquid is soaked up and mixture remains moist. Spread evenly on sheet tray and cool. Cut into individual shapes and re-warm individually.

For the Glazed Carrots

5   *pounds carrots, peeled and waffle cut*
    on a mandoline
1   *quart sugar*

1   *quart water*
½   *pound butter*
    chives, chopped

ROAST GOOSE, CONTINUED

ADD all in a large pot. Bring to a boil and cook carrots till done. Reserve carrots and continue to reduce liquid till thick and syrupy, about 30 minutes. Before serving, add carrots to liquid and garnish with freshly chopped chives.

For the Chestnuts

1 quart chestnuts, cleaned	*2 cups water*
2 cups sugar	*3 vanilla beans*

DISSOLVE sugar with water in saucepot over medium heat. Add chestnuts. Slowly simmer till chestnuts are soft but not crushed. Remove chestnuts and continue reducing water till syrupy. Pour over chestnuts in bowl. When re-heating, heat chestnuts in the syrup till bubbly.

For the Cranberry Sauce

1 bag fresh cranberries	*½ cup sugar*
1 cup cranberry vinegar (substitute red wine or raspberry vinegar)	*1 pint demi sauce (reduced stock)*

REDUCE cranberries, vinegar, and sugar in a saucepan till thick and syrupy. Add demi and continue boiling till thick and sauce-like. If sauce becomes too thick, thin it out with stock or water.

Lark entry

Frozen Grand Marnier Soufflé

with Framboise Accents

Ingredients

2½ cups sugar
 1 cup water
18 egg yolks
 2 quarts whipped cream (from 1½ cups
       heavy cream)

red food coloring
½ cup Grand Marnier
     cocoa powder
     Framboise Accents (recipe follows)

Preparation

MIX sugar and water in a saucepot and bring to a boil. Cook unitl mixture reaches 250 degrees on a pastry thermometer. While sugar is boiling, whip egg yolks in a Kitchen Aid or other mixer til light and fluffy. Slowly add the sugar mixture while whipping on Speed 2. Continue whipping til cool, approximately 10 minutes. Fold into whipped cream. Add coloring and Grand Marnier. Place in star-tipped pastry bag and pipe into cocoa powder-lined aluminum soufflé cups. Freeze.

WHEN ready to serve, remove the flan to a small serving plate and accent with the Framboise Sauce.

Makes 18 two-ounce servings

Wine Suggestion: Kir Royale (Champagne and Framboise)

For the Framboise Accents

4 cups fresh raspberries
    (preferably organic)
1 cup sugar

MIX together in a bowl and crush berries. Let stand for 5 minutes. Strain through chinois.

Stroh's workers posed with beer kegs and signs and bottles, c. 1890.

Tribute

Tribute Restaurant

31425 West Twelve Mile Road
Farmington Hills, MI 48334
248-848-9393
www.tributerestaurant.com

Lunch Monday – Friday
11:30am – 2:00pm
Dinner Tuesday – Saturday
5:00pm – 9:30pm

Tribute

Executive Chef Don Yamauchi
Larry & Toni Wisne, Owners

The capricious nature of business requires restaurants to compete amongst each other for diners. While this may be true from a dollars and cents perspective, certain restaurants acknowledge no competition and simply try to do things in a wholly original, unfettered way. If this sounds vain or pompous, you are mistaking the attitude because this is not a game for the fainthearted. Poseurs will be spotted immediately. But if one possesses the requisite knowledge base, training, resources, and that extra intangible of rare creativity, then sleep comes easy at the end of the night. They are living true to themselves.

We can assume this is the attitude of Tribute, a restaurant unlike any other in Michigan, or, as stated by the *New York Times* a few years ago, "Tribute may be the best restaurant between New York and Chicago; it is certainly the finest in Detroit." Why? Because not one element—from the stunning architecture, interior design, art, wine collection, and obsessive staff, both front and back of the house—was overlooked. This also means highly-acclaimed Executive Chef, Don Yamauchi, is given free rein to obtain exactly what he needs from anywhere in the world, to be prepared completely as he sees fit.

Tribute diners often choose one of Yamauchi's tasting menus including the twenty-one-course Gourmet Tasting Menu offering his version, Tribute's version, of an unforgettable dining experience. Think Foie Gras Torchon, Golden Osetra Caviar, Chef's Salad with Deviled Quail Eggs and Smoked Salmon and Sliced Beef and Brie, Lamb Carpaccio, Tuna Tartare, and Red Wine Braised Short Rib.

Ala carte entrées from a recent menu featured Soy Marinated Salmon and Tartare; Roasted Sea Bass accompanied by Brandade, Fried Artichoke, Peruvian Chips, Jerusalem Artichoke, and Red Bell Pepper Oil; and Venison Saltimbocca including Venison Loin, Venison Pastrami, Mozzarella, Basil, Eggplant, and Mushroom Cream. These are the sort of innovative, exquisitely detailed dishes Tribute diners come to expect on a nightly basis. Ultimately, a chef's table for eight is available in the bustling kitchen.

The wine cellar currently holds an astounding 2,200 different labels, assembled and managed by Sommelier Antoine Przek. To call it "award-winning" does not do justice to this expert collection.

 Best of Award of Excellence

Foie Gras and Monkfish Liver Torchon

Ingredients

Fig Purée (recipe follows)
Foie Gras (recipe follows)
orange sections (for garnish)
Honey Sauce (recipe follows)
Monkfish Liver (recipe follows)

pickled ginger
sansho pepper
optional garnishes: micro greens, five-spice powder

Preparation

SPREAD the Fig Purée on one side of serving plate and lay ¼-inch disks of Foie Gras on top garnished with orange segments. On the other side, spread the Honey Sauce and lay ¼-inch disks of the Monkfish Liver, garnished with pickled ginger and sansho pepper. Extra garnishes: micro greens, five-spice powder.

Serves 4

Wine Suggestion: A. Margaine, Demi-Sec, Champagne, France, NV

For the Fig Purée

½ cup dried figs
½ cup port wine
    salt & pepper

IN A small pot boil the figs and port together. When the figs are soft, purée in a bar blender, season with salt and pepper, and pass through a fine sieve. Cool the purée down and reserve.

For the Foie Gras

8 ounces duck liver
1 quart water
3 ounces salt
3 ounces sugar

1 orange, zested, juiced
    salt & pepper
    five-spice powder

IN A small pot, combine the salt, sugar, and water and heat until all is dissolved. Add the zest and juice of one orange and cool the liquid down. Store the liver in the liquid overnight. PREHEAT oven to 250 degrees. Remove the liver from the brine and clean the liver, removing as many veins as possible. Season the liver with salt, pepper, and five-spice powder, and place on an oiled sheet tray. Bake in oven until slightly warm. Mold in plastic wrap and store in the cooler until needed.

For the Honey Sauce

¼ cup honey
2 tablespoons fresh orange juice

1 teaspoon arima sansho pepper
1 teaspoon orange zest

HEAT ingredients in a small pan just until all the juice is incorporated. Strain through a fine sieve and place in a squirt bottle.

For the Monkfish Liver

8 ounces monkfish liver
2 cups milk

2 ounces fresh tarragon
salt & pepper

CLEAN the monkfish liver, and place in the milk overnight refrigerated. Rinse the monkfish and season with salt and pepper. Place the monkfish on top of the tarragon and steam for 6 minutes. Let the liver cool slightly and roll in plastic wrap. Store the liver in the freezer until needed.

Tribute kitchen

Tribute dining room

Watermelon Soup

Ingredients

6 cups watermelon, roughly diced
6 leaves fresh green basil
⅛ teaspoon salt

⅛ teaspoon sugar
pinch ground black pepper
¼ cup water

Preparation

IN A bar blender or food processor, place all the ingredients. Blend or purée until most of the chunks are gone. Reserve. Place cheesecloth over a fine strainer and pass the soup through. Let the soup pass through on its own without squeezing the cloth. Chill thoroughly.
MAKE sure to serve the soup in chilled bowls.

These are some of the garnishes we use at the restaurant:

goat cheese
black pepper
gooseberries

cucumber
cilantro
extra virgin olive oil

Other possible garnishes:

tequila
vodka
basil
parsley

jalapeno
mango
Champagne

Serves 4

Wine Suggestion: Kim Crawford, Sauvignon Blanc, Marlborough, New Zealand

SCALLOP, FLUKE AND TUNA SASHIMI
with Yuzu Vinaigrette

Ingredients

1   ounce micro mâche
1   tablespoon radish, julienne
    Yuzu Vinaigrette (recipe follows)
    salt & pepper
4   ounces live scallops, thinly sliced

4   ounces fluke, thinly sliced
4   ounces yellow fin tuna, thinly sliced
1   tablespoon salmon roe, divided evenly
    for 4 plates

Preparation

MIX the micro mâche and the julienne of radish in a small bowl. Toss the salad with the Yuzu Vinaigrette and season with salt and pepper to taste. Divide the scallop, fluke, and tuna evenly between four plates. Drizzle the top of the fish with about 1 tablespoon of the Yuzu Vinaigrette (or to taste) and garnish the top with the salmon roe.

Serves 4

Wine Suggestion: Bodegas Dios Baco, Amontillado, Sherry, Jerez de la Frontera, Spain, NV

For the Yuzu Vinaigrette

¼   Vidalia onion, grated
½   finger of ginger root, grated
⅔   cup soy sauce
¾   cup yuzu juice
⅔   cup sugar

1   teaspoon togarashi
1¼ cups grapeseed oil
¾   cup sesame oil
    fresh ground pepper

COMBINE grated onion, grated ginger, soy sauce, yuzu juice, sugar, and togarashi in a small bowl. Slowly drizzle in oils, whisking constantly. Add pepper to taste.

Yield: 2 cups

LOBSTER BARIGOULE

Ingredients

3 raw lobster tails, each cut into 6 pieces
4 tablespoons carrots, small dice
4 tablespoons celery, small dice (can substitute celery root, or pascal)
4 tablespoons mushrooms, small dice
6 pearl onions, peeled and cut in half
1 small garlic clove, sliced thin

5 tablespoons extra virgin olive oil, divided
3 cups chicken stock
4 tablespoons cold butter
⅛ teaspoon thyme leaves
1 teaspoon parsley, chopped
salt & pepper

Preparation

IN A saucepot sweat the carrots, celery, mushroom, onion and garlic in about 3 tablespoons of the olive oil. Add the chicken stock and let reduce on medium heat until ½ cup of chicken stock is left. Lower the heat and add the butter to the reduced stock and stir until butter is incorporated. Season stock with salt and black pepper. Add lobster pieces while stirring (try not to boil the liquid after adding the lobster, this will make it a little tough. The slower and more gently the lobster is heated the better for the texture.) Add thyme leaves and chopped parsley.

TO SERVE, portion the barigoule into six small cups with three pieces of lobster each. Drizzle the remaining 2 tablespoons of olive oil on top of the portioned barigoule.

Serves 6

Wine Suggestion: M. Chapoutier, Grenache Blanc, La Bernardine, Chateauneuf-du-Pape, Rhone, France

Men on frame of barn at barn raising, c. 1900.

Bacco
Ristorante

29410 Northwestern Highway
Southfield, MI 48034
248-356-6600
www.baccoristorante.com

Lunch Mon – Fri 11:30am – 2:00pm
Dinner Mon – Fri 5:30pm – 10:00pm
Dinner Saturday 5:30pm – 11:00pm
Closed Sunday

Bacco Ristorante

Chef / Owner Luciano Del Signore

The likes of Italian super chef Mario Batali splashed over books, magazines, television, and several restaurants around the U.S., has helped propel the understanding and appreciation of Italian food into perhaps, the #1 global cuisine. Batali, to his credit, would certainly admit that "helped" may be an overstatement. In fact, there are dozens of Italian-American restaurant chefs serving world-class food every night in this country. They are the chefs on the ground, turning heads (and palates), plate by delicious plate; moving once exotic food, cooking techniques, and presentations, and even the way courses are served, into the mainstream. Metro Detroit's leading Italian-cuisine innovator is Luciano Del Signore, chef/owner of Bacco Ristorante in Southfield. *Gourmet* magazine, *Style Magazine*, and the peerless James Beard Foundation have all lauded his exceptional interpretations of traditional Italian, as well as the truly imaginative food he prepares.

On Bacco's antipasti menu, you will find impeccable renditions of carpaccio, both tuna and beef, Italian sausages served with caramelized onions, balsamic, and gorgonzola, and zuppetta studded with mussels, clams, shrimp, and chile. Del Signore's flair is seen in the elegant Capesante Dorate al Profumo di Tartufo (pan roasted day boat scallops, porcini truffle cream, sprinkled with shaves of Parmigiano), or Insalata di Rucola e Finocchi (arugula, fennel, toasted walnuts, orange sections, and lemon oil).

From linguine in Little Neck clam sauce, to roasted eggplant lasagnette, and tagliatelle with lamb ragout, the Le Paste menu is loaded with winners. But, one glance at the meat and fish offerings and you'll discover the heart and soul of any Del Signore menu. Foremost are the preponderance of veal dishe, starting with a grilled prime veal chop served simply with chopped tomatoes and rosemary oil; onto veal tenderloin paired with Taleggio cheese, black truffles and porcini sauce, and finally two scaloppini dishes: Scaloppine al Limone (lemon, white wine, parsley), and Saltimbocca (prosciutto di Parma, sage, white wine, and demi glace). Beef filet, lamb chops, sea bass, and salmon paired accompanied by clams, shrimp, mussels, and tomato fumé, round out the Secondi Piatti menu.

Of course, the name Bacco is derived from Bacchus and this house's décor is unmistakably vin-spired complemented by original jazz-themed paintings on the white walls. The tiled dining room is contemporary and deftly managed by Alberto DeSantis. Sommelier Matthew Bricker is responsible for Bacco's astounding cellar of Italian wine. His palate and breadth of knowledge are the result of numerous tours of Italy's wine regions.

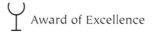

Award of Excellence

ZUPPA DI FARRO
(Italian Whole Grain Soup)

Farro is an ancient grain of Italy with loads of history and packed with Vitamin E and fiber. The legend goes that eating farro promotes a certain, how shall we say, sexual prowess. It was the main staple food of the ancient Roman Legion. Real Italian farro can be found on the Internet and has a good shelf life.

Ingredients

- 1 cup olive oil
- 4 ounces pancetta diced
- 2 onions, diced
- 1 clove garlic, minced
- 4 bay leaves
- 6 carrots, minced (use food processor)
- 6 ounces canned crushed tomatoes

- 2 quarts chicken stock
- 3 cups farro, soaked in water overnight in fridge, then drained
- 1 teaspoon fresh picked thyme
- salt & pepper
- olive oil, young harvest
- toasted Italian bread, for garnish

Preparation

IN A soup pot add olive oil and pancetta and sauté till pancetta is golden brown. Add onions, garlic, bay leaves and carrots and sauté till tender. Add crushed tomatoes and chicken stock, bring to simmer then add drained farro and simmer for 1 hour. Season with thyme, salt and pepper and continue to simmer for 10 minutes.

TO SERVE, place in hot bowl and drizzle with young harvest olive oil. Garnish with toasted Italian bread.

Serves 6

Wine Suggestion: Italian Chardonnay, Jermann, Lageder or Antinori

Melanzane alla Parmigiana
(Tepid Eggplant Parmigiano)

This dish is my version of a classic; the ingredients are the same, I just assemble them differently. I made it to be much lighter to be used as a first course. This dish is a lot of fun to make and gets great reviews from those who eat it. I only peel half of the eggplant because I think some skin adds a new texture to the dish and great flavor. You can find buffalo mozzarella at most Italian markets, make sure it is from Campagna and has a government approved DOP marking on the package. This dish should be served warm, not hot.

Ingredients

- 4 large eggplants, half-peeled, diced in 1-inch squares
- ½ cup olive oil
- ½ cup fresh basil leaves, chopped
- ½ cup grated Parmigiano Reggiano (the real thing, please)

- 2 6-ounce balls buffalo mozzarella, whipped in a food processor
- 2 cups Basic Tomato Sauce (recipe follows)
- salt & pepper
- fresh or fried basil leaves for garnish

Preparation

PREHEAT the oven to 450 degrees. In a large bowl, add eggplant and olive oil and toss very well. Place on sheet pan and roast in oven till eggplant is dark golden and tender. Let cool for 5 minutes and transfer back to a large bowl. Add basil, Parmigiano cheese and Tomato Sauce and gently toss.

TO SERVE, spoon eggplant into bowls and top with whipped buffalo mozzarella, garnish with fresh basil leaf or fried basil leaf (hot oil 1 minute on each side).

Serves 6

Wine Suggestion: Barbara di Asti, Contratto, Coppo or La Spinetta

For the Basic Tomato Sauce

- ½ cup olive oil
- 2 cloves garlic minced
- 1 teaspoon chile flakes
- 2 bay leaves

- ½ onion, diced
- 1 16-ounce can Italian peeled tomatoes (crushed by hand)
- salt and pepper to taste

IN A saucepan add olive oil, garlic, chile flakes, and bay leaves. Sauté on medium-low heat till garlic is golden. Add onion and continue to cook till onions are transparent. Add tomatoes and season with salt and pepper. Simmer for 20 minutes and set aside.

Spaghetti al Salmone

This is my favorite way to eat salmon and a way to get those ever so popular omega-3 fatty acids. I think chile lends a lot of flavor to the dish, but can be adjusted based on sensitivity to heat. Norwegian salmon or farm raised can be substituted for wild salmon. I do not recommend serving grated cheese with this pasta dish. In Italy, we only use grated cheese for pastas that don't have delicate fish.

Ingredients

¼ cup olive oil
1 clove garlic, minced
16 ounces wild salmon, skinned, remove and discard dark flesh, dice in ½-inch cubes

6 ounces dry white wine
1½ cups Basic Tomato Sauce (see recipe under Melanzane alla Parmigiana)
1 pound dry spaghetti
¼ cup flat leaf parsley, chopped

Preparation

BRING a large pot of salted water to boil. In a large skillet add olive oil and garlic, cooking on medium-low heat till garlic is golden. Add salmon and sauté on high heat for 3 minutes. Add white wine and Tomato Sauce, simmer for 5 minutes and set aside. Boil spaghetti 1 minute less than instructed on package (very al dente), drain and add to sauce. Cook on high heat for about 1 minute till spaghetti absorbs liquid, stirring constantly. Add parsley.
TO SERVE, place pasta on plates first, and top with salmon sauce.

Serves 4

Wine Suggestion: Soave, Anselmi, Michele Castellani or Pieropan

Costoletta di Vitello Valdostana
(Veal Chop Valdostana)

The name Valdostana comes from the region Val D'Aosta and is famed for its dairy products, so the use of butter and cheese here come as no surprise. The recipe is, however, a relatively new development.

Ingredients

- 6 16-ounce veal chops
- 9 ounces imported Fontina cheese marked Val D'Aosta, cut into 6 pieces
- 6 slices Prosciutto de Parma
- 6 feet butcher twine, cut into foot lengths
- ½ cup olive oil
- 4 shallots, minced

- 2 sprigs fresh rosemary
- ¼ cup brandy
- ¼ cup red wine
- 1 cup demi glace (found at local high-end restaurant)
- ¼ cup unsalted butter
- salt & pepper

Preparation

PREHEAT the oven to 400. Cut a pocket into the side of the veal chops and set aside. Wrap each piece of Fontina cheese with prosciutto on all sides to contain the cheese. Stuff each chop with the prosciutto/Fontina squares and tie the chops with the butcher twine. Heat 2 large skillets to high heat. Season both sides of the chops with salt and pepper, place 3 chops to each pan and brown well on one side, flip the chops and finish in the oven for 10 minutes. Take chops out of pans and let rest for a few minutes while making sauce.

IN one of the same pans used to cook the chops, un-cleaned but drained of the oil, add fresh olive oil, shallots, and rosemary sprigs and sauté on medium heat for 5 minutes. Add brandy, red wine and demi glace, and reduce on high heat till thickened. Finish with butter and strain.

TO SERVE, plate the chops with your favorite roasted potatoes and sautéed asparagus with olive oil, salt and pepper. Top with the sauce.

Serves 6

Wine Suggestion: Brunello di Montalcino, Altesino, Palazzo or Argiano

BUTTERMILK PANNA COTTA
with Mango Vanilla Gelée

Here's a tip on blooming gelatin sheets: Place sheets one at a time into ice water and soak for 5 to 8 minutes. Take out, squeeze off excess water, and the gelatin is ready to use.

Ingredients

8 ounces cream

3½ ounces sugar

1 orange, zest of

2 sheets gelatin, bloomed

8 ounces buttermilk

1 vanilla bean, split and scraped

Mango Vanilla Gelée (recipe follows)

thin slices of mango, for garnish

Preparation

BRING cream, sugar, orange zest, and vanilla bean to a boil in a saucepan. Turn off heat and let stand for 20 minutes. Bring back to boil, turn off, add bloomed gelatin sheets and whisk till dissolved. Add cold buttermilk then strain the mixture through a fine mesh sieve. Portion into 6 ramekins, cover and refrigerate overnight.

Prepare Mango Vanilla Gelée and pour a thin layer over set panna cotta. Refrigerate for another hour.

TO SERVE, place ramekins on plate with a folded napkin and garnish with thinly sliced mango fan.

Serves 6

Wine Suggestion: Torcolato, Maculan

Mango Vanilla Gelée

8 ounces mango purée

4 ounces water

3 ounces sugar

½ vanilla bean, split and scraped

3 sheets gelatin, bloomed

BRING mango purée, water, sugar, and vanilla bean to a boil in a saucepan, turn off and whisk in bloomed gelatin sheets. Strain through fine mesh sieve.

Robert and Margaret Menzies Homestead, Vanderbilt, 1900.

Rugby Grille
at the Townsend

100 Townsend Street
Birmingham, MI 48009
248-642-7900
www.townsendhotel.com

Sunday – Thursday 6:30am – Midnight
Friday & Saturday 6:30am – 1:00am

Rugby Grille
at the Townsend

Executive Chef James Barnett

Restaurants and hotels have a long and testy relationship complicated by the fact that certain top chefs don't want to be perceived as just another food-service option for hotel guests, no matter the level of accommodations. Yet, there are many exceptions including the Rugby Grille, perfectly content to share space and acclaim with Birmingham's incomparable Townsend Hotel.

Opulent is the one word we can't avoid when describing Rugby Grille. From the bountiful fresh cut flowers, crystal chandeliers, turtle-shell green leather chairs, lush carpeting, and Italian tile, the lobby, intimate dining room, and overall ambiance promise a rare dining experience.

Rugby Grille Executive Chef, Jim Barnett, a Johnson & Wales College grad and former executive chef for the Matt Prentice Restaurant Group's top restaurants, including Coach Insignia and No. VI Chop House, oversees a staff lead by Chef de Cuisine David Gilbert who learned his craft with restaurants such as French Laundry and Mansion on Turtle Creek. It's no wonder Zagat Restaurant Guide recently called Rugby "one of the top ten restaurants in the United States."

On the Starters menu we find Black Truffle and Lobster Risotto, Steak Tartar (served tableside), Townsend Caviar Service ("000" Malossol Osetra), Seafood Platter (Scottish Smoked Salmon, Oysters, Shrimp, and Lobster Medallion), and Maine Lobster Salad, to name a few.

Entrées—or Composed Plates, as they are called at Rugby—include a quartet of seafood dishes starting with Norwegian Salmon, Citrus Roasted Black Cod, Maine Diver Scallops, and a tableside preparation of East Coast favorite, Sauté of Dover Sole "A La Meunière. Moving on, the meat dishes feature Millbrook Farm's Rack of Lamb (served with Parmigiano-Reggiano and white truffle infused polenta), Veal Bolognaise (sautéed veal served over fresh porcini bolognaise, fricassee of cipollini onions, tomato confit, and Italian pancetta), and the simple, elegant Oven Roasted Amish Chicken. Filet mignon, prime New York strip, and Delmonico steak are offered with a choice of sauces. Any entrée can be accompanied by one of ten-plus vegetable and potato selections. Each night, a Chef's Tasting Menu and featured special entrée are offered.

Lastly, a worldly selection of artisan cheeses encourages diners to pause before or after dessert. Items such as Profiteroles and Chocolate Caramel Mousse Pyramid assure that dessert will be impossible to resist.

Mario Plaza, Rugby Grille's General Manager, also serves as its wine director overseeing a stellar list assembled with the help of Master Sommelier, Ron Edwards.

CITRUS ROASTED BLACK COD

with Curried Jumbo Lump Maine Crab Meat Crépinette, Carrot Ginger Reduction And Batonnet of Honey Glazed Carrots

Ingredients

2 6-ounce Alaskan black cod fillets, skinned, pin bones removed
2 ounces clarified butter
sea salt
Citrus Powder (recipe follows)
Lump Maine Crab Meat Crépinette (recipe follows)

Carrot Ginger Reduction (recipe follows)
Honey Glazed Carrots (recipe follows)
pea tendrils, for garnish

Preparation

HEAT clarified butter in a 10-inch sauté pan over medium heat. Season black cod fillets with sea salt. Cook black cod 4 minutes, until lightly golden brown. Turn over and repeat on other side for an additional 4 minutes. Dust top of fish evenly with Citrus Powder.

WARM Crab Meat Crépinettes in low oven. Place 2 ounces of Carrot Ginger Reduction on bottom of each plate. Place warm crépinette over sauce. Add black cod on top of crépinette. Add Honey Glazed Carrots around edge of sauce. Garnish with pea tendrils.

Serves 2

Wine Suggestion: A dry Alsatian Gewürztraminer or Riesling is the way to go with this dish.

For the Citrus Powder

1 orange
1 lemon
1 lime

REMOVE zest of orange, lemon, and lime. Dry in low oven until all moisture is removed from zest. Grind to fine powder and reserve.

For the Lump Maine Crab Meat Crépinette

2 whole eggs
½ cup flour
¼ cup milk
¼ cup water
¼ teaspoon salt

1 tablespoon melted whole butter
4 ounces Maine jumbo lump crab
2 tablespoons curry powder
2 ounces Mascarpone cheese

PLACE eggs, flour, milk, water, and salt into a stainless steel bowl. Mix well for 30 seconds. Scrape down sides. Blend for 15 seconds more. Cover and let sit for 1 hour. This helps the flour absorb more of the liquids. Next, warm a small crêpe pan. Coat inside of pan with melted whole butter. Place 2 ounces of crépinette batter into bottom of crêpe pan and cook until golden brown. Flip crêpe and cook other side until golden brown. Remove from pan and reserve.

WHIP the curry into the Mascarpone and then gently fold in the crab. Add 2 ounces of the filling to each crépinette and roll into a small purse.

For the Carrot Ginger Reduction

4 ounces fresh carrot juice	2 ounces heavy cream
½ ounce fresh ginger juice	4 ounces butter

IN A small saucepot reduce the carrot juice and ginger juice to 2 ounces. Add the heavy cream and bring to a simmer for 5 minutes. Remove from heat and add butter slowly, whisking constantly. Adjust seasoning and set aside in a warm place.

For the Honey Glazed Carrots

2 medium size carrots, en battonets (cut in thin sticks)	1 ounce clover honey
1 cup fresh orange juice	2 tablespoons butter

PLACE ingredients in small saucepot over medium heat. Bring liquid to a simmer. Reduce heat to low, and cook until liquid has reduced to a glaze.

SAUTÉ OF DOVER SOLE A LA MEUNIÈRE
with Roasted Fingerling Potatoes and Haricot Vert Almandine

Far and away, the Rugby's signature dish. We always start with the biggest fish we can find and prepare it at the absolute last minute to keep it moist and perfect.

Ingredients

1 24 – 26 ounce Dover sole from Holland, cleaned, skinned
all-purpose flour
salt & pepper
1 tablespoon grapeseed oil
2 ounces butter
2 sprigs fresh thyme

Haricot Vert Almandine (recipe follows)
Roasted Fingerling Potatoes (recipe follows)
Beurre Blanc (recipe follows)
lemon wedges, for garnish

Preparation

PREHEAT oven to 375 degrees. Heat a large sauté pan until pan is very hot. Dust Dover sole with all-purpose flour and season with salt and white pepper. Add grapeseed oil to hot sauté pan. Add Dover sole to oil and sauté until golden brown. Flip Dover sole and add fresh thyme and whole butter. Place in 375-degree oven for 12-14 minutes.

WHEN ready to serve, remove bones from Dover sole and place fillets on plates. Place Haricot Verts and Fingerling Potatoes on plates. Sauce the Dover sole with the Beurre Blanc and garnish with fresh lemon wedges.

Serves 2

Wine Suggestion: French Chardonnay, whether it's a Grand Cru Chablis, or a white Burgundy, that's the ideal choice for this dish.

For the Haricot Vert Almandine

1 tablespoon shallots, finely chopped
grapeseed oil
1 ounce butter

3 ounces haricot vert
1 ounce fresh toasted sliced almonds

HEAT medium size sauté pan with grapeseed oil. Add shallots and cook until translucent. Add whole butter and haricot vert. Add freshly toasted almonds. Season with salt.

For the Roasted Fingerling Potatoes

3 ounces tri-color heirloom fingerling potatoes

½ tablespoon extra virgin olive oil
salt & pepper

Sauté of Dover Sole A La Meunière, continued

TOSS the potatoes in olive oil, salt and pepper, and roast on a baking sheet in a 350-degree oven for 15 minutes.

For the Beurre Blanc

1 tablespoon shallots, finely chopped	2 tablespoons heavy cream
1½ tablespoons black peppercorns	2 tablespoons fresh thyme
3 tablespoons white wine	½ cup butter, cut into ½ inch cubes
3 tablespoons white wine vinegar	salt & white Pepper

PLACE shallots, black peppercorns, white wine, and vinegar in a small saucepan. Reduce over medium heat until liquid is almost gone. Add heavy cream and fresh thyme and simmer to a boil for 30 seconds. Remove from heat and add butter slowly, whisking constantly. Adjust seasoning and set aside in warm place.

Braised Wagyu Beef Short Rib

with Braised Red Cabbage, Fondue of Bartlett Pear, and Salad of Fall Vegetables Finished with a Red Beet Infused Sauce

The rich, fattiness of the Wagyu (Kobe-style beef) is what makes this dish. If your butcher can locate some, you'll understand why.

Ingredients

- 4 6-ounce Wagyu beef short rib portions
- 2 tablespoons grapeseed oil all-purpose flour
- 1 tablespoon French five spice
- 2 quarts of veal stock
- 2 large red beets, juiced

- Fondue of Bartlett Pear (recipe follows)
- Red Cabbage (recipe follows)
- Fall Vegetable Salad (recipe follows)
- Red Beet Infused Sauce (recipe follows)
- fresh baby arugula or watercress, for garnish

Preparation

PREHEAT oven to 250 degrees. Dust short ribs with all-purpose flour and French Five Spice. In a large braising pan place 2 tablespoons of grapeseed oil. Over medium-high heat, color short ribs to golden brown. Remove excess oil from pan. Cover short ribs with veal stock. Cover braising pan with aluminum foil and place in a 250-degree oven for 6 hours or until tender with a fork. Remove short ribs and keep warm.

COMBINE braising sauce with the juiced red beets and reduce liquid by half, or until nappe. Keep sauce warm for service.

TO SERVE, place a Bartlett pear half on each plate, offset to one side. Add warmed Red Cabbage on top of pear. Add braised short ribs on top of red cabbage. Place dressed Fall Vegetable Salad on opposite end of plate. Place sauce down the middle of plate. Garnish with fresh baby arugula or watercress.

Serves 4

Wine Suggestion: Super Tuscan from Italy

For the Fondue of Bartlett Pear

- 2 Bartlett pears
- 1 quart clarified butter
- 1 quart simple syrup

PEAL and seed Bartlett pears. Cut lengthwise in half. Poach in simple syrup for 10 minutes. Place pears directly into clarified butter and continue to cook for 15 more minutes. Place cooked pears between 2 baking sheets and press for 1 hour.

For the Red Cabbage

2	bacon slices	750	ml good red wine
	olive oil	2	cups honey
1	onion, brunoise (matchstick-size	4	heads medium size cabbage,
	slices)		chiffonade
8	apples, small dice	3	tablespoons red wine vinegar
375	ml Port	2	potatoes, grated

PREHEAT oven to 300 degrees. Render bacon in olive oil. Add onion and sweat; add apples, wait 30 seconds, add Port, red wine, and honey and reduce by half. Add cabbage and cook until wilted then add vinegar. Mix well, and cover. Place in 300-degree oven and cook until nearly dry. Add grated potato and cook until dry.

For the Fall Vegetable Salad

1	parsnip, chopped	1	red beet, chopped
1	green apple, chopped	1	yellow beet, chopped
1	large carrot, chopped		

SEASON with extra virgin olive oil. Roast fall vegetables in low oven until golden brown.

Big Rock Chophouse

245 South Eton Street
Birmingham, MI 48009
248-647-7774
www.bigrockchophouse.com

Lunch
Mon – Fri, 11:00am – 4:00pm
Sat, Noon – 4:00pm
Dinner
Mon – Tues, 4:00pm – 10:00pm
Wed – Thurs, 4:00pm – 11:00pm
Fri – Sat, 4:00pm - Midnight

Big Rock Chophouse

Executive Chef Jeff Rose

Along, long time ago, before Birmingham's old train depot became its chicest restaurant, the Grand Trunk line from Royal Oak west to Bloomfield Hills ran through the center of Birmingham alongside the street that would eventually become Woodward Avenue. By the late 1920s, as automobile traffic increased and Detroit's expansion pushed westward, the State of Michigan asked Grand Trunk to relocate their tracks so they could upgrade the roadway. In exchange the state built them the depot—that would be a restaurant—in 1931, drawing 25,000 people to the inauguration. History lesson aside, all of Metro Detroit knows we are talking about the Big Rock Chophouse.

Regulars flock to Big Rock Chophouse for more reasons than ultra fine food served in an eclectic Montana hunting lodge setting. Beer lovers know about the onsite brewery producing award-winning micro-brew beers. Night clubbers head upstairs to Got Rocks Ultra Lounge, the cosmopolitan martini and cigar bar attracting an "A List" crowd, many of them arriving in Ferraris and Maseratis. Meeting and party planners utilize Big Rock's event facilities for groups up to four hundred people. Oenophiles reserve The Boulder Wine Cellar for exotic wine dinners prepared by Executive Chef Jeff Rose, truly one of Michigan's top young culinary talents. And, The Stone Terrace is hard to beat on a summer afternoon to gather with sun-worshipping friends for a frothing ale.

But food is the foremost reason to visit Big Rock Chophouse and Chef Rose created a menu with just the right balance of a first-rate steakhouse complemented by more exotic fare. Prior to Big Rock, he spent six years under the tutelage of James Beard Foundation award-winner Takashi Yagahashi at Tribute in Farmington Hills, so we know Rose has the needed skills to branch out from classic steak house fare. For example, Tuna Mignon Dusted with Sesame Seeds and Wasabi Green Onion Glaze, or Seared Hudson Valley Foie Gras with Roasted Pear Financier, Muscat and Maple Reduction.

The Chophouse's signature dish is certainly Bone-In Filet Mignon with Sautéed Swiss Chard and White Cheddar Roasted Garlic Mashed Potatoes. Though meat lovers will also be tempted by Three Double Cut Rib Lamb Chops served with Ratatouille and Kalamata Olives and a Zinfandel Sauce.

The lesson here is not to be misled by all the goings-on around you. The Big Rock Chophouse is an ultra fine dining restaurant flaunting a *Wine Spectator* award-winning wine list, with premium cigars waiting upstairs. For those so inclined, it doesn't get any better than that.

Award of Excellence

CAJUN STEAK BITES

The Cajun Spice mix can be left on your spice shelf until it is gone, and then you can make some more. A BIG ROCK CHOPHOUSE secret recipe, it can be used on steaks, chicken, and fish.

Ingredients

6 ounces tenderloin tips, cut into bite-sized pieces

½ teaspoon olive oil

1 teaspoon Cajun Spice Mix (recipe follows)

Preparation

HEAT a small fry pan. Add a few drops of oil, add the beef tips. Season with salt and pepper. Cook to desired temperature, and add about one teaspoon of Cajun Spice and mix evenly. For a spicier dish add more Cajun Spice.

Wine Suggestion: Kenwood Jack London Vineyards Cabernet Sauvignon

For the Spice Mix

4 ounces paprika

1½ ounces onion powder

1 ounce garlic powder

1½ ounces ground cayenne pepper

1 ounce ground white pepper

1 ounce ground black pepper

1 ounce dry thyme

1 ounce dry basil

COMBINE all ingredients.

Yield:1 ½ cups

Seared Salmon with Mushroom Ragoût

Ingredients

    4 *8-ounce salmon filets*
       olive oil
       Mushroom Ragout (recipe follows)

Preparation

PREHEAT oven to 350 degrees. In a medium size pan sear the salmon over high heat with a few drops of olive oil. Flip, drain the oil, and place in 350-degree oven until done, about 7 minutes. Top with Mushroom Ragoût. Serve with rice or potato.

Serves 4

Wine Suggestion: Argyle Reserve Pinot Noir

For the Mushroom Ragoût

1 *tablespoon butter*	4 *green onions, sliced*
1 *jalapeño, chopped*	2 *red peppers, roasted, peeled, diced*
2 *shallots, chopped*	2 *yellow peppers, roasted, peeled, diced*
2 *cloves garlic, chopped*	1 *tablespoon sherry vinegar*
4 *cups shiitake mushrooms, quartered*	3 *tablespoons olive oil*
¼ *cup tomato concassé*	*salt and pepper to taste*

IN A medium sized pan, sweat the jalapeño, garlic, and shallot in the butter. Add the mushrooms and cook until tender. Add the rest of the vegetables and cook lightly. Finish with the vinegar and oil, salt and pepper. Keep warm for service.

BIG ROCK CHILI

This is the only chili around made from fresh tenderloins – it's a lunchtime favorite!

Ingredients

3 pounds ground tenderloin
   salt & pepper
1 large onion diced
1 red pepper diced
1 yellow pepper diced
1 small jalapeño diced
3 tablespoons chili powder

1 tablespoons oregano
1 teaspoon cumin
½ teaspoon cayenne
12 ounces beer
1 cup Bloody Mary mix
2 14.5-ounce cans diced tomatoes
1 can black beans

Preparation

IN A large pot brown off the ground tenderloin. Strain any excess fat. Season with salt and pepper. Add all other ingredients and simmer for about an hour until all vegetables are soft and all flavors are combined.

Serves 6

Beverage Suggestion: Big Rock Chophouse's own Russian Imperial Stout

BEEF SHORT RIBS

This is one of our customer favorites. Typically, this is just a fall/winter dish but it is so popular that we keep it on the menu all year round.

Ingredients

24 ounces 2-bone short ribs	1 cup diced onion
salt & pepper	1 bay leaf
flour, for dusting	2 cups Port wine
vegetable oil	4 cups red wine
½ cup diced carrot	8 cups beef or veal stock
½ cup diced celery	

Preparation

PREHEAT oven to 350 degrees. Season the short ribs with salt and pepper. Dust them in flour. Place in a hot sauté pan with a little vegetable oil and cook until golden brown on all sides. Place them in a deep baking dish. In the same sauté pan add the vegetables and bay leaf. Cook about half way and add to the short ribs. Add Port and reduce by half. Add red wine and reduce by half. Add beef stock and bring to a simmer. Let cook for 5 minutes and add liquid to the short ribs. Cover with foil and place in a 350-degree oven for 5 hours. Ribs should be fork tender when done. Let rest before removing from pot.

Serves 2

Wine Suggestion: Ridge "Paso Robles" Zinfandel

Big Rock Chophouse interior

Cherry Blossom

Cherry Blossom
JAPANESE RESTAURANT

43588 West Oaks Drive
Novi, MI 48377
248-380-9160
www.cherryblossom.biz

Lunch
Monday – Saturday 11:30am – 2:00pm
Dinner
Monday – Thursday 5:30pm – 10:30pm
Friday and Saturday 5:30pm– 11:00pm
Sunday 4:00pm – 10:00pm

Cherry Blossom

Shigeru Yamada, Partner

Undoubtedly, a survey of chefs in the United States would show an overwhelming amount of them to be fanatic lovers of sushi. There's just something about impeccably fresh fish and plain rice served in the traditional style of Japan, with little other than wasabi and ginger and the heady influence of sake, that calls to food professionals like nothing else. Perhaps, it's the wondrous knife skills used by genuine sushi chefs, or the minimalist approach to presentation, or even the foreignness of chop sticks—perpetually offering the novice a chance to inadvertently fling something at a tablemate.

Furthermore, sushi's fabulously healthy; a point not lost on the millions of Americans seeking to control their weight, cholesterol intake, and reliance on processed food. Michiganders, in particular, know their great state ranks depressingly low nationwide in obesity rankings. Adhering to a diet based on the foods of Japan has proven to lessen the incidence of cancer, heart disease, and diabetes in numerous studies.

All of which leads to Cherry Blossom in Novi, the creation of Shigeru Yamada, a veteran manager and owner of several Japanese restaurants in Metro Detroit. Yamada opened Cherry Blossom in 1992 with two partners and a desire to improve cultural relations between the U.S. and Japan. Good things happen around the dinner table, and a great meal, no matter the type or ethnicity, brings people together. Of course, with the opening of Cherry Blossom, he also sought to provide Japanese ex-patriots, and all sushi lovers on the west side of Detroit, with world class Japanese food.

Sushi yes, but there's more to love at Cherry Blossom. The extensive menu is a delight of both familiar Japanese foods—teriyaki, tempura, delicately fried shrimp—and a great many other authentic dishes, fascinating in their creativity and visual beauty. From appetizers of barbecued river eel (Unagi Kabayaki), broiled whole capelin fish including roe (Shishamo), and chilled tofu served with grated ginger, green onion, and bonito flakes (Hiyayako), the offerings track through fresh seafood and vegetables served with vinegar (Sunomono), over grated Japanese Horseradish (Aemono), or with soy and sesame paste (Nuta). Hands-on diners can cook their own beef, duck, chicken, or seafood in the Nabemono style, or choose king crab or sea urchin served with rice and broth in a ceramic pot.

To be sure, sushi and sashimi play the central role at Cherry Blossom. Impeccably fresh servings of tuna, yellowtail, whitefish, salmon, mackerel, octopus, and eel prepared by gifted, first-rate sushi chefs, are offered in a dozen or so combinations, each as beautiful as they are delicious.

A generous list of sake and wine is available. There truly is nothing amiss at this elegant, inviting, friendly restaurant; a perfect choice for novices to Japanese cuisine or seasoned culinary professionals.

ENOKI BACON

Ingredients

2 slices bacon	1 tablespoon vegetable oil
⅛ pound enoki mushrooms	lemon wedges

Preparation

WRAP each strip of bacon around ½ of enoki mushrooms. Heat oil in sauté pan and sauté bacon until cooked. Cut in half and serve with lemon.

Serves 2

Wine Suggestion: Yamadanishiki (semi-dry Sake), or Sauvignon Blanc

---

SHIITAKE HAKATA
(Stuffed Shiitake Mushrooms)

Ingredients

2 shiitake mushrooms	oil for deep-frying
½ cup cornstarch	⅛ pound sliced onion
¼ pound ground chicken	2 tablespoons Ponzu Sauce
¼ teaspoon salt	grated spicy daikon radish
⅛ teaspoon black pepper	chopped green onion
1 teaspoon chopped onion	chili paste, optional
½ egg yolk	

Preparation

DUST mushrooms in cornstarch. Mix ground chicken, pepper, salt, chopped onion, and egg yolk in bowl. Evenly divide the chicken mixture and place in each mushroom. Dust again with cornstarch and deep fry. Scatter sliced onions on serving plate and place mushrooms on top. Add grated daikon radish and chopped green onion to Ponzu sauce to dip. To spice up, you may add chili paste into grated radish.

Wine Suggestion: Otokoyama (dry Sake), or Pinot Grigio

Cherry Blossom

SAKURA ROLL

Sakura means "cherry blossom" in Japanese.

Ingredients

¼ cup chili sauce
¼ cup mayonnaise
1 cup Sushi Rice, cooked, chilled (recipe below)
1 sheet Pink Soy Bean Paper
1 teaspoon sesame seed
1 ounce smelt fish eggs
1 ounce tuna, cut in strips the same length as seaweed

1 ounce yellowtail, cut in strips the same length as seaweed
1 ounce salmon, cut in strips the same length as seaweed
2 thin slices of avocado
   soy sauce

Preparation

MIX chili sauce and mayonnaise in small bowl to make a spicy sauce. Spread Sushi Rice over soy paper at approximately ¼ inch thick then sprinkle sesame seeds over rice. Spread chili sauce and mayonnaise mixture in the middle and place smelt eggs, tuna, yellowtail, salmon, and avocado over sauce. Carefully roll with bamboo roller. Slice into 5 pieces and serve with soy sauce.

Serve as an appetizer or main course with miso soup.

Wine Suggestion: Karatamba (dry Sake), or Hess Select Chardonnay

For the Sushi Rice

2½ cups rice
1 sheet konbu, 4 inches square
2½ cups water

4 tablespoons vinegar
3 tablespoons sugar
2 teaspoons salt

COVER rice with cold water in a large bowl and stir with hand momentarily. Drain off the cloudy water, add more fresh water, and repeat process 5 or 6 times until water is clear. Drain very well.

MAKE several ½-inch cuts along all sides of the konbu. Place water in a bowl, add konbu and soak for approximately 1 hour. Drain, reserving water. In a large saucepan add rice and konbu-infused water, discarding konbu. Cook rice according to instructions on package. Allow to cool. Mix vinegar, sugar, and salt in a small bowl. Add to cooked rice and mix thoroughly.

SUNOMONO COMBINATION
(Sashimi in Vinegar Sauce)

Fresh, sushi-quality seafood is crucially important to this, and all sashimi recipes.

Ingredients

1 piece shrimp	2 ounces cucumber, peeled and sliced thinly
1 slice octopus	
1 slice mackerel	1 teaspoon sesame seed
1 slice surf clam	Vinegar Sauce (recipe follows)
2 ounces seaweed	

Preparation

PUT all ingredients except sesame seeds into deep 12-ounce non-metallic bowl. Pour Vinegar Sauce over seafood and sprinkle with sesame seeds.

Wine Suggestion: Hot Sake Shochikubai (semi-dry Sake)

For the Vinegar Sauce

7 cups water	3 cups rice vinegar
1 cup mirin (sweet rice wine)	3 ounces dried shaved bonito
1 cup light soy sauce	

ADD water, mirin, soy sauce, and vinegar to sauce pan and bring to boil. Add bonito, turn off heat and allow to cool down to room temperature. Strain, preserving liquid. Keep this sauce chilled. Serve as an appetizer or seafood salad. Serve cold.

KAMO NABE

Ingredients

7   cups water
½   sheet seaweed
1   ounce shaved dried bonito
1   cup soy sauce
1   cup mirin (sweet rice wine)
1   pound duck meat in ⅛-inch slices
¼   wedge Chinese nappa, cut in bite-size
    pieces

¼   medium size carrot, cut in bite-size
    pieces
1   bunch green onion, cut in bite-size
    pieces
4   shiitake mushrooms, cut in bite-size
    pieces
1   3.5-ounce package enoki mushrooms
1   7-ounce package wheat or egg noodles

Preparation

BOIL water in deep pot. Add seaweed and bonito for 1 minute. Turn off heat and allow to steep for 30 minutes. Remove seaweed and bonito from pot. Add soy sauce and mirin and bring to boil again.

ADD duck to boiling soup. Allow to cook for several minutes, removing fat as it forms on surface. Add vegetables and cook until just tender. Add noodles and serve.

IF planning this dish as a main course, cook it at the table using a cassette fuel stove. Preheat the broth in your kitchen and, at the table, begin adding duck, carrot, mushrooms, etc., in the order of cooking time needed, ending with the noodles. Refill as you eat and enjoy both eating and cooking at the same time. At the end, if you still have soup with no duck or vegetables left, make a plain noodle soup.

Wine Suggestion: Hot Sake Ozeki (dry Sake), or Ravenswood Cabernet Sauvignon

Five Lakes Grill

424 North Main Street
Milford, MI 48381
248-684-7455
www.fivelakesgrill.com

Monday – Thursday 4:00pm – 10:00pm
Friday and Saturday 4:00pm – 11:00pm

Five Lakes Grill

Chef / owner Brian Polcyn

The adage about teachers being unable to cut it in the real world is sufficiently ludicrous to avoid comment, but it does offer an opportunity to spotlight that rare (perhaps, crazy) breed of chefs who spend days teaching at culinary school and evenings running a restaurant. Each job is exhausting, emotionally and physically, demanding long hours on the feet and plenty of after-hours catch-up work. It's hard to imagine then, how Brian Polcyn, chef / owner of the Five Lakes Grill, and Schoolcraft College Culinary School instructor, also simultaneously managed to co-author the definitive book on charcuterie, raise five kids, and earn his pilot's license. Who is this guy? And, why do *The New York Times*, *Atlantic Monthly*, *Gourmet*, *Bon Appetite*, *Playboy*, *Hour Detroit*, and *Wine Spectator* refer to him as one of the nation's top chefs?

We need only look at Polcyn's work in Metro Detroit's top restaurants, including The Golden Mushroom, The Lark, Pike Street, Chimayo, and Acadia. Or the awards to his credit: three gold medals and a silver medal from The American Culinary Federation, The Hiram Walker Corp. naming him a Rising Star in American Cuisine, his first runner-up finish in the semi-annual American Culinary Gold Cup Bocuse d' Or competition seeking America's top native-born chefs, and the fact that he's cooked several times at the James Beard House in New York. Chef, educator extraordinaire—of this we are certain.

At first menu glance, Five Lakes Grill promises a unique dining experience in the form of numerous preparations of charcuterie, Polcyn's passion and subject matter at Schoolcraft. Count them: salume, duck terrine, smoked pork loin and belly, salted and smoked seafood, garlic sausages—seemingly every menu item is accompanied by some form of this ancient and intricate culinary skill. Roast Saddle of Rabbit comes with spinach and pine nut sausage; even an appetizer of Hand Rolled Potato Gnocchi in Gorgonzola Cream makes room for house-made pancetta.

Yes, there are inviting contemporary fish, fowl, beef, and venison entrées, but how can one avoid Lamb Shank Cassoulet, Brisket of Milk Fed Veal, or The Glorious Pig: A Selection of Roasted Smoked Loin, Pork Confit and Josephine's Kielbasa with Granny Smith Apple and Potato Gratin, Shallot Confit, Root Vegetables, Hard Cider Reduction and Sweet Potato Hay? These are rare treats even in the world's most acclaimed restaurants, and Five Lakes dispenses them with an air of nonchalance.

Once a month, Five Lakes prepares special dinners based on Southern Italy, Southwest France, Spain, Wild Game, to name a few from the 2007 Calendar of Events. Year round, a Five Wines and Five Appetizers promotion is offered on Tuesday evenings for just $20. General Manager Craig Madigan also manages the Five Lakes wine list, and serves as sommelier. The list is hard to beat in terms of breadth and selection of small estate wines.

 Award of Excellence

GRILLED VEGETABLE TERRINE

Go out to the garden and pick the freshest, most ripe items and apply them to this recipe. Whatever you choose, make sure the first layer will encompass the entire terrine; this will help hold it together. Also be sure not to use a mold that is bigger than a quart.

Ingredients

1   eggplant, peeled and sliced ⅛ inch
2   zucchini, sliced ⅛ inch
2   yellow squash, sliced ⅛ inch
½   cup olive oil (for the vegetables) salt & pepper
1   tablespoon fresh garlic, chopped
3   tablespoons water
2   teaspoons granulated gelatin

¼   cup Balsamic vinegar
¾   cup extra virgin olive oil (for the vinaigrette)
1   tablespoon fresh garlic, chopped
3   all night tomatoes
8   ounces goat cheese, room temperature
1   red pepper, roasted, peeled and sliced into 1-inch strips lengthwise

Preparation

PRE-HEAT the grill. Toss the eggplant, zucchini, and yellow squash in the olive oil, and season with salt and pepper. Grill on both sides being careful not to burn. Cook until just soft, remove and set aside to cool.

PREHEAT oven to 350 degrees. Put water in a small bowl, drizzle gelatin over water, allow to bloom (absorb into the water). Set aside. Whip together Balsamic vinegar, extra virgin olive oil and garlic making a vinaigrette, season with salt and pepper. Set aside. Place bloomed gelatin in a 350-degree oven for 5 minutes or until dissolved, pour into vinegar and oil mixture, set aside but keep warm.

LINE a 1-quart terrine mold with plastic wrap, lay the eggplant slices widthwise into the mold allowing ends to overhang. Brush the interior with vinaigrette. Continue the same process with the zucchini and yellow squash. Lay the all night tomatoes down the center connecting them end-to-end. Spread the softened goat cheese down the center, place the roasted pepper on tip of the goat cheese, and drizzle with vinaigrette. Fold the eggplant and squash flaps over the top and brush with remaining vinaigrette. Cover with remaining plastic wrap and refrigerate over night. When completely cold, remove from the mold, remove plastic and slice ¼-inch thick. Serve with a simple salad or just by itself.

Serves 8

Wine Suggestion: Husch Sauvignon Blanc, Mendocino

CHERRYWOOD SMOKED TROUT

with Heirloom Tomatoes, Organic Micro Greens and 35-Year-Old Balsamic Vinegar

The trout we use at the restaurant comes from a small farm just south of Traverse City. I like to smoke it with cherrywood, which is abundant in that part of Michigan. The organic micro herbs are grown by the Werp family farms in nearby Leelanau County; making this a real community dish.

Ingredients

12 fresh whole boneless rainbow trout
    about 8 ounces each
    Smoked Trout Brine (recipe follows)
 3 large heirloom tomatoes
¼ cup extra virgin olive oil

¼ cup fresh basil leaves, sliced
    salt & pepper
24 ounces organic micro greens
    olive oil
    35-year-old balsamic vinegar

Preparation

PLACE trout in a non-reactive container and pour Smoked Trout Brine over. Insure that the fish stay submerged by using a plate or rack. Brine under refrigeration for 8 hours. Remove fish from brine and rinse well under cold water. Pat dry with paper towels, place on a rack for 3 hours.

PREHEAT smoker to 200 degrees. Hot smoke over cherry or other wood for 2 hours or until internal temperature reaches 145 degrees. Remove and allow to cool overnight.

CUT the tomatoes to a suitable size. Toss with olive oil, salt, pepper, and basil. Place a little on each plate. Toss organic greens with a little olive oil, salt, and pepper and place on plates. Remove skin from trout and place a nice-sized piece on top of greens, drizzle with balsamic.

Serves 12

Wine Suggestion: Brys Estate Riesling, Old Mission Peninsula

For the Smoked Trout Brine

 1 gallon water
18 ounces kosher salt
 2 ounces brown sugar
 2 tablespoons pickling spice

 2 ounces honey
 2 cloves fresh garlic
 1 cup onion, sliced thin

MAKE the brine by combining all ingredients, being sure to dissolve salt and sugar.

GRILLED YELLOW FIN TUNA
with Tomato Beurre Blanc and Saffron Aioli

This dish has a Mediterranean influence and is great to eat outside, right off the grill. Be careful not to overcook the tuna.

Ingredients

6 *7-ounce portions center cut tuna*
   salt & pepper

Buerre Blanc Sauce (recipe follows)
Saffron Aioli (recipe follows)

Preparation

PREHEAT the grill. Season the tuna with salt and pepper. Grill over high heat about 2 to 3 minutes per side depending on the thickness. Tuna should be served medium rare. Sauce the plates with Tomato Beurre Blanc, place the fish on top and finish with Saffron Aioli.

Serves 6

Wine Suggestion: Wyncroft "Avonlea Vineyard" Chardonnay, Lake Michigan Shore

For the Tomato Buerre Blanc

2 *ounces shallots, chopped*
¼ *cup dry white wine*
¼ *cup white wine vinegar*

2 *tablespoons tomato paste*
2 *tablespoons heavy cream*
8 *ounces unsalted butter, softened*

COMBINE shallots, wine, vinegar, and tomato paste in a non-reactive skillet. Simmer over high heat until reduced to almost a paste. Add cream to combine. Beat in the softened butter at a gentle simmer. Strain the sauce through a fine mesh strainer. Set aside in a warm spot until service.

For the Saffron Aioli

3 *medium sized garlic cloves*
1 *pinch coarse salt*
2 *egg yolks*
6 *strands saffron*

1 *cup extra virgin olive oil*
1 *tablespoon lemon juice*
   salt & pepper

WITH the side of a French knife mash garlic cloves with a pinch of salt, forming a paste. Place garlic mixture in a bowl, add saffron and egg yolks and, with a wooden spoon, work the mixture into a paste. Slowly add olive oil while stirring. When half the oil is in, add the lemon juice. Add remaining oil and stir until thick.

Chocolate Pâté with Praline and Raspberries

Pâté usually is used in charcuterie terminology; that's why I like to use it when referring to desserts. Change things up a bit. The principle is the same but ingredients are different.

Ingredients

1⅓ cups water
½ cup sugar
12 ounces soft butter
2 cups cocoa powder
12 ounces bittersweet chocolate, melted
1 orange, zested

2 tablespoons Grand Marnier
2 whole eggs
4 egg yolks
Praline Powder (recipe follows)
raspberries

Preparation

COMBINE the water and sugar in a saucepan, stirring to dissolve. Heat to just the boiling point then cool. Cream the butter and cocoa in a food processor, scraping down the sides often. Slowly add the sugar water. Add the melted chocolate, scrape the sides down, add zest, Grand Marnier, then eggs and yolks, scraping the sides down often. Fold in Praline Powder. Line a 1¼-quart terrine mold with plastic food wrap. Fill the mold with the chocolate mixture, cover and refrigerate overnight. Slice and serve with raspberries.

Serves 8

Wine Suggestion: Jackson-Triggs Ice Wine, Niagara, Canada

For the Praline Powder

½ cup sugar
2 tablespoons water
¾ cup sliced almonds

PLACE the sugar in a heavy-bottomed saucepan with water, stirring until dissolved. Over medium heat cook the sugar until it is smooth and lightly brown. Stirring continuously, add the almonds and cook another minute. Pour out onto an oiled marble slab or Silpat, allow to cool. Pulverize in a food processor to a fine powder.

Restaurant Villegas

villegas

1735 Grand River Avenue
Okemos, MI 48864
517-347-2080
www.restaurantvillegas.com

Monday – Thursday 5:00pm – 10:00pm
Friday – Saturday 5:00pm – 11:00pm

Restaurant Villegas

Chef / owner Eric Villegas

The meteoric rise of television cooking shows has been nothing less than shocking to TV producers, advertisers, and just about everyone else, but no one more than the chefs who cook on the shows and soon find themselves hounded for autographs. The celebrity factor has served to attract both very qualified restaurant chefs, as well as some telegenic, media savvy personalities seeking personal stardom without first-rate cooking skills. (If you watch them handle a whisk or knife closely, you can spot the difference.) The point being, not everyone cooking on television is a world-class chef.

Eric Villegas, chef / owner of Restaurant Villegas in Okemos—and star of the nationally broadcast PBS show Fork In The Road with eric Villegas—is the genuine article. Yes, he is a gifted talker and personable to the point of flamboyant, but cooking is his primary calling. And, loyalty to produce and foodstuffs of his beloved state of Michigan is an obsession.

Restaurant Villegas looks the part of a contemporary, big-city restaurant. The dining room is stylish and understated yet offers glimpses of kitchen activity, including the wood-fired oven dispensing with caramelized onion and Michigan grown Anjou pear pizzas. But there's playfulness to Villegas, as well. What comparably acclaimed restaurant would offer potato frites, potato chips, and fried popcorn shrimp alongside Foie Gras (on steamed brown bread with dried cherries and local maple syrup) on the appetizer menu? Of course, those fries are served with black and white truffle aioli, the chips are hand cut and accompanied by hickory smoked tomato ketchup, and the elegant cocktail sauce served with the shrimp uses more of those smoked tomatoes.

Entrées on a recent winter menu also made good use of the restaurant's smoker, including 18-Hour Hickory Smoked Beef Brisket (with garlic mashed Yukon Gold potatoes, broccolini, finished with horseradish cream), and 14-Hour Hickory Smoked Pork Shoulder (with wood roasted vegetables and jalapeno cream). Another highlight: Atlantic Cod Poached in Olive Oil with Garlic Confit and Thyme, Served on a Stew of Roasted Bell Peppers. Every dish on the menu possesses a certain swagger of bold and satisfying flavors. Even the dessert menu where Spice Cake is accompanied by oranges, dates, and handcrafted cinnamon ice cream.

Restaurant Villegas features a hip bar just a few steps in the door serving a wide range of martinis, interesting beers, local hard cider, and distinctive wines-by-the-glass from a *Wine Spectator*-awarded wine list.

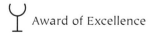 Award of Excellence

MICHIGAN WILD RAMP QUICHE
with Raw Milk Cheddar & Roasted Garlic

Because the baking time of quiche is so short, raw vegetables would never have time to cook properly so I have always found it far better to cook the vegetables ahead of time, bringing them to their peak flavor and texture potential. This makes a far tastier quiche without the watery pitfalls.

Ingredients

4   cups whole ramps, cleaned and
    chopped
3   tablespoons extra virgin olive oil
    sea salt
    freshly ground black pepper

Pâté Brisée, (recipe follows)
½   cup raw milk cheddar, freshly grated
    Quiche Custard (recipe follows)
2   tablespoons Parmesan cheese, freshly
    grated

Preparation

PREHEAT the oven to 350 degrees. In a preheated sauté pan large enough to hold the ramps add 1 tablespoon olive oil followed by the ramps. Sauté the ramps over medium heat, seasoning with the salt and pepper for 10-15 minutes until the ramps have nicely browned caramelized edges and are tender. Remove from pan and let cool.

SPREAD the grated cheddar cheese evenly over the bottom of the prepared Pâté Brisée and follow with the cooled ramps. Pour the Quiche Custard into the quiche shell to within ¼ inch of the top of the crust and scatter the Parmesan over the top. Place the quiche in the middle-center of the preheated oven and bake 25 - 30 minutes, or until custard puffs. Allow to cool 10 minutes before serving. Serve warm or room temperature.

Serving 8

Wine Suggestion: Bel Lago Chardonnay

For the Pâté Brisée

3   cups all purpose flour
1   cup unsalted sweet butter

½   teaspoon sea salt
¾   cups ice water

IN A large bowl, combine the flour with butter, salt, and ½ the water. Mix lightly with your fingertips until pastry forms in pea-sized pieces. You should be able to see chunks of butter, and the pastry should be moist enough to begin to stick together. If the pastry is too dry, add the necessary remaining water. Turn the pastry out onto a lightly floured work surface, dust with flour, and knead until the pastry is smooth, about 3 to 4 times. Transfer to a plastic bag and form pastry into a disk. Refrigerate a minimum of 30 minutes, or as long as 3 days.

For the Quiche Custard

- 4 eggs
- 1 cup heavy whipping cream
- ¼ cup Roasted Garlic Purée (recipe follows)

Clancy's fancy hot sauce
sea salt

MIX the eggs, cream, and garlic together with a whisk until smooth. Season to taste with the salt and hot sauce.
NOTE: Makes approximately 1 pint of custard good for 1 8-inch round quiche crust.

For the Roasted Garlic Purée

- 1 pound garlic, fresh, whole heads (see note)
- ½ cup extra virgin olive oil

sea salt
freshly ground pepper
mixed herbs, optional

PREHEAT the oven to 375 degrees. Peel the outermost layers of skin off the heads of garlic leaving an intact whole head free of any scrap. Cut off the top one-third of the heads to open the cloves. Save the small pieces of garlic for another use. Put the heads, cut sides up, in a small baking dish and pour olive oil over them. Season with salt, pepper, and the herbs, if desired. Cover tightly with foil or lid and place in the oven. Roast until about three-fourths cooked, about 45 minutes. Uncover and return to the oven until the cloves begin to pop out of their skins and brown, about 15 minutes. Let cool. When cool enough to handle easily, squeeze the roasted garlic into a small bowl. Press against the skins very well to get out all the sweet roasted garlic you can. Add the oil from the baking dish and mix well until a paste forms.
GARLIC NOTE:
When choosing garlic, look for well-formed heads with cloves that have grown tightly together. Avoid sprouted garlic or heads that have dark bruises or soft spots; these must be removed or they will affect the taste of the entire head. Although I prefer hard neck garlic (where the center of the garlic heads contain the hard garlic stalk) it's generally not seen in commercial groceries because of the short shelf life. For my taste the hard neck varieties have a wider variety and wealth of flavor compared to their soft necked cousins but this recipe works with both varieties. If you're interested in hard-necked varieties of garlic your best bet would be to frequent your local farmers markets and request them.

Baked Michigan Navy Beans
with Smoked Bacon, Chiles, and Cocoa

Ingredients

1	pound navy beans, picked over, rinsed and soaked overnight in cold water
6	cups cold water
½	cup boiling water
1	large pasilla chile, whole
¼	cup lard
2	large red onions, diced
1	pound smoked bacon, chopped
¼	teaspoon chipotle chile, ground
¾	cup maple sugar, preferably from Michigan
½	cup Roasted Garlic Purée, (see recipe under Quiche in this section)

¼	teaspoon nutmeg, ground
¼	teaspoon cloves, ground
¼	teaspoon cumin, ground
¼	teaspoon sweet paprika, ground
⅓	cup tomato paste
1¼	cups stout beer, preferably from Michigan
3	cups chicken broth, or similar to finish the beans
2	ounces cocoa powder, unsweetened
1½	teaspoons sea salt, or to taste
½	teaspoon black pepper, or to taste

Preparation

PREHEAT oven to 350 degrees. Drain and rinse the beans. In a large saucepan, cover the beans with the cold water and bring to a boil. Reduce heat to low, cover and simmer until tender, anywhere from 30 minutes to 1 hour. You want the beans tender but not falling apart.

Meanwhile, soak the pasilla in the ½ cup of the boiling water until softened, about 20 minutes. Drain the pasilla. Discard the stem, seeds, and water. Mince the chile.

HEAT lard in a large heavy-bottomed casserole or bean pot. Add onions and cook over moderate heat until softened, about 2 - 3 minutes. Add bacon and cook until softened, 2 to 3 minutes longer. Stir in the minced pasilla, chipotle powder, maple sugar, Roasted Garlic Purée, nutmeg, cloves, cumin, paprika, and tomato paste into the bacon and toast the ingredients a bit to intensify the flavors for another 2 to 3 minutes. Top off with the beer and the broth.

DRAIN the navy beans and add them to the casserole, stir to blend. Cover and place the casserole in the preheated oven until the sauce has thickened, about 1 hour. If you like your beans thicker remove the cover after 30 minutes.

Taste the beans and adjust seasonings. Stir in the cocoa powder, season with salt and pepper and serve.

Serves 12

Wine Suggestion: Peninsula Cellars Cabernet / Merlot

GREAT LAKES WHITEFISH MEATBALLS
Tossed with Eden Organic Spaghetti in a Simple Tomato Sauce with Lemon & Dill

Ingredients

1 pound freshwater whitefish fillets, all
skin and sinews removed
3 tablespoons fresh breadcrumbs
1 whole egg, lightly beaten
½ cup Wisantigo Parmesan, finely grated
2 tablespoons lemon zest, fresh
2 tablespoons fresh dill, chopped
2 tablespoons Roasted Garlic Purée (see
recipe under Quiche in this section)
1 teaspoon Clancy's fancy hot sauce, or
similar

sea salt
freshly ground lack pepper
all-purpose flour, for coating
soy bean oil, preferably from Michigan
Simple Tomato Sauce & Pasta (recipe
follows)
dill fronds, for garnish, optional
extra virgin olive oil

Preparation

CUT the freshwater whitefish fillets into chunks and pass through a meat grinder with a medium die. In a medium-sized bowl, combine the ground whitefish with the fresh breadcrumbs, egg, cheese, lemon zest, dill and Roasted Garlic Purée. Combine until the mixture forms a thick homogenous paste. Lightly season with salt, pepper and hot sauce.

USING a 2-ounce scoop, form the whitefish mixture, rolling between your palms to form round-shaped "meatballs." You should have approximately one dozen. Fill a deep heavy pan no more than halfway with the soybean oil. Heat the oil over medium-high heat until it reaches 350 degrees.

ROLL each whitefish ball into the all-purpose flour to coat, shaking off any excess. Using a slotted spoon, carefully lower the whitefish meatballs into the hot oil and cook until they are a light golden brown and cooked through, about 4 - 5 minutes. Remove with the same slotted spoon and leave to drain on a serving platter lined with paper towels. Season with salt and pepper while hot. Repeat until all the whitefish mixture has been used. Keep warm in a low oven while preparing the sauce and the pasta.

TO SERVE, mound the Simple Tomato Sauce & Pasta on a large serving platter or individual serving plates and top with the whitefish meatballs.

Garnish with the optional fresh dill fronds and some more drizzles of extra-virgin olive oil.

Serves 4

Wine Suggestion: Chateau Chantal Pinot Grigio

For the Simple Tomato Sauce & Pasta

3 tablespoons olive oil
1 28-ounce can tomatoes, whole &
   peeled, then chopped by hand
1 tablespoon Roasted Garlic Purée (see
   recipe under Quiche in this section)
1 teaspoon Clancy's fancy hot sauce, or
   similar
   sea salt
   freshly ground black pepper

drizzle extra virgin olive oil
½ bunch fresh parsley, finely chopped
2 tablespoons lemon juice, freshly
   squeezed
4 portions EDEN organic spaghetti,
   freshly cooked, al dente
¼ cup reserved pasta cooking water,
   optional

IN A medium saucepan, heat 3 tablespoons olive oil over medium heat. Add the tomatoes, the Roasted Garlic Purée, and the hot sauce. Season to taste with the sea salt and pepper. Add a drizzle of extra-virgin olive oil and cook tomatoes for about 8 to 10 minutes. Sprinkle in the chopped parsley and lemon juice and quickly blend. Taste and adjust seasonings if necessary.

Add the cooked spaghetti to the sauce and mix well. If the mixture seems a bit dry carefully add some of the pasta cooking water to create more of a sauce-like consistency.

My Paella of Aspen Hills Rabbit and Michigan White Shrimp

Ingredients

2 cups extra virgin olive oil, or as needed
1 whole red bell pepper, cut in strips
2 cups Michigan white shrimp, peeled & de-veined
1 whole naturally-raised Aspen Hills rabbit, or similar, cut into pieces
½ teaspoon sweet paprika
½–1 tablespoon rosemary, chopped, with additional sprigs as garnish
   sea salt
   freshly ground black pepper

1 teaspoon pure La Mancha saffron
½ pound green beans, cut into 1-inch pieces
½ pound broad beans, cut into 1-inch pieces
1 whole tomato, peeled, seeded and chopped
4½ cups broth, or water, divided
1¼ pounds short grain rice
   lemon wedges and rosemary sprigs, for garnish

Preparation

HEAT ¼ to ½ cup of the oil in a pan. Add the strips of pepper and fry until they start to soften. Add and sauté the shrimp over medium heat until rare, remove and reserve. Add rabbit and cook over medium heat until golden brown, adding more oil, as necessary. Add paprika, chopped rosemary, saffron, salt and freshly ground pepper.

PUSH the meat out to the edges of the pan and add the beans and tomatoes in the center, mixing them well. Add half the water or broth, making sure to cover the pan until it is half full. Simmer for approximately 30 minutes until most of the water has evaporated.

ADD the rice, distributing it evenly over the pan and fry for a few minutes, moving it around in the pan. Add the rest of the water/broth and cook for about 15 minutes.

TOP the paella with the prepared shrimp and gently stir into the rice. Season to taste with more of the salt and freshly ground pepper and cook for another 5 minutes or until the rice is tender and the rabbit is cooked through. Cover the pan and let it rest for 5 minutes before serving. Garnish with sprigs of rosemary and lemon wedges.

Serves 6

Wine Suggestion: Zafarana Vineyards Semi-Dry Riesling

The Farm

The Farm Restaurant

699 Port Crescent Road
Port Austin, MI 48467
989-874-5700
www.thefarmrestaurant.com

Open Seasonally
Open Mother's Day
Full Time after Memorial Day
Tuesday – Saturday 5:00pm – 10:00pm
Sunday Brunch 8:30am – 1:00pm
Sunday Dinner 4:00pm – 9:00pm

The Farm

Chef / owner Jeffrey Gabriel

Chefs around the world are frequently asked what spark or event is responsible for their lifelong love of cooking. Was it a mother? Grandmother? The pastry display at a local bakery? The answers are so varied and unique as to remain unhelpful but, oh what a wonderful thing it would we be if we were able to recreate the experience for all children. Just imagine a world where the stove was the most popular appliance and not the television. Think of the ramifications for small farmers if pre-teen culinarians sought to learn how herbs or zucchini are grown, and how chickens or lambs are raised.

Certified Master Chef Jeffrey Gabriel, Schoolcraft College culinary instructor and chef / owner of The Farm Restaurant in Port Austin, writes about his moment of truth, "When I learned I could take chicken bones, vegetables, herbs, and water and create a broth that was clean, aromatic, flavorful, nutritional, and full bodied, I was addicted to the field of cookery." We see that it was the alchemy of cooking that drew him in. The moment when various unrelated ingredients magically become something else in a pan. Based on his twenty-year tenure at Schoolcraft, we can assume that he is skillfully preparing his students to be culinary mystics, as well.

A further scan of Gabriel's lengthy list of degrees and accomplishments reveals that he possesses a Certified Master Gardner diploma from Michigan State University. All of which is fine and good until one realizes The Farm Restaurant is a seasonal restaurant, wholly dependent on the herbs and produce grown on premise. Now we're getting somewhere.

If the distance between farm and table is only a matter of feet with the skilled hands of a Master Chef in between, soups like Spring Asparagus and Tomato Tarragon (from a recent menu) promise to be otherworldly. Gabriel's entrée selections include regional fare, leading with Pan Seared Great Lakes Whitefish with an Array of Cous Cous, Rock Shrimp, Cabbage, Fresh Tomatoes Served with Potato Chive Sauce; followed by House Smoked BBQ Chicken Breast Supreme Presented with Warm German Potato Salad and Spring Vegetables; and Mediterranean Mixed Grill with Lamb Chops, Marinated Chicken, and Andouille Sausage Presented with Grilled Vegetables and Basmati Rice Pilaf. The other dishes are similarly distinct and inviting.

This is a restaurant to remember and seek out when summer's bounty is reaching perfect ripeness. Wine and full beverage service is certainly available at all times. Off season, chef gabriel takes in both experienced and novice cooks for hands-on cooking classes leading to elaborate dinners at the end of the day.

ROASTED ARTICHOKE
with Brie and Grainy Mustard Beurre Blanc

Ingredients

4 fresh artichokes, trimmed
4 slices lemon
   water, with salt and lemon juice as
   needed
6 ounces Brie cheese

butter, melted as needed
salt & pepper
Grainy Mustard Beurre Blanc (recipe
follows)

Preparation

PREHEAT oven to 350 degrees. Cut the bottom of the artichokes and remove the choke in the center. Tie a slice of lemon on the cut surface of the artichoke. Simmer the artichokes in the seasoned water until they are tender, approximately 20 minutes. Shock the artichokes in ice water. Place the artichokes on a cookie sheet and stud them with small pieces of the Brie cheese. Brush them with butter and sprinkle with seasoning. Place them in a 350-degree oven for about 10 minutes, or until the cheese melts. Pour the Grainy Mustard Beurre Blanc in the center of the artichoke, and advise guests to pull the leaves and dip them in the sauce with the melted cheese.

Serves 4

For the Grainy Mustard Beurre Blanc Sauce

1 ounce shallots, minced
2 ounces white wine
½ ounce lemon juice
½ ounce cider vinegar

½ cup heavy cream
6 ounces butter, cubed and soft
   salt & white pepper
2 teaspoons grainy mustard

COMBINE shallots, wine, lemon juice, and vinegar in a saucepan and reduce. Add heavy cream and reduce slightly. Gradually whisk in the butter, strain. Add mustard and adjust the seasoning to taste with salt and white pepper.

VEGETABLE STRUDEL
with Spinach and Boursin Cheese

Ingredients

3 tablespoons olive oil
1 cup green onions, small dice
3 cloves garlic, minced
1 cup red peppers, small dice
1 cup carrots, small dice
1 cup celery, small dice
2 cups mushrooms, sliced
2 quarts fresh spinach, chopped
4 cups couscous, steeped
2 tablespoons fresh dill, chopped fine

½ cup Boursin cheese
1 cup Feta cheese
½ cup Parmesan cheese, shredded
salt & pepper
phyllo pastry as needed
clarified butter as needed
1 teaspoon total, mixture of sesame, poppy, and fennel seeds
Vegetable Demi-glaze (recipe follows)

Preparation

HEAT olive oil and sauté the onions, garlic, peppers, carrots, and celery until tender. Add the mushrooms and spinach, cook until almost dry, and remove from heat. Blend in the couscous, dill, and cheeses. Adjust the seasoning and cool in the refrigerator.

PREHEAT oven to 400 degrees. Place one sheet of phyllo dough on the table and brush it with butter and fold in half. Place 1½ cups of the cooled filling on the pastry and roll as a strudel. Brush top with butter, sprinkle top with seeds, and bake for 20 minutes or until golden brown. Serve with Vegetable Demi-glaze and vegetable garnish.

Serves 6

For the Vegetable Demi-glaze

1 tablespoon olive oil
½ cup carrots, small dice
½ cup celery, peeled small dice
1 cup leeks, medium dice
½ cup onions, small dice
2 cloves garlic, minced
2 tablespoons tomato paste

½ cup red wine
1 sprig thyme
1 bay leaf
1½ quarts strong vegetable stock
arrowroot slurry, as needed
salt & cayenne pepper, as needed

HEAT olive oil and sauté carrots, celery, leeks, and onions until the carrots begin to caramelize. Add the garlic and the tomato paste. Add red wine, thyme, and bay leaf. Bring to a simmer and reduce by half. Add the vegetable stock and simmer 5-10 minutes. Thicken slightly with the arrowroot slurry and remove the bay leaf and thyme sprig. Straining is optional. Adjust the seasoning.

LAKE MICHIGAN SALMON EN CROUTE
with Beurre Blanc

Ingredients

1½ pounds salmon fillet
1 cup white wine
1½ teaspoons lemon juice
¾ teaspoon chervil, chopped
1 teaspoon dill, chopped
1 pound raw shrimp
8 ounces salmon trimmings
3 eggs
2 cups heavy cream

dill, minced, to taste
6 phyllo sheets
clarified butter, as needed
breadcrumbs as needed
crepes, prepared as needed
butter, melted, as needed
Beurre Blanc Sauce (recipe follows)
3 tablespoons American caviar

Preparation

COMBINE white wine, lemon juice, chervil, and dill in a bowl. Add salmon fillet and marinate to 6-8 hours in the refrigerator. Combine raw shrimp, salmon trimmings, and eggs in the food processor and grind. Add heavy cream and dill. Purée until smooth and reserve.

PREHEAT oven to 400 degrees. Brush one sheet of phyllo dough lightly with clarified butter. Sprinkle with breadcrumbs. Repeat 6 times, placing each sheet of phyllo atop the last. Cover top layer of phyllo with the prepared crepes. Spread with ¼-inch layer of reserved puréed shrimp/salmon mixture. Place reserved marinated salmon filet on top. Roll to enclose fillet. Brush with butter. Place on parchment-lined sheet tray. Bake at 400 degrees for approximately 20 minutes.

JUST before serving add American caviar to the Beurre Blanc Sauce and serve with the salmon roulade slices.

Serves 4

For the Beurre Blanc Sauce

4 ounces white wine
1 ounce cider vinegar
1 ounce lemon juice
2 ounces shallots, minced

1 cup heavy cream, reduced by ⅓
12 ounces butter
salt & pepper

COMBINE white wine, cider vinegar, lemon juice, and shallots in a saucepan. Heat to boiling and reduce until almost dry. Add the reduced cream. Over low heat, slowly whisk in the butter. Adjust seasoning with salt and pepper and keep warm for service.

Pan Seared Whitefish

with an Array of Israeli Couscous, Rock Shrimp, Cabbage, Snow Peas, and White Wine Potato Sauce

Ingredients

4 whitefish fillets, skin on
   seasoning, as needed
   dusting flour, as needed

clarified butter and oil mix, as needed
Array (recipe follows)

Preparation

PREHEAT oven to 400 degrees. Season the fish fillets and dust with flour. Heat a large sauté pan with some clarified butter and oil. Brown the fish fillets on the flesh side only. Remove the fillets and place on a sheet tray in the oven, skin side down, so the skin will stick to the tray. Roast in the oven for about 6 to 8 minutes.

TO SERVE, remove the skin from the whitefish by peeling it off. Arrange the array on a serving plate and place the whole fillet on top.

Serves 4

For the Array

2 cups Napa cabbage, cut chiffonade
1 cup snow peas
¾ cup tomato concassé
   olive oil
⅓ cup white wine
1 cup chicken stock

1 cup Israeli couscous, precooked
2 cups rock shrimp, raw
¾ cup mashed potatoes
½ cup chives, sliced
   salt & pepper

TAKE a clean sauté pan and sauté the cabbage, snow peas, and tomato concassé for 2 minutes in a small amount of olive oil. Then add the wine, stock, couscous, shrimp, mashed potatoes, and chives. Season with salt and pepper. Cover and let steam until the shrimp are cooked, approximately 3 minutes.

FIERY GRILLED BEEF SALAD

Ingredients

1 pound beef steak (marinated in soy
   sauce and oil for 2 hours)
2-3 stalks lemongrass hearts, minced
1 small red onion, finely sliced
½ pound pickling cucumbers, peeled and
   finely sliced

1 tomato, cut in half and finely sliced
½ cup fresh mint, loosely packed
   Salad Dressing (recipe follows)
   lettuce, as needed to line platter

Preparation

GRILL the marinated steak on both sides until medium-rare. Let rest for 5 minutes. Slice
the steak across the grain very thin. Transfer the meat with its juices into a mixing bowl and
toss with the remaining salad ingredients, except the lettuce. Add the dressing and toss well.
Arrange the lettuce on a serving platter and top with salad.

Serves 4

For the Salad Dressing

¼ cup cilantro, chopped
2 tablespoons serrano chilies, chopped
   (approximately 4 chilies)
3 cloves garlic, chopped
2 tablespoons palm sugar or granulated
   sugar

1½ tablespoons fish sauce
    salt & white pepper as needed
½ cup fresh lemon juice

COMBINE all of the ingredients for the dressing in a blender and blend well.

Main Street, Ann Arbor, 1870.

eve

Kingsley & Fourth Avenue
Ann Arbor, MI 48104
734-222-0711
www.evetherestaurant.com

Tuesday – Thursday 5:30pm – 10:00pm
Friday & Saturday 5:30pm – 11:00pm
Sunday 5:00pm – 9:00pm
Wine bar open later
Closed Monday

eve

Chef / Owner Eve Aronoff

In the main, professional chefs fall into two camps: minimalists who cook with the shortest list of ingredients seeking to highlight just a few key flavors, and others with an alchemist's attitude—a little of this, pinch of that—intent on deeper, more complex tastes. When taken to the highest level, each approach can be equally appetizing, and difficult, but those chefs who choose the latter route often do so for unexpected reasons. Ann Arbor's Eve Aronoff, chef and owner of eve: The Restaurant, calls upon the ingredients she uses in her restaurant to "not only transform the taste of a dish, but bring up memories and images of places you've dreamed about going to, dreams, and romantic ideals." She is a food artisan using texture and contrast to express nuance in flavor, mouth feel, and eye appeal.

The descriptions in eve's menu are beautifully written and fun. One does feel taken on a world tour of her favorite places. An appetizer named Inspired Nachos features fried wontons covered with black beans, three cheeses including goat Gouda, and cilantro-lime salsa. Stir Fried Smoked Duck is served with paper-thin slices of duck breast sautéed with apples, pears, and sweet potatoes over bibb lettuce and sweet fig / walnut vinaigrette. Or, Slow Roasted Berkshire Pork Shank arrives dusted with Moroccan spices over lentil broth finished with crème fraîche and fresh mint.

A look behind the curtain reveals a Paris Le Cordon Bleu background with degrees in French Cuisine and Wines and Spirits. Eve also has a Bachelor of Arts degree in Comparative Literature from Brandeis University. She understands words with the same skill as food, so it's no surprise to discover she authored an acclaimed cookbook in 2006 simply titled *eve: Contemporary Cuisine – Methode Traditionnelle.*

The restaurant interior has brick walls and arches with wooden chairs and floors and globes of electric light dropping randomly from the high ceiling. Four bar stools face a stainless bar just inside the front door. Tables are covered smartly in white tablecloth. Wine lovers can choose from over forty wines served by the glass and a carefully selected list of ultra food-friendly wines with a wide range of both old and new world. eve maintains an "excursion" list of bottles under $30 offering great values. The by-the-glass list is "designed to give people an opportunity to learn about wine or just to taste and enjoy wines that might be too esoteric or extravagant to order by the bottle." Incidentally, Eve is currently studying for the wine world's highest professional achievement, a Master of Wine designation.

The restaurant is located just a couple blocks north of Ann Arbor's vibrant downtown in the historic Kerrytown district, home to the Ann Arbor Farmer's Market, long considered one of Michigan's best.

MOROCCAN SCALLOPS
with Carrot Lime Purée and Crème Fraîche

Ingredients

8 large, fresh sea scallops, preferably dry scallops that have not been frozen, soaked, or injected with saline
2 tablespoons extra virgin olive oil
   kosher salt
   freshly ground black pepper
   Moroccan Spice (recipe follows)

   Moroccan Seasoned Flour (recipe follows)
   extra virgin olive oil
1½ cups Carrot Lime Purée (recipe follows)
1 cup Crème Fraîche (recipe follows)

Preparation

SEASON scallops evenly and generously in the following order: with kosher salt, lightly with freshly ground black pepper, and moderately with Moroccan Spice. Dredge in Moroccan Spice Flour, shake off excess and set aside.

HEAT oil in large non-stick sauté pan and sear the scallops over high heat, making sure that they have enough space and are not crowded, as this will cause the scallops to steam instead of being able to sear properly. Move once to ensure that scallops don't stick to pan. Lower heat to medium-high and continue cooking for about 2 minutes – turn the scallops and repeat process. Because the scallops are cooked so quickly, the extra virgin olive oil, which has a low smoke point, will actually help develop a deeper, richer color without burning.

SPOON 2 concentric circles first of Carrot Lime Purée and second Crème Fraîche in center of each plate and then place scallops overlapping sauce.

Serves 4

Wine Suggestion: Zind Humbrecht Gewürztraminer Wintzenheim

For the Moroccan Spice

2 tablespoons plus 2 teaspoons ground cumin
2 tablespoons plus 2 teaspoons ground ginger
¼ cup ground coriander
1 tablespoon plus 1 teaspoon freshly ground pepper
1 tablespoon cayenne

1 teaspoon urfat isot (Turkish pepper)
1 teaspoon ground cloves
¾ cup plus 2 tablespoons ground allspice
2 tablespoons plus 2 teaspoons ground cinnamon
   kosher salt

COMBINE well and store in an airtight container in a cool, dry place.

Yield: about ¾ of a cup

For the Moroccan Seasoned Flour

1 cup Moroccan Spice (recipe above)	6 teaspoons kosher salt
1 cup flour	½ teaspoon urfat isot (Turkish pepper)

COMBINE well and store in an airtight container in a cool dark place.

Yield: about 2 ¼ cups

Carrot Lime Purée

Many cultures and cuisines make a variation of this sauce, but this recipe is adapted from Steve Raichlen's *Miami Spice Cookbook*. It is extremely flavorful and versatile and seems like it goes with just about anything.

1 green bell pepper, roughly chopped	10–12 cloves garlic
1 cup onions, roughly chopped	1–2 teaspoons sugar
¾ cup fresh lime juice	⅛–¼ cup water
½ cup light olive oil	kosher salt
1 pound carrots, peeled and rough chopped	freshly ground black pepper

PLACE bell peppers, onions, and lime juice in food processor. Slowly add olive oil while food processor is running to emulsify. Add carrots, garlic, and sugar. Add a small amount of water, if necessary, to loosen up sauce. Season with kosher salt and freshly ground black pepper.

For the Crème Fraîche

1 cup sour cream
1 cup whipping cream

IN A mixing bowl, stir together sour cream and whipping cream until smooth. Cover and keep at warm room temperature for 15 hours. Refrigerate 24 hours before serving.

Yield: 2 cups

MICHIGAN CORN PUDDING

Ingredients

1¼ cups half & half	2 tablespoons sugar
1¼ cups heavy cream	1 quart fresh corn kernels, scraped from cob
5 eggs, beaten until light and fluffy	
¼ cup salted butter	½ cup scallions, cut on long thin bias
¼ cup flour	1½ tablespoons salted butter
2¼ teaspoons kosher salt	½ cup panko
1 pinch cayenne pepper	1½ cups smoked mozzarella, shredded

Preparation

PREHEAT oven to 350 degrees. Grease a 2 ½-quart baking dishes. Bring cream and half & half to a boil. Melt ¼ cup butter in saucepan and add ¼ cup flour whisking over the heat until smooth and small bubbles form. Add cream and half & half to flour/butter mixture and whisk to combine. Bring to a simmer, making sure no lumps form, and remove from heat. Add beaten eggs gradually and season with salt, pepper, cayenne, and sugar. Fold in corn and scallions.

DIVIDE evenly into greased pans. Bake at 350 degrees in water bath, until just set, approximately 45 minutes. Melt 1½ tablespoons of butter and toss with panko.

SPRINKLE mozzarella over pudding and then sprinkle buttered panko over the top of each pan.

Serves 8

Wine Suggestion: Domaine Jacques Prieur Chambertin
Gary Farrell Russian River Chardonnay

Michigan Rabbit Braised in Cèpe Cream
with Polenta Biscuits and Roasted Farmer's Market Carrots

This is a pretty decadent dish. Cèpes may not always be available, and buying them fresh is somewhat of a splurge – so feel free to substitute your favorite mushrooms or even just to season the sauce with a handful of the precious cèpes. We have made this sauce with almost every combination of mushrooms you could think of and it is always delicious.

Ingredients

2 whole rabbits
kosher salt
freshly ground black pepper
Chili Mélange (recipe follows)
Chili Mélange Seasoned Flour (recipe follows)
olive oil

4 quarts Cèpe Cream, divided (recipe follows)
Roasted Farmer's Market Carrots (recipe follows)
Polenta Biscuits (recipe follows)
Crème Fraîche (see recipe under Moroccan Scallops in this section)

Preparation

PREHEAT oven to 250 degrees. Cut each rabbit into 5 pieces (4 legs and saddle) discarding ribs or setting aside for another use such as making a stock. Season rabbit generously with kosher salt, freshly ground black pepper, and lightly with Chili Mélange. Dredge in Chili Mélange Seasoned Flour and shake off excess. Brown rabbit in olive oil over medium-high heat until just golden. Remove from pan immediately, and pour off excess oil, leaving caramelized bits in pan. Add Cèpe Cream to pan, reserving 1 quart for dressing the rabbit just before serving. Stir to incorporate caramelized bits into sauce and bring to a gentle simmer. Gently place rabbit into sauce – the sauce should come about ¾ of the way up the rabbit – spoon some sauce over the rabbit to coat it. Bring to a low simmer and cover with a tightly sealed lid (Le Creuset© casserole pans are ideal) or cover tightly with professional grade film wrap, and then foil and place in 250-degree oven. Cook until rabbit is extremely tender and almost falling off the bone, about 3½ hours. Remove the rabbit and either add additional sauce to thicken and deepen the flavor, or remove braising liquid/sauce to make into soup, and bring fresh sauce to a simmer. Adjust seasoning and dress the rabbit with sauce. Finish with chopped fresh herbs.

SERVE rabbit dressed with remaining Cèpe Cream. Accompany with Roasted Farmer's Market Carrots and Polenta Biscuits. Garnish with Crème Fraiche.

Serves 4

Wine Suggestion: Paternaster Rotondo Aglianico Del Vulture
L. Mawby Talismon Sparkling Wine

eve

For the Chili Mélange

If you can't find some of the chiles included in the recipe – don't worry about it – it will still be delicious.

2 tablespoons ground chili powder
2 tablespoons ground paprika
2 tablespoons ground coriander
1 tablespoon garlic powder
1 tablespoon plus 1 teaspoon ground cumin
3 tablespoons ground cayenne

2 teaspoons crushed red pepper
3 teaspoons dried oregano
2 tablespoons kosher salt
2 teaspoons freshly ground black pepper
½ teaspoon ground ancho chile
¼ teaspoon urfat isot (Turkish pepper)*
¼ teaspoon ground habanero chile

COMBINE well and store in an airtight container in a cool, dry place.

Yield: about 1 cup.

For the Chile Mélange Seasoned Flour

2 cups all-purpose flour
⅓ cup Chili Mélange (from recipe above)

2 teaspoons kosher salt

COMBINE well and store in an airtight container.

Yield: about 2½ cups.

For the Roasted Farmer's Market Carrots

2 bunches thin, tender carrots, most of stem removed, leaving about 2-inches, rinsed, scrubbed and dried (about 1 pound)

extra virgin olive oil
kosher salt
freshly ground black pepper

PREHEAT oven to 450 degrees. In a large mixing bowl, drizzle carrots with extra virgin olive oil and season generously with kosher salt and freshly ground black pepper and toss together. Carrots should be moist and glistening, but not oily. Place on sheet tray and drizzle again with extra virgin olive oil.

ROAST in oven, shaking pan occasionally, until carrots begin to caramelize and blister. They should still hold their shape; time varies with size of carrots, about 15–20 minutes.

For the Cèpe Cream

3 tablespoons fresh shallots, minced
3 tablespoons fresh garlic, minced
3 pounds cèpes or favorite assortment of wild and cultivated mushrooms
1 tablespoon kosher salt
  freshly ground black pepper
1⅓ cups sherry (we use Lustau Amontillado Sherry)
6 cups chicken stock or broth
1 quart heavy whipping cream

1 quart sour cream
2 cups Parmigiano Reggiano or aged provolone, grated, (At the restaurant, we use equal parts of each)
1 cup fresh herbs, chopped - such as flat leaf parsley, chives, chervil, basil, rosemary, thyme (Avoid cilantro and rosemary as they may overpower the flavor of the other herbs)

SWEAT shallots and garlic with some kosher salt over medium-low heat. Add mushrooms and raise heat to medium-high until mushrooms exude liquid. Simmer until liquid is almost completely gone. Season generously with kosher salt and freshly ground black pepper. Deglaze with sherry and cook for a few minutes, or until sherry is incorporated with mushrooms. Add chicken stock and cream and reduce until mixture thickens and coats the back of a spoon, about 20–30 minutes. Temper with sour cream by adding some of the sauce to the sour cream and then adding sour cream back into the sauce. Simmer until slightly thickened. Add cheese and fresh herbs, adjust seasonings and then immediately remove from heat. Garnish with Crème Fraîche.

Yield: about 4 quarts

For the Polenta Biscuits

½ cup plus 2 tablespoons finely ground cornmeal
½ cup plus 2 tablespoons flour
3 tablespoons plus 1 teaspoon sugar
1½ teaspoons baking powder

1 teaspoon salt
1 egg
¾ cup plus 1 tablespoon half and half
⅔ stick butter, melted, cooled to room temperature

PREHEAT oven to 350 degrees. Lightly grease 6 of the 12 cups of a large 1-cup measure muffin tin. Combine dry ingredients in a large bowl and make a well in the center. Combine liquid ingredients in a separate mixing bowl. Pour liquids into well, and stir until barely combined. Spoon batter into muffin tins and bake until just set and golden, about 15 to 20 minutes.

Yield: 6 large biscuits

SUGARED MINT LEAVES

We always serve these mint leaves to conclude the meal – they are our version of an "after dinner mint" and are very refreshing and rejuvenating after a long, hard night of eating.

Ingredients

12 large, hardy mint leaves (As big and in as pristine condition as possible.)
 1 egg white, whisked just to mix and loosen slightly
¾ cup sugar

Preparation

PREPARE small sheet tray lined with parchment paper. Pour sugar onto dinner plate. Place egg white in small mixing bowl or cup and whisk together lightly, just to incorporate. Using a pastry brush, brush mint leaves, one at a time, with egg white, coating both sides lightly but evenly. Set mint leaf, one at a time, onto plate with sugar; lift sugar and pour over mint leaf. Turn and repeat so mint leaf is thoroughly coated. Place leaves onto prepared sheet tray as you finish – as you lift, allow excess sugar to fall off back onto plate. Let mint leaves dry, uncovered, in cool dry place for a minimum of 2 hours.

Serves 4

Wine Suggestion: Chateau de Stony Muscat de Frontignan

Sugared Mint Leaves

Michigan Agricultural College Forestry Class, Roscommon County, 1910.

The Earle Uptown

300 South Thayer
Ann Arbor, MI 48104
734-994-0222
www.theearle.com/uptown

Tuesday – Thursday 5:00pm – 10:00pm
Friday and Saturday 5:00pm – 11:00pm
Closed Sunday and Monday

The Earle Uptown

Executive Chef Shelley Caughey Adams
Dennis Webster, Owner

In light of the spectacular attention given to the cooking of Spain, North Africa, Italy, India, Asia, as well as other regions of the world, French cuisine seems, well, passé. Current trends exalt bold, exotic flavors cooked over aromatic wood or poaching liquids, or even the nouveau vacuum pack techniques employed by chefs who wouldn't dare compromise the integrity of certain ingredients. The sauces and techniques known to France are still used in almost every serious kitchen but they are hidden away, as if a naughty child who has been banished to the basement when guests arrive.

Hogwash! The culinary world owes its soul to France and no serious culinary critic questions the fact that French chefs and the country overall, still cook better than anyone else. And, in Michigan, no restaurant is prouder to embrace the French theme than The Earle Uptown in Ann Arbor. In fact, owners Dennis and Mary Lou Webster and Executive Chef, Shelley Caughey Adams shamelessly opened Uptown at the height of French-bashing in 2003 to fulfill a mutual dream.

Adams is a Culinary Institute of America grad and former understudy to Ed Janos and Jimmy Schmidt, perhaps Michigan's two grandest culinary names, and sticklers for sound technique. Indeed, a careful scan of recent Uptown menus reveals she doesn't shy away from France's more demanding dishes including Bouillabaisse, Gateaux de Crabe, Artichaut Gratine, Confit aux Poireaux Asiatique (in phyllo with orange sauce), and Assiette de Pates, all of which appear on her list of hors d'oeuvres.

More purely Gallic treasures appear among the Plats Principaux. Leading off, Tournedos Rossini (beef tenderloin with foie gras, Madeira, and truffle), Carre d'Agneau Dijonnais (roasted lamb chops), Medallions de Veau aux Morilles (veal with morels), and the French favorite fish, Loup de Mer au Fenouil (with fennel and Pernod enhanced beurre blanc), to name only a few of several enticing dishes. Porterhouse, New York strip, and Delmonico steaks are offered with a choice of three sauces and side dishes including asparagus, sautéed wild mushrooms, redskins, pommes frites, or pomme dauphines..

Uptown's Sommelier is Steve Goldberg, a longtime employee of the Webster's other restaurant, The Earle. Goldberg was instrumental in building The Earle's cellar into the envy of Ann Arbor and he is rapidly doing the same with Uptown.

BROILED ARTICHOKE
Stuffed with Goat Cheese

There is a wide variety of goat cheese available. Be sure to choose a mild chèvre so as not to overpower the artichoke's subtle flavor.

Ingredients

4 *whole artichokes*
   juice of 1 lemon wedge
6 *ounces goat cheese, softened at room*
   temperature
2 *tablespoons olive oil*

2 *tablespoons basil, chopped*
1 *tablespoon rosemary, chopped*
   salt & black pepper
   spring greens

Preparation

PREP one artichoke at a time and then drop in simmering water with lemon juice. Cut 2 inches off the top of an artichoke until all dark green is removed and only the artichoke bottom with fuzzy choke remains. Simmer until tender in the lemon water. Let cool. Using a teaspoon, carefully remove the fuzzy choke and discard. If desired, you can refrigerate the artichoke bottom at this point and use later.

CREAM goat cheese. Add olive oil and mix until blended. Add herbs and fold in. Season to taste. (Be careful, as goat cheese is already a little salty). Refrigerate until firm.

PREHEAT oven to 375 degrees. Form goat cheese into 4 discs and gently place one disc into each artichoke bottom. Place onto baking pan and bake in oven for 5- 10 minutes until hot. Place under broiler briefly to brown. Serve surrounded by spring greens tossed with your favorite vinaigrette.

Serves 4

Wine Suggestion: Serve with a French red such as Domaine de L'Espigoutte (Cotes du Rhone) or an Italian red such as Avignonesi (Vino Nobile de Montepulciano).

SEARED SEA SCALLOPS
with Leeks and Saffron

The delicate flavor of scallops combines with leeks, cream, and a touch of saffron, and is one of our most praised appetizers at The Earle Uptown. When you try this at home, be careful not to overcook the scallops.

Ingredients

1 cup leeks, washed well & sliced	scant tablespoon chives, fine chop
3 tablespoons butter	1 pound sea scallops (approximately16
1¼ cups heavy cream	scallops)
salt & pepper (white & black)	olive oil
2 pinches saffron	

Preparation

SAUTÉ leeks in butter on low heat until tender. Add cream and bring to a boil. Turn down to simmer and let thicken. Add salt and white pepper to taste. Add saffron and simmer 60 seconds. Add chives.

AS you are preparing the sauce, heat a small amount of oil in a sauté pan until smoking. Sprinkle sea scallops with salt and black pepper. Sear scallops until medium golden brown. FLIP scallops and turn heat down to medium and finish cooking.

POUR sauce onto serving platter and place seared scallops on top.

Serves 4

Wine Suggestion: Serve with a sparkling white or Champagne such as Veuve Clicquot, or a dry Ries-ling such as a J.J. Prum Kabinett (Germany) or even a white Burgundy such as a Meursault from the house of Matrot.

BROILED LOUP DE MER

with Tarragon and Pernod

This is a very pretty, colorful dish and one that is quick to prepare, especially if the tomato purée is prepared a day before.

Ingredients

4 *large tomatoes*	8 *loup de mer fillets*
1 *cup water*	*salt & black pepper*
½-⅔ *cup whole grain mustard*	½ *cup Pernod*
¼ *cup heavy cream*	5 *tablespoons tarragon, lightly chopped*

Preparation

CORE and chop tomatoes. Place in pot with water and simmer until extremely soft. Push tomatoes through a wire mesh strainer or food mill and set aside. Mix mustard and cream until blended. Sprinkle fish fillets with salt and pepper, then coat them with mustard-cream mixture. Broil (or bake) until done. While fish is in oven, heat tomato purée with Pernod. Simmer until lightly thickened. Add salt to taste and tarragon. Put fish fillets on platter and pour sauce around. Garnish with chopped tarragon.

Serves 4

Wine Suggestion: Serve with a white Bordeaux such as Vieux Chateau Gaubert (Graves) or a Spanish red such as Sierra Cantabria, Rioja (Tempranillo).

The Earle Uptown

109

DUCK BREAST
with Caramelized Pineapple and Ginger

Duck continues to be one of the most popular entrées at both of our restaurants. Throughout the years we have prepared many variations; this is one of our favorites.

Ingredients

4 *duck breasts, boneless and skinless*	2 *cups Vouvray white wine*
salt & black pepper	2½ *cups beef stock*
olive oil	10 *2-inch slices fresh ginger, peeled and*
12 *tablespoons butter, divided*	*thinly sliced*
12 *tablespoons brown sugar*	4 *teaspoons dried currants*
32 *fresh pineapple wedges, approximately*	
¼-inch thick	

Preparation

SPRINKLE duck breasts with salt and pepper. In a large pan, heat oil until smoking. Add duck breasts and sear on high heat. When well browned, flip the duck breasts and reduce heat to medium. Sauté until desired doneness (we recommend medium rare).

IN another pan place 4 tablespoons butter and the brown sugar. Add pineapple wedges and caramelize them over high heat. Turn over and caramelize the other side of the wedges. Remove pineapple wedges from pan and set aside. Leave sugar and butter in pan and add wine, beef stock and ginger. Bring to a boil and let reduce over high heat until almost syrupy. Remove ginger and add remaining butter, currants, and salt to taste. Swirl butter in over medium heat. Slice duck and place on plate(s) surrounded by the caramelized pineapple wedges. Pour the sauce over and around the duck.

Serves 4

Wine Suggestion: Serve with a French Alsatian white such as Domaine Weinbach Gewürztraminer or a Pinot Gris such as the one from MacMurray produced in the Russian River Valley of California.

Bistro On the Boulevard

Chef / Owner Ali Barker

Separated by the picturesque St. Joseph River, the cities of Benton Harbor and St. Joseph anchor the southwest corner of the state in a region praised for its production of peaches, apples, pears, plums, grapes, and cherries; all of which ripen to perfection due to Lake Michigan's moderating influence. Yet cooks around the world owe the cities a huge debt for another reason: the fabulous line of counter top appliances produced by KitchenAid™. How many flawless loaves of bread were birthed in a KitchenAid™ stand mixers? Billions, no doubt.

We're not done yet. St. Joseph deserves recognition for Bistro On the Boulevard's Ali Barker, the chef who opened Union Square Café with Danny Meyer in 1985. Fine diners know the Café is still New York City's most highly rated Zagat restaurant and might just be the restaurant that redefined American Cuisine.

Many Michiganders may not realize that Barker is a Favorite Guest Chef at the James Beard Foundation (appearing there five times), or that he's been cited by the *New York Times* and *USA Today* as one of the first to introduce a chef's table in restaurant kitchens. His former restaurant in Cleveland, Piperade, was named "One of the nation's best new restaurants" by *Bon Appetit* magazine shortly after Barker opened it with his wife Marcie.

An Ali Barker menu is equal parts urban savvy, classic training, and fresh, local, seasonal ingredients. While The Bistro offers fabulous views of Lake Michigan, setting suns, and the lighthouse on Silver Beach, its essence is unmistakably French. For Starters, Barker offers Escargot Thiebault (garlic-infused, pastis and cream over sautéed spinach), Sautéed Veal Sweetbreads (spinach with warm bacon sherry vinaigrette), and French Onion Soup Gratinée. But we find unexpected dishes, as well—Grilled Andouille Sausage with Portabella Mushroom Tempura (spicy roasted red pepper and cumin aioli), Fried Calamari (graham cracker crusted with lemon black pepper aioli), and Signature Black Bean Soup (drizzle of sherry)—also compete for attention. Barker verve is found amongst the inviting entrée offerings, including Glazed Whitefish (roasted garlic sunflower seed and sweet red onion compote), Great Lakes Walleye Murat (diced potatoes, artichokes, and red wine demi glace), and Seared Sweet Sea Scallops (wild mushroom compote, lobster broth, and angel hair pasta). Several bistro-style duck (confit), chicken (roasted), lamb (roasted rack), and beef (rib eye, filet, and NY strip) round out the menu.

Wine Spectator has honored The Bistro in the past with its *Award of Excellence* for having one of the most outstanding wine lists in the world. Barker offers prix fixe and taster's menus, paired with wine for those who want a true culinary legend to make the hard decisions for them.

The Bistro is attached to The Boulevard Inn, a spacious all-suite hotel sitting on bluff above the lake.

QUICK TOMATO BISQUE

Sinfully delicious, and even more sinfully easy to make!

Ingredients

¼ cup extra virgin olive oil
1 small onion, diced
2 cloves garlic, minced
2 cups dry white wine
2 28-ounce cans chopped peeled Italian
   tomatoes

1 teaspoon dried oregano
1 teaspoon dried basil
1 cup heavy cream
   salt & pepper
6 leaves fresh basil, cut in chiffonade for
   garnish

Preparation

HEAT the oil in a 2-quart saucepan over medium heat. Add the onions and garlic. Cover, reduce heat and sweat until the onions are translucent, about 3 minutes. Add the wine, bring to a boil and reduce wine by half. Add the tomatoes, dried oregano, and dried basil and simmer for about 45 minutes. Add cream and bring to a boil. Purée bisque in food processor or with immersion blender. Check seasoning and serve with fresh basil chiffonade.

Serves 6

BARLEY RISOTTO
with Merguez Sausage and Peppers

A twist on classic risotto, the barley adds an unexpected nutty flavor and hearty texture.

Ingredients

½   pound Merguez sausage
2   red peppers
2   yellow peppers
¼   cup olive oil, plus extra for coating
      peppers
2   tablespoons unsalted butter
2   shallots, minced
2   garlic cloves, minced

¼   pound pearl barley
1   cup red wine
1   pint chicken stock
      salt & pepper
3   tablespoons Parmigiano Reggiano
      cheese, divided in half
1   tablespoon parsley, chopped

Preparation

BAKE the Merguez in a 400-degree oven for 20 minutes. Meanwhile, coat the peppers in olive oil and bake them in a 400-degree oven for 15 minutes. Remove the peppers and place in a paper bag, or bowl covered tightly with plastic wrap. When cool, peel the skin, remove seeds and julienne the peppers. Reserve. Chop the cooked Merguez into small pieces. Reserve.

HEAT the oil in a heavy bottom 4-quart saucepan over high heat for 1 minute. Add the butter. When the butter has completely melted, add the shallots and garlic and sweat them without browning for about 1 minute. Add the barley and stir until it is completely coated with oil and butter. Reduce the heat and add the wine and stir until it is absorbed. Proceed to add the chicken stock in ⅓-cup increments, stirring after each addition until absorbed. The barley will increase about three times in size. Season to taste with salt and pepper. Stir in the sausage and the peppers and half the cheese. Divide the risotto into 6 warmed bowls and garnish with remaining cheese and chopped parsley.

Serves 6

Wine Suggestion: Spanish Garnacha

ROASTED LOIN OF LAMB
Stuffed with Ratatouille

The Provençal-style vegetables infuse bright flavors into the meat, as well as offer a striking plate presentation

Ingredients

10 tablespoons olive oil, divided	salt & pepper
½ eggplant, diced	1 tomato, diced
1 small onion, minced	1 clove garlic, minced
½ zucchini, diced	½ cup white wine
½ yellow squash, diced	2 12-ounce loins of lamb, cleaned

Preparation

PREHEAT oven to 425 degrees. Heat a large sauté pan with 4 tablespoons of olive oil. When you can smell the aroma of olives, add the eggplant and onion and cook over high heat for 2 minutes. Add zucchini and yellow squash and cook for an additional 1 minute. Season with salt and pepper. Add 2 more tablespoons of oil, if necessary, then add tomatoes and garlic. Cook for 2 minutes and then add wine. Bring to a boil, reduce heat to simmer for 2 – 3 minutes until wine has evaporated. Season with salt and pepper to taste. Cool thoroughly.

USING a long, flat knife, make a 2-inch incision in the lamb at one end/side. Carefully hollow out the loin without tearing the outer walls of the meat. It is a little tricky so take your time. When completed, spoon the ratatouille into the loin – don't overfill as it could burst! Take 3 or 4 toothpicks to seal the open end. Season both sides with salt and pepper.

HEAT a 10-inch sauté pan and add 4 tablespoons of olive oil. When hot, place the loins in the pan and brown over high heat for 2 minutes. Turn and cook for another minute. Place in the 425-degree oven for 5 minutes. Let the meat rest for 10 minutes before slicing.

Serves 4

Wine Suggestion: Côtes du Rhone

Osso Bucco
with Oranges and Green Peppercorns

A soul-satisfying dish that continues to stand the test of time.

Ingredients

4 1-pound osso bucco portions
1 teaspoon kosher salt, divided
½ teaspoon freshly ground pepper
   flour for dredging
3 tablespoons olive oil
¼ cup brandy

1 cup white wine
¼ cup orange juice concentrate
3 cups veal stock
3 cups carrots, peeled and sliced
1 tablespoon green peppercorns
1 orange, peeled and cut into supremes

Preparation

PREHEAT oven to 375 degrees. Season the osso bucco with ½ teaspoon salt and ¼ teaspoon pepper and dredge each of them in flour. Heat the olive oil in a 12-inch skillet or Dutch oven over medium high heat and brown the osso bucco on both sides. Transfer the osso bucco to a platter and reserve.

POUR all the fat from the pan. Deglaze the pan by adding the brandy, white wine, and orange juice concentrate. Bring to a boil, scraping with a wooden spoon all the brown bits adhering to the pan. Cook over high heat until the liquid is reduced by half. Add the veal stock to the pan and bring to a simmer. Season with the remaining salt and pepper. Return the osso bucco to the pan, cover and braise in the oven for 1 hour.

UNCOVER the pan and add the carrots and peppercorns. Cook an additional hour, or until the meat is fork-tender and the carrots are completely cooked. Remove the pan from the oven and transfer the osso bucco to a serving platter and keep warm. Skim off the fat and cook the remaining liquid over high heat to reduce slightly, approximately 4 – 5 minutes. Stir in the orange segments. Ladle the sauce over the meat and serve.

Serves 4

Wine Suggestion: Barbera d'Alba or Gigondas

Butch's Dry Dock

BUTCHs

44 East Eighth Street
Holland, MI 49423
616-396-8227
www.butchs.net

Lunch
Monday – Saturday 11:00am – 3:00pm
Dinner
Monday – Thursday 5:00pm – 9:00pm
Friday & Saturday 5:00pm – 10:00pm
Closed Sundays

Butch's Dry Dock

Executive Chef Adam Smith
Bruce "Butch" TerHaar, Owner

Butch

Above all others, grape nuts in the United States read *Wine Spectator* and *Wine Enthusiast* for current reviews, tasting notes, and information on the wine world. Realizing the integral role wine plays in the restaurant industry, these magazines also monitor wine lists and carefully bestow awards to deserving restaurants. A good many of the establishments appearing in this book are recipients of such honors including Holland's best restaurant, Butch's Dry Dock, recently awarded *Wine Enthusiast's Award of Unique Distinction.* Only one other restaurant in Michigan earned a similar rating. In addition, the *Wine Spectator* placed Butch's Dry Dock in a select group of seven in Michigan granted its *Best of the Award of Excellence* grade in 2005. The influential magazine also made mention of Butch's unique plan offering diners an advantageous discount should they choose a bottle from the retail side of the operation to be served at dinner. A miniscule $5 corkage fee is added.

It should come as no surprise that proprietor Bruce "Butch" TerHaar is a first-rate oenophile and world traveler, regularly organizing wine tours and buying trips to Burgundy and other favorite haunts in France for his patrons. He is Holland's version of the Pinot Pied Piper.

First-rate would also serve to describe Adam Smith, the chef responsible for assuring that food and elegant dining share equal billing with wine at Butch's Dry Dock. No worries here. In fact, Chef Smith's menu is a model of wine friendliness ranging from Mediterranean-inspired seafood, to artisanal cheese, duck pâte, even Shrimp Fondue calling insistently for a glass of flinty Meursault. Diners looking to pair a big California Cab or Bordeaux will gravitate to either the Top Sirloin (grilled and glazed with fresh sage butter), Roasted New Zealand Lamb Rack (caressed with blackberry-mint glaze), or Filet Mignon (cornmeal spiced and pan seared, topped with gorgonzola butter), each of them served with Asiago roasted garlic Yukon Gold potatoes.

First time visitors to Holland will instantly be enchanted by this lakeside city, named recently by *Money Magazine* as one of the top five places in the United States to retire. Old-world influences include the annual Tulip Festival in May and the two-week Dutch Winterfest shortly after Thanksgiving. Also of note, nearby beaches are some of the best in Michigan.

 Best of Award of Excellence

Butch's Dry Dock

Shrimp Fondue with Pistou Gruyère Alfredo

Ingredients

2 ounces onion, diced
1 stalk celery, diced
2 tablespoons clarified butter, divided
½ tablespoon garlic, minced
1 ounce white wine
2 cups heavy whipping cream
2 tablespoons corn starch

2 tablespoons water
   Pistou (recipe follows)
4 ounces Gruyère cheese, shredded
8 13 / 15 weight shrimp, peeled,
   deveined, tail on
12 thin slices baguette
   salt & pepper

Preparation

SAUTÉ onions and celery until translucent in 1 tablespoon clarified butter. Add minced garlic for 1 or 2 minutes and then deglaze pan with white wine. Add heavy cream and bring to a boil. Strain well through a chinois and then bring to boil again. Mix cornstarch and water in separate bowl and slowly whisk in to cream mixture, and then return to boil. Whip in Pistou and Gruyère until fairly smooth.

SAUTÉ shrimp in sauté pan with remaining tablespoon of clarified butter until completely cooked. Combine with Alfredo and serve with baguette slices.

Serves 4

Wine Suggestion: Ken Forrester Chenin Blanc, Stellenbosch, South Africa

For the Pistou

¼ cup fresh basil leaves
¼ cup fresh parsley
1 tablespoon pine nuts, toasted

1 tablespoon olive oil
1 tablespoon tomato paste

COMBINE all pistou ingredients in a food processor and purée until paste. Set aside.

Java Chili Rubbed Salmon
with Tomato Provençal

Ingredients

6 8-ounce salmon fillets, skinless	1½ tablespoons ancho chili powder
12 ounces diced roma tomatoes	1½ tablespoons kosher salt
1 tablespoon garlic, minced	2 tablespoons brown sugar
1 tablespoon sugar	1 teaspoon ground black pepper
4 ounces balsamic vinegar	1 tablespoon clarified butter
¼ cup freshly ground coffee beans	

Preparation

PREHEAT oven to 350 degrees. Combine tomatoes, garlic, sugar and vinegar in a bowl and set aside.

MIX coffee, ancho chili powder, salt, brown sugar, and black pepper thoroughly in a bowl and coat show side of each salmon fillet with rub. Heat skillet over medium high burner with the clarified butter. Sear coated side of salmon. Flip and finish in 350-degree oven until medium rare, approximately 8 minutes.

PLACE diced tomatoes, garlic, sugar, and vinegar in sauté pan and warm. Cover each salmon fillet generously with tomato sauce and serve.

Serves 6

Wine Suggestion: River's Edge Pinot Noir

GRILLED BEEF TENDERLOIN
with White Truffle Roasted Tomato Sauce

Ingredients

6 choice cut 6-ounce beef tenderloins	½ red onion, medium dice
2 pounds Roma tomatoes, cored, quartered	1 teaspoon clarified butter
1 tablespoon fresh basil, minced	1 tablespoon balsamic vinegar
1 tablespoon fresh oregano, minced	1½ teaspoon roasted garlic, minced
2 tablespoons white truffle oil	¼ cup Cabernet Sauvignon
1 yellow pepper, cleaned, medium dice	ground black pepper

Preparation

PREHEAT oven to 350 degrees. Combine tomatoes, basil, oregano, and truffle oil in a bowl, then spread evenly on a parchment paper-covered sheet tray and roast for 30 minutes. While tomatoes are roasting, sauté peppers and red onion in 1 teaspoon clarified butter for 3 minutes. Then add vinegar, garlic, and ground pepper and continue sautéing until vinegar evaporates. Deglaze with Cabernet, bring to boil, and add roasted tomatoes. Simmer for 5 minutes then purée with stick blender.

GRILL beef tenderloins to your desired doneness. Serve with sauce, a favorite vegetable, and potato.

Serves 6

Wine Suggestion: Lava Cap Cabernet Sauvignon Reserve

FLOURLESS CHOCOLATE CAKE

Ingredients

½ cup sugar
⅓ cup water
½ cup butter
12 ounces bittersweet chocolate chips

⅓ cup Cointreau or Grand Marnier
6 eggs
fresh raspberries
whipped cream

Preparation

PREHEAT oven to 325 degrees. Grease a spring form pan and cover it in aluminum foil. Combine sugar and water in a sauté pan, bring to a simmer. In a stainless bowl melt butter and chocolate in a water bath until smooth then add Cointreau and the water and sugar mixture. Mix well then add eggs one at a time while continuing to stir.

POUR into spring form pan and bake on a sheet pan with water bath for 45 minutes. When cool, cut and serve with raspberries and whipped cream.

Serves 10

Wine Suggestion: Warre's Optima 10 Year Tawny Port

The Dining Room
at Clearbrook

Contemporary Classic Cuisine

6494 Clearbrook Drive
Saugatuck, MI 49453
269-857-2000
www.clearbrookdining.com

Seasonal Dining
see next page for schedule

The Dining Room at Clearbrook

Executive Chef Rob Guerrero
Jim & Candy Jeltema, Co-owners

Detroit looms so imposingly in the minds of most out-state Michiganders, it is easy to forget that some regions of the state are as many as 600 miles away and identify much more closely with Wisconsin or, in the extreme southwest corner of the state, Chicago. In fact, the Windy City has a long and storied history with places like Saugatuck, and each year sends untold thousands of tourists to the city's art galleries, beaches, golf courses, boutiques, and yes, restaurants.

The Dining Room at Clearbrook Golf Club in Saugatuck ranks as Michigan's best restaurant south of Grand Rapids. Golfers should also know that Clearbrook's "olde course" dates from 1926 and frequently hosts some of Michigan's most prestigious professional and amateur tournaments, and that award-winning flower and herb gardens adorn the grounds. Herbs and flowers for use in the kitchen and dining room, by the way, because dining is our concern, and no less than *Gourmet Magazine* says, "The fare at Clearbrook FAR surpasses that of most private clubs."

Executive Chef Rob Guerrero and Sous Chef Jeff Kudrna create new menus everyday for their loyal customer base. Influenced by the cooking of the American Southwest, Asia, and France/Continental, the chefs are obsessive about freshness, working closely with area farmers, and often visiting Saugatuck's popular Farmer's Market.

A recent menu of First Dishes featured Roasted Creamy Tomato Soup with Gorgonzola Morel Relish and Chive Oil; Scallop Shrimp & Peppered Salmon Bouillabaisse; and Seared Lamb Loin Au Poivre accompanied by Julienned Carrot, Leek, Red Pepper Medley and Roasted Garlic Relish.

Longtime guests – the Dining Room opened in 1985 – regularly look forward to Traditional Table-side Caesar Salad before launching into any of the hand-cut, house-aged, certified Angus beef steaks, or other Primary Dishes. Notable among them: Griddled Fresh Canadian Walleye, Pan-seared Breast of Duck & Pheasant Confit Ragout, and Pistachio Encrusted Rack of Lamb. A prix fixe Chef's Tasting Menu is available served with two glasses of vintage wine.

The Dining Room's wine list grew from a respectable fifty labels to over 200 in the past few years, anchored by many of California's most storied wineries. Wonderful garden views are enjoyed from every table.

The Dining Room is open nearly year-round: Seven nights a seek from mid-June through mid-September, and then weekends only until Valentines. Re-opening Easter and weekends beginning in May.

Award of Excellence

FIGS, BLEU CHEESE, AND WALNUTS IN PHYLLO CANAPÉS

This hors d'oeuvre allows your creativity to shape the item. It works for any season.

Ingredients

2 ounces walnuts
1 clove garlic
4 ounces good bleu cheese
4 ounces dried figs

2 ounces Port wine
salt & pepper
3 sheets of thawed phyllo dough
melted butter

Preparation

PULSE walnuts and garlic in a food processor a few times. Add bleu cheese and figs. Pulse a few times. Add port wine, while processor is running. Salt and pepper to taste.

CAREFULLY separate each sheet of phyllo, and brush with melted butter. Fill with fig and cheese filling and roll, cut, or form into desired shape (purses, rolls, raviolis, etc.) Brush with a bit more butter and place in the refrigerator for 1 hour.

PREHEAT oven to 350 degrees, and bake for 10-15 minutes, until golden brown. Serve immediately from the oven.

Yield: 10–14 canapés

Wine Suggestion: Argyle Pinot Noir, Rivers Edge Pinot Noir

Front entry at Clearbrook

The Dining Room at Clearbrook

BLUEBERRY, PEACH, AND WATERCRESS SALAD
with Candy Onions in Dijon Tarragon Vinaigrette

Between 2002 and 2005, we wrote new menus weekly for The Dining Room (we're smarter now, only monthly!) and this was one of our best-received summer salads.

Ingredients

- 1 *pint blueberries*
- 3 *ripe peaches*
- 2 *cups watercress*
- 1 *Vidalia onion*

- 1 *head Bibb lettuce*
- *Dijon Tarragon Vinaigrette (recipe follows)*

Preparation

RINSE the blueberries, peaches, watercress, and lettuce. Peel and thinly slice the onion. Place in bowl. Gently tear the watercress into 2-inch pieces and add to bowl. Gently slice the peaches into wedges and add to bowl, along with the blueberries.

TO SERVE, peel the leaves of Bibb lettuce and place two on each plate. Add half of the dressing to the bowl with the fruit and watercress mixture. Toss gently. Taste. The salad should be well coated but not swimming. Divide the salad between the plates and serve.

Serves 4

Wine Suggestion: Poet's Leap Dry Riesling

For the Dijon Tarragon Vinaigrette

- 2 *tablespoons Dijon mustard*
- 2 *tablespoons fresh tarragon*
- 1 *tablespoon sugar*
- 2 *ounces red wine vinegar*

- 3 *ounces olive oil*
- 3 *ounces vegetable or canola oil*
- *salt & pepper*

PLACE the mustard, tarragon, sugar, and vinegar in a bowl. Mix well and let sit for a couple of minutes. Combine oils and slowly add to vinegar mixture, while whisking vigorously. Adjust seasoning and set aside.

Thai Chicken Salad on Crostini

This is a good party hors d'oeuvre or an amuse-bouche prior to dinner. Mixture may be warmed prior to placing on crostini.

Ingredients

3 chicken breasts
1 ounce sesame oil
1 ounce fresh ginger, minced
3 cloves garlic, minced
1 teaspoon chile flakes (or one sliced Thai chile)

3 ounces raisins
8 ounces coconut milk
2 ounces peanut butter
1 ounces honey
1 French baguette
   olive oil

Preparation

BOIL chicken in salted water until fork-tender. Remove to a bowl and shred with a fork. Heat the sesame oil in a sauté pan, until it shimmers. Add ginger, garlic and chili flakes. Stir for 1 minute over medium heat, then add raisins. Stir for 1 minute. Add coconut milk and bring to a boil. Remove from heat and add peanut butter and honey. Add the chicken. Cover and refrigerate.

PRE-HEAT oven to 350 degrees. With a serrated knife, thinly slice (¼-inch slices) a good French baguette. Brush with olive oil and kosher salt. Bake for about 15 minutes on a baking sheet, until golden brown.

SERVE the chicken salad with (or on) the crostini.

Yield: 20 canapés

Wine Suggestion: Trimbach Gewürztraminer, Gundlach-Bundschu Gewürztraminer

WARM TOMATO TORTE, WILTED SPINACH, & APPLE SALAD
Tossed with Hot Bacon Vinaigrette, Bleu Cheese, and Toasted Walnuts

This is the quintessential dinner party salad. VERY impressive! And, although it seems like a lot of work, your guest reaction will justify the effort!

Ingredients

1 sheet of puff pastry cut into 6 pieces	1 ounce fresh basil, chopped
1 6-compartment muffin pan (4 ounces each)	1 ounce fresh oregano, chopped
	pinch salt and pepper
1 ounce garlic, minced	Wilted Spinach & Apple Salad (recipe follows)
8 ounces tomato juice	
12 ounces half & half	Hot Bacon Vinaigrette (recipe follows)
12 ounces heavy cream	3 ounces bleu cheese, crumbled
8 whole fresh eggs	3 ounces walnuts, toasted

Preparation

PREHEAT oven to 350 degrees. Sprinkle a little flour on a clean surface. Using a rolling pin roll out puff pastry squares about 1" larger on all four sides. Spray the inside of each muffin compartment. Gently place the rolled pastry squares each in a muffin form. Dampen your fingers with a little water. Press into place and seal any overlapping folds of pastry with a press from your slightly wet fingers. Using a paring knife, trim the edges so the puff pastry is level with the top of pan. Now cut pieces of waxed paper to line the inside of the pastry cups, fill each with dry beans, and bake for 15 minutes or until the shells are golden brown. Gently remove the shells from the pan, then the beans from the wax paper, then the wax paper from the shells. Set aside.

WHILE shells are baking, combine the garlic, tomato juice, half & half, and heavy cream in a small pot and heat at medium. While this cream mix is heating, whisk the eggs and herbs until combined in a medium-size mixing bowl. Once bubbles form around the edge of the cream in pan, slowly pour it into the egg mix. Season with salt and pepper.

SPRAY each muffin pan cup again, and place a baked shell back into each cup. Slowly fill each shell almost to the top with the cream and egg mix. Now place the muffin pan inside of a baking dish, so that it rests directly on the bottom of the baking dish. Fill the baking dish with hot water so the water rises about two-thirds of the way up the muffin pan. Bake at 350 degrees for 35-40 minutes, or until the mix has just set in the middle (gently shake the muffin pan – the egg mixture should wiggle very slightly in the center). Once the tarts have cooled slightly, remove them from their pan by running a paring knife around the outside of each shell.

TO SERVE, toss the Spinach & Apple Salad thoroughly in the Hot Bacon Vinaigrette and divide onto 6 large salad plates. Place a warm torte on top of the wilted warm greens. The bleu cheese and walnuts are for garnish on the greens, so sprinkle on until gone.

Serves 6

Wine Suggestion: Grgich Hills Estate Grown Napa Valley Fumé Blanc or St. Supery Sauvignon Blanc

For the Wilted Spinach & Apple Salad

>   1   *pound spinach, torn in half*
>   ½   *red onion, julienned*
>   2   *Ida Red apples, sliced*

TOSS the spinach, onion, and apple slices in a bowl and hold for service.

For the Hot Bacon Vinaigrette

>   4   *ounces bacon, julienned*   1   *ounce balsamic vinegar*
>   1   *ounce garlic, minced*   1   *tablespoon Dijon mustard*
>   1   *ounce onion or shallot, minced*   1   *cup extra virgin olive oil*
>   1   *ounce red wine*   *salt and pepper*
>   4   *ounces chicken stock*

COOK the bacon in small sauté pan over medium heat until the bacon is crispy and has rendered a good amount of fat. Add garlic and shallot and cook for 1-2 minutes. Add red wine and reduce until almost evaporated then add chicken stock and balsamic vinegar. Take off heat and whisk in the Dijon mustard, then whisk in the olive oil slowly. Now salt and pepper to taste and set aside somewhere warm.

Pan-seared Sea Scallops

with Three-Pepper Quinoa, Yellow Beet Purée, and Grapefruit

This recipe is a super four-person primary dish for seafood at home without having the house smell of fish! Fresh scallops are tender delicacies that always sell whenever we place them on our menu at The Dining Room.

Ingredients

2 grapefruits, peeled and segmented
olive oil
12 sea scallops, fresh and cleaned (2 inches each, buy more if smaller)

salt & pepper
Yellow Beet Purée (recipe follows)
Three-Pepper Quinoa (recipe follows)
1 shallot, minced

Preparation

CUT the skin of the grapefruit to expose the flesh. Using a smaller knife, slice in between the membrane of each segment to release as much flesh as possible. Toss with a tablespoon of olive oil and set aside.

PLACE sauté pan on high heat. Lay scallops on paper towel and pat dry. Season with salt and pepper and add just enough oil to cover the bottom of the pan. Have an empty coffee cup nearby. Once the oil is hot and begins to smoke, carefully pour oil into the cup, and return the pan to the burner. Keep the heat high, and slowly add the scallops. Don't move the pan. Let the scallops sauté for about 2-3 minutes until golden brown. Flip the scallops, then cover and reduce the heat to medium. (If scallops start to overly brown, add a small amount of water/white wine to the pan.) Check scallops for doneness. They should be firm to the touch, and look opaque in the center.

WHILE the scallops are covered and cooking, ladle a small pool of Yellow Beet Purée on the center of the 4 plates. Moving the ladle in a circular motion spread the purée over most of the plate. This may require a little more sauce. Using a spoon, divide the Three-Pepper Quinoa equally among the plates, placing it right in the center of the purée. Place the cooked scallops around the quinoa, and top with grapefruit sections and minced shallot.

Serves 4

Wine Suggestion: Sonoma-Cutrer Russian River Ranches Chardonnay

For the Three-Pepper Quinoa

2 cups quinoa
2 cups water

¼ each of yellow, red, and green peppers, minced
salt & pepper

BOIL water with salt and pepper. Add quinoa, bring to boil and let cook for about 10 minutes. Strain through a fine mesh strainer. Add minced peppers, taste, and adjust seasoning if needed. Keep warm.

For the Yellow Beet Purée

1 ounce olive oil	¼ teaspoon cinnamon
2 shallots, minced	¼ teaspoon ginger
1 clove garlic, minced	2 ounces white wine
2 small yellow beets, peeled, cooked, diced	8 ounces chicken stock
¼ teaspoon cumin	2 teaspoons fresh thyme, rough chopped (optional)
¼ teaspoon coriander	

PLACE small pot on medium heat. Add oil, shallots, and garlic before pan gets too hot. Stir occasionally. Once hot, add the diced beets. Sauté 5 minutes. Add the spices and cook 1 minute more continuing to stir. Add wine, bringing to boil for 1 minute then add the chicken stock and thyme. Again bring to boil, and reduce heat to simmer for 15 minutes. Place beets and liquid into blender and purée until smooth. Through a fine mesh strainer, strain back into the pot and season with salt and pepper. Keep warm.

Garden View

Peppered Flank Steak over Sweet Potato Gratin

This is a delicious steak & potato meal, especially in the middle of our quite long Michigan winter. Add a wedge of iceberg, 1000 Island dressing, with a French baguette and butter.

Ingredients

2 flank steaks, 12-16 ounces each
1 cup peppercorns, crushed

2 ounces high quality olive oil
Sweet Potato Gratin (recipe follows)

Preparation

HEAT a skillet or large sauté pan over medium heat. Roll the steaks in peppercorns. Once the pan is hot, add olive oil and sear the steaks. Don't turn too often, probably about 5 minutes on each side for medium rare, depending on the thickness of the meat. Take the steaks out of the pan and let rest for 2-3 minutes. Slice ¼-inch to ⅜-inch thick, against the grain, and fan the slices out over a serving of the Sweet Potato Gratin.

Serves 4

Wine Suggestion: Cline Zinfandel

For the Sweet Potato Gratin

3 fresh sweet potatoes, peeled & sliced
  very thin
1 cup heavy cream

salt & pepper
sweet butter
2 cloves garlic, minced

PREHEAT oven to 400 degrees. Place sweet potatoes in bowl and cover lightly with the mix of heavy cream with salt & pepper. Grease a small cake pan with sweet butter. Lay potato slices north and south to cover the bottom of pan. Season lightly with salt & pepper. Lay the next layer of sweet potato slices east and west, again lightly seasoning with salt & pepper. Continue alternating layers until all slices are used. When finished layering, pour a small amount of the cream from the bowl into the cake pan – enough so when pressure is applied to the top of the potatoes the cream will just cover them. Top with minced garlic and cover with plastic wrap followed by aluminum foil and bake for 35-45 minutes. Cut into large squares before serving, then diagonally to form a serving-sized triangle.

The 1913 Room

The 1913 Room.

Amway Grand Plaza
187 Monroe, N.W.
Grand Rapids, MI 49503
616-774-2000
www.amwaygrand.com

Lunch
Monday – Friday 11:30am – 2:00pm
Dinner
Monday – Thursday 5:30pm – 10:30pm
Friday – Saturday 5:00pm – 10:30pm
Closed Sunday

1913 Room

Chef de Cuisine Christian Madsen

Since 1937, the American Automobile Association (AAA) has employed field inspectors to visit the hotels, motels, and restaurants they list in their travel publications to ensure a certain level of quality. In 1963, the inspectors implemented a simple rating system that led to the Diamond Rating Process they now use to rate over 60,000 hotels and restaurants. Remarkably, only one Michigan restaurant has ever been given AAA's highest designation—the Five Diamond award—and it's not in Detroit. In fact, the 1913 Room in the Amway Grand Plaza Hotel has won the honor five years running.

The operative word at the 1913 Room is "opulence." Outside of Paris, you don't see restaurants like this anymore; starting with the massive chandeliers, floor-to-ceiling tasseled indigo draperies, golden walls, and table finery modeled after Louis XVI's own service. Any number of French kings (queens, and handmaidens, for that matter) would take instantly to the bill of fare, as well.

Indeed, Chef de Cuisine Christian Madsen's menus evoke the best in dining from any era. If classic is the name of the game, it's tough to improve on Roasted Breast of Pheasant and Leg Confit served with Brioche Bread Pudding, Lacinato Kale – an Italian heirloom variety of history's most popular green vegetable – which Madsen finishes with an Apple Cider Gastrique. Or picture (and savor) the colorful nouvelle fish plate, Grilled Barramundi with Beet Tapioca, Swiss Chard and White Port Sauce, offering a fresh take on root vegetables, simple chard, and Port's white version. His appetizer offerings include Gewürztraminer Poached Foie Gras, Escargot Bourguignonne, White Truffle Risotto, and Braised Beef Short Ribs with Soft Poached Egg and Umami Broth, amongst others.

The dining room is meticulously run by Maitre D'Hotel Denis Cerezo. A prominent wine station stands at the entrance from which Cerezo and his staff serve many of the twenty-eight wines by-the-glass. The wine list features a fabulous selection of European whites, and an equally impressive collection of California red wines. First time diners will be surprised to find that The 1913 Room entrance is located at the far end of The Grill at 1913, an elegant steakhouse and surely one of west Michigan's best.

CELERIAC CREAM WITH MAPLE POPCORN

This is a soup featured on our autumn menu. The popcorn garnish is a surprise that people really enjoy. At the restaurant we had to pop extra to accommodate all the requests for more.

Ingredients

2 tablespoons unsalted butter
1 cup Spanish onion, minced
3 pounds celeriac (celery root), rinsed, peeled, diced in 1-inch cubes
2 cups chicken stock

2 cups heavy whipping cream
½ teaspoon freshly ground nutmeg
   salt & pepper
1 cup Maple Popcorn (recipe follows)

Preparation

IN A heavy-bottomed saucepan over low heat, melt butter and add onion. Sauté until translucent, about 4 minutes, then add celeriac and sauté over low heat for 10 minutes. Add chicken stock and simmer for 15 – 20 minutes, stirring occasionally, until celeriac is soft. Slowly add cream, stirring constantly until cream is incorporated into broth and well heated. Add nutmeg, salt, and pepper to taste. Purée in blender or food processor using caution. Strain. Adjust seasoning as desired. Ladle or pour into serving bowls. Garnish with Maple Popcorn.

Serves 8 (4-ounce servings)

Wine Suggestion: Wehlener Sonnenuhr, Riesling Spatlese, J.J. Prum, Mosel

For the Maple Popcorn

1 cup popped popcorn (air popped is best, microwave popcorn is not recommended)
4 tablespoons maple syrup

pinch sea salt
pinch celery seed
pinch Piment d' Espelette

IN A heavy bottomed 1-quart saucepan, reduce maple syrup over medium heat until reduced by half. Combine with all other ingredients. Cool.

SALAD OF FRISÉE AND BELGIAN ENDIVE
with Vanilla Poached Pears and Pear Nectar Vinaigrette

Ingredients

Vanilla Poached Pears (recipe follows)
1 large head frisée, washed well and hand torn from core
1 head Belgian endive, leaves washed and cut into fine julienne

2 ounces Bleu d' Auvergne cheese, crumbled
freshly ground pepper
Pear Nectar Vinaigrette (recipe follows)

Preparation

ARRANGE 3 poached pear quarters into a triangle shape in the center of each chilled salad plate. Toss together lettuce, bleu cheese, and vinaigrette and gently place on top of the poached pears.

For the Vanilla Poached Pears

3 Bosc pears, peeled, cored, quartered, stored in lemon water until ready to poach
3 cups water
⅔ cup white sugar

1 cup Chardonnay
1 vanilla bean, split
1 teaspoon black peppercorns
1 stick cinnamon

IN A non-reactive 2-quart saucepan, combine all ingredients except pears and bring to a simmer. Add pears, cover, and simmer until pears are tender, about 30 – 40 minutes. Cool to room temperature with pears remaining in poaching liquid. Remove pears with a slotted spoon. Strain poaching liquid and reserve liquid. Refrigerate pears until ready to assemble salad. May be done up to three days in advance.

For the Pear Nectar Vinaigrette

1 cup reserved pear poaching liquid
1 cup pear nectar
2 tablespoons Champagne vinegar
¾ cup sour cream

2 tablespoons crème fraîche
2 limes, juiced
salt
¼ cup canola oil

IN A heavy bottomed 1-quart saucepan, combine poaching liquid and pear nectar and cook over medium heat until reduced by half. Cool. Combine with all other ingredients (except oil) in a food processor and blend well. Continue blending and slowly drizzle in canola oil. Refrigerate and reserve.

4 Servings

Wine Suggestion: Zafarana Vineyards Late Harvest Riesling, Old Mission Peninsula

ROASTED BREAST OF PHEASANT

with Leg Confit, Brioche Bread Pudding, Braised Kale, and Apple Cider Gastrique

Ingredients

2 8-ounce pheasant breasts, boned but not skinned

8 ounces pheasant meat, connective tissue removed, cut into small dice

½ cup heavy whipping cream

1 egg white

½ tablespoon kosher salt

½ teaspoon freshly ground pepper

2 tablespoons olive oil

1 tablespoon unsalted butter

1 sprig sage

1 sprig thyme

1 sprig rosemary

   Brioche Bread Pudding (recipe follows)

   Braised Kale (recipe follows)

   Apple Cider Gastrique (recipe follows)

2 ounces pheasant confit, for garnish

Preparation

IN A pre-chilled food processor, combine diced pheasant meat, cream, egg white, salt, and pepper and process until smooth. Carefully pull back skin on pheasant breasts and divide pheasant mousse under skin. Refrigerate until ready to cook. May be prepped one day in advance.

PREHEAT oven to 375 degrees. In a sauté pan over medium heat, combine oil and butter. Carefully place seasoned pheasant breast, skin side down, into the pan and sauté until golden brown, about 5 – 6 minutes, basting occasionally. Carefully turn pheasant over, and add herb sprigs to pan and sauté for 3 – 4 additional minutes. Place pheasant breasts, herbs, oil, and melted butter into a small roasting pan and roast in oven until 165-degree internal temperature is reached on a meat thermometer, approximately 8 – 10 minutes. (Alternatively, if the sauté pan is oven-friendly, place directly in oven, though cooking time will be shorter.) Allow to rest out of the oven for at least 10 minutes before slicing.

TO SERVE, place a serving of Brioche Bread Pudding on a warm plate. Place a small pile of Braised Kale in center of bread pudding. Slice pheasant into 8 – 10 slices per breast, and arrange 4 – 5 slices on top of kale. Spoon Apple Cider Gastrique around plate and garnish each plate with pheasant confit.

Serves 4

Wine Suggestion: Chateau-Chalon, Vin Jaune, De Longue Garde, Reserve Catherine De Rye

Roasted Breast of Pheasant, continued

For the Brioche Bread Pudding

2 cups brioche, cubed
1 Granny Smith apple, peeled, cored,
  and small diced
½ cup golden raisins, soaked overnight
  in hot water, then well drained

4 eggs
6 ounces whole milk
⅓ cup plus 2 tablespoons white sugar
½ tablespoon ground cinnamon
½ tablespoon ground nutmeg

PREHEAT oven to 350 degrees. In a large mixing bowl, combine brioche, apple, and raisins. In a separate bowl, whisk together eggs and milk, then slowly whisk in sugar, cinnamon, and nutmeg. Pour egg mixture over bread and fruit mixture, and combine well. Place in a pre-greased loaf pan, cover with aluminum foil, and bake on center rack for 50 – 60 minutes. Cool and cut into squares or rounds for serving. Reheat for 5 – 7 minutes at 350 degrees on a greased pan.

For the Braised Kale

1 bunch kale, leaves torn from stems,
  well washed, and dried
2 tablespoons unsalted butter

2 tablespoons chicken stock
salt & pepper

IN A large sauté pan, over medium heat, melt butter, and then add kale, stirring constantly, for 4 – 5 minutes. Add stock and season, then cook an additional 4 – 5 minutes, or until kale is tender, but not mushy. Reserve.

For the Apple Cider Gastrique

¼ pound unsalted butter
1 cup shallots, sliced
⅓ cup garlic, sliced
¼ cup white sugar

2 cups apple cider
1 quart pheasant or chicken stock
¾ cup apple cider vinegar
salt & pepper

IN A 2-quart saucepan over medium-low heat, melt butter, add shallots and garlic and sauté for 3 – 4 minutes. Add sugar and stir for 10 – 15 minutes, until sugar and butter have become golden brown caramel. Carefully add apple cider and stock. Turn up heat to medium and cook until liquid is reduced to half its original volume. Stir in vinegar, season with salt and pepper, strain and keep warm over low heat until ready to serve.

San Chez
A Tapas Bistro

San Chez

A TAPAS BISTRO

Authentic Food~And Fun~From Spain.

38 West Fulton
Grand Rapids, MI 49503
616-774-8272
www.sanchezbistro.com

Monday – Thursday
7:00am – 10:00pm
Friday 7:00am – Midnight
Saturday 10:00am – Midnight
Sunday
9:00am – 10:00pm

San Chez:
A Tapas Bistro

General Manager / owner Dan Gendler

In the unhappy annals of blighted urban areas the world over, very often it takes a restaurant to infuse life. In the case of Grand Rapids, the magic formula was perfected by San Chez, a Tapas Bistro that opened in 1992 and transformed the down-trodden area south of Fulton Street. Owner Dan Gendler was intent on breathing some big city energy into Grand Rapids. He loved the themed restaurants in Chicago at the time, and especially some of the dining spots situated in old warehouse districts. Well, decrepit buildings and weed infested lots is what he found around the building he chose in Grand Rapids, on the corner of Commerce and Fulton.

It's hard to imagine now. San Chez Bistro is a fabulous success story for all the right reasons. Beautiful high-vaulted tin ceiling supported by mosaic pillars, sandblasted brick walls, the mesmerizing activity of an open kitchen, and the one intangible so sought after by every restaurant: people, lots of people - eating, laughing, and not wanting to leave. No wonder tapas are called the fun food from Spain.

The San Chez Bistro menu is a marvelous piece of writing and design. Diners are instantly encouraged to order one or two of several Starter plates mixing and matching Spanish cheeses, meats, breads, and olives to share at the table with a first round of drinks. And, one can sense in other diners a *when in Rome* (or Madrid) attitude because everyone seems to be reaching across tables to grab a bite of an unfamiliar sheep's milk cheese, or handful of spicy olives.

But tapas is the reason there is a line forming at the door and San Chez serves up an amazing variety of hot and cold dishes from Spain, Morocco, the Middle East, and even Cuba. In all, over 100 items from both sides of the Straits of Gibraltar are served in the 450-seat restaurant.

Marinated artichoke hearts grilled, sautéed, or in a casserole with asparagus and cheese lead us into the hot items. We also find classic banderillas, the most tempting a marinated scallop and bacon skewer served with mixed organic greens and habanero, and a grape mango chutney. Crab, cod, crayfish, duck, and lamb figure into other dishes. Indeed, the menu demands decisiveness.

Both red and white sangria feature prominently on the Drinks menu. The wine list is relatively brief but includes wines from nearly all regions of Spain. Savvy diners (or indecisive diners) can opt for flights of wine.

Baba Ghanoush

Because this is an Arabic name from a language that does not use the English letters, you will find it transliterated and spelled many different ways. The best baba ghanoush will always have a wonderful nutty and smoky flavor from the roasting and/or grilling process.

Ingredients

2 pounds eggplant, about 1 large size or 2 medium size	3 tablespoons olive oil, divided
2 tablespoons tahini	3 ounces red onion, diced
2 cloves fresh, minced garlic	6 ounces tomato, diced
1 lemon, juiced	3 ounces pitted black olives
pinch cumin	12 strips Preserved Lemon (recipe follows)
½ teaspoon chef's salt	4-6 loaves pita bread cut into triangles

Preparation

PREHEAT oven to 400 degrees. Pierce eggplant in several places and place under broiler or on grill for 10 to 15 minutes, turning often to get a bubbly, slightly charred skin evenly around the eggplant. Roast at 400 degrees for an additional 30 to 40 minutes, until flesh begins to become soft. Scoop out the flesh, and discard the skin. Very lightly squeeze out any excessive liquid from the flesh of the eggplant. Combine eggplant, garlic, tahini, lemon juice, cumin, chef's salt, and 1½ tablespoons of the olive oil in a food processor and purée. Garnish with onion, tomato, black olives, and Preserved Lemon. Serve with pita bread.

Serves 6 – 8

Wine Suggestion: Cerrosol Esperanza, Rueda, Spain

For the Preserved Lemon

- 4 lemons, quartered
- ¾ cup kosher salt

MIX salt and quartered lemons in airtight container. A ziplock bag works well. Make sure to squeeze out all air to ensure that mold growth is inhibited. Store in dark place for two months—not in the refrigerator. Cut each quarter into four strips when ready to use.

Mezze Café Hummus

This is a classic Mediterranean spread. Sometimes we have fun with it and purée in a little roasted red peppers, pesto, or sundried tomato for a twist. Mezze Café is a sister restaurant to San Chez Bistro.

Ingredients

1 15-ounce can garbanzo beans, drained, reserving liquid
1 tablespoon plus 1 teaspoon olive oil
½ lemon, juiced
1 medium clove garlic, minced

2 teaspoons tahini, (can substitute peanut butter or crushed sesame seeds)
chef's salt
pita bread

Preparation

PURÉE all ingredients until as smooth as possible. Add reserved liquid until desired consistency is reached. Season to taste with salt. Serve chilled with pita or other flat bread or favorite crackers.

Serves 6

Wine Suggestion: Cerrosol Esperanza, Rueda, Spain

Mezze Café Hummus

Fire Roasted Mussels with Harissa Sauce

San Chez Bistro owner and president, Dan Gendler writes, "Chef Casey and I had a dish similar to this in Chicago at a Moroccan restaurant. We wanted to make it quicker and easier to make and to eat, so we used the larger green-lipped mussels on the half shell instead of the smaller blue/black variety, but both make a wonderful tapa/mezze."

Ingredients

42 half-shell mussels, preferably New
    Zealand Greenlips
9 ounces Mussel Dust (recipe follows)

6 ounces olive oil, divided
6 ounces Harissa Sauce (recipe follows)
1 lemon

Preparation

RUB mussels with the Mussel Dust, and place into a smoking hot sauté pan with 1 ounce of olive oil. Sear the mussels until slightly crisp. Heat the Harissa Sauce in a small saucepan. Serve the Harissa Sauce in a soufflé cup with the lemon wheel as a garnish. Surround the cup with the mussels.

Serves 4

Wine Suggestion: Pircas Negras Organic Syrah, Argentina

For the Mussel Dust

4 ounces Calypso Rub
4 ounces Spanish paprika
2 ounces salt

4 ounces ground cumin
2 ounces cayenne pepper

COMBINE all ingredients and mix well. Store in a tightly sealed container.

For the Harissa Sauce

¼ ounce chile de Arbol
1 lemon
1 tablespoon fresh garlic, chopped
1 teaspoon chef salt
3 cups olive oil
1 cup salsa (favorite store-bought is
    fine)

1½ tablespoons ground cumin
1 tablespoon chicken base
1½ tablespoons Spanish paprika
1½ cups water

SOAK the chiles in very hot water for about 10 minutes. Cut the whole lemon into small pieces without peeling or de-seeding. Once the chiles are rehydrated, de-stem and dice them into small pieces. Purée the chiles and lemon pieces in a food processor. Add all remaining ingredients into processor and continue puréeing until evenly blended.

PAELLA

If you find that you and your family really enjoy cooking and eating paella, then we highly recommend the book *Paella* by Penelope Casas. This is an amazing sourcebook full of tips, tricks, and a history of paella and its many ingredients.

Ingredients

16 ounces vegetable, seafood, or chicken stock
1 tablespoon olive oil
3 ounces Spanish onion, diced
1 ounce green onion, chopped
3 ounces Roma tomato diced,
3 ounces canned pimento
3 ounces peas
1 teaspoon fresh garlic, chopped
2 teaspoon fresh parsley, chopped

½ teaspoon saffron threads
½ teaspoon spicy smoked paprika
⅛ teaspoon white pepper
10 ounces or slightly less, meat, poultry, shellfish, vegetables in any combination
5 ounces Arborio rice
½ teaspoon kosher salt
¼ lemon

Preparation

PREHEAT oven to 400 degrees. Heat the stock so that it is hot, but not boiling, and reserve keeping it warm. Heat the olive oil in the paella pan on medium to high temperature. Add the onions, tomatoes, peas, and pimentos and sauté until the vegetables are tender. Add the garlic, parsley, and the spices; mix evenly into the vegetables. Add in the main ingredients, your choice of meat, poultry, shellfish, and/ or vegetables. Cook lightly. Add the rice and incorporate it evenly into the mixture. Add the reserved stock, 8 ounces at a time, mixing it well with the rice and other ingredients. Add salt to taste. Bring the stock to a boil, stirring and rotating the pan occasionally. When the rice is no longer soupy but sufficient liquid remains to continue cooking the rice (about 5 minutes) transfer to the oven and cook, uncovered, about 15 minutes in a 400-degree oven. The rice should be al dente (tender but firm). Remove to a warm spot, cover with foil and let sit for 5 to 10 minutes to finish cooking. Juice the quarter lemon over the paella and mix it up with a pair of serving spoons.

Serves 4

Wine Suggestion: Mar de Frades Albarino, Rias Baixas, Spain

The Sardine Room

2536 Henry Street
Muskegon, MI 49441
231-755-5008
www.sardineroom.com

Lunch and Dinner
Monday – Thursday: 11:00am–11:00pm
Friday & Saturday 11:00am–Midnight
Sunday, Dinner only 4:00pm–9:00pm

The Sardine Room

Chef / co-owner Chris Anderson
Dave Biesiada, Co-owner

For all the excited chatter about the California gold rush, it's interesting to note that Michigan's timber era created more millionaires by far than California's gold. Muskegon alone, with its deepwater port, counted forty millionaires during the height of the lumber rush due to the log-friendly and lengthy Muskegon River, which offered a direct waterway to Chicago. Often overlooked between west Michigan's stylish southern beach communities and the resort towns of northern-lower Michigan, the coastal city of Muskegon is surprisingly diverse and, owing to its lumber era exploits, still swaggers a bit.

Muskegon's restaurant scene took a Paul Bunyan leap forward in November of 1998 with the opening of the Sardine Room on Henry Street in the West Village Plaza. As is the case in so many successful restaurants, the Sardine Room owners also serve as manager and chef. In fact, Dave Biesiada and Chris Anderson have been friends since high school. Their restaurant experience amounts to over forty years combined and the menu they created is a unique take on the best of contemporary American cuisine, from Chicago to New Orleans. It all adds up to one of the premier restaurants in west Michigan drawing diners from Pentwater, Ludington, Grand Haven, Holland, and even Grand Rapids. And, with a mere eighty seats, when the Sardine Room is really cranking they pack the place like, well…, sardines.

A beautiful marble bar with half a dozen bar stools and a stunning twenty-foot arched mural created by Michigan artist Michael Pfleghaar greet diners as they enter, offering an ideal place to enjoy an aperitif while a table is readied. Designer Tyler Deveroux utilizes soft earthy tones, vintage French artwork, displays of wine, and modern light fixtures all offset by a huge stone fireplace in the dining room to create a sophisticated yet comfortable interior. Longtime diners also look forward to warmer weather when there's thirty more seats scattered under hanging baskets of hibiscus on the outdoor patio.

The menu is temptingly eclectic. Chef Anderson's style may best be described as "upscale American comfort food with Asian and Latin influences." What could be more reassuring than Center Cut Pork Chops with Jack Daniels Glaze and Apple Chutney? Classic takes on filet mignon, NY strip, chargrilled lamb chops also round out the dinner entrées, along with BBQ Ribs, and even the Italian dish Osso Bucco. Depending on the season, seafood lovers will have a choice of Macadamia-crusted Grouper, Whitefish with Lemon Caper Butter, Sesame Seared Ahi Tuna, and the house specialty of fried Lake Perch, amongst other enticing offerings.

The Sardine Room wine list is reasonably priced and diverse. They host a Wine School on the third Monday of every month where guests can taste through a flight of five or six wines and nibble on light hors d'ouevres.

Mixed Greens with Apples, Pecans, and Gorgonzola

The pecan vinaigrette dressing has a very sweet, unique flavor and goes very well with any bitter greens, vegetables, or strong cheeses.

Ingredients

- 1 head iceberg lettuce
- 1 head romaine lettuce
- 4 ounces spring mix of greens
- 1 green apple, chopped into ¼-inch squares

- 1 cup roasted pecans (roasted in the oven for 10 minutes at 400 degrees)
- 1 cup crumbled Gorgonzola cheese
- ½ cup sweet red bell pepper, diced
  Pecan Vinaigrette (recipe follows)

Preparation

CHOP the iceberg and romaine to desired size then combine and toss with other greens, apple, whole roasted pecans, gorgonzola, and red pepper. Toss salad with Pecan Vinaigrette and serve.

Serves 4

Wine Suggestion: Rocky Gully Dry Riesling

For the Pecan Vinaigrette

- 2 cups whole or chopped pecans
- 2 cups granulated sugar
- 1 cup red wine vinegar
- 1 cup rice wine vinegar

- 1 tablespoon kosher salt
- ½ tablespoon dry tarragon leaf
- 2 cups vegetable oil
- 1 cup olive oil

IN A large mixing bowl combine all dressing ingredients and whisk until the dressing is fairly emulsified.

Yield: about 5 cups

BRANDY BUTTERED SEA SCALLOPS

This is a simple but amazing dish offering bold, rich buttery flavor to one of the treasures of the sea. Serve with a favorite rice dish or vegetable for a complete meal.

Ingredients

1 *pound fresh sea scallops*	¼ *cup brown sugar*
salt and pepper	3 *ounces brandy*
3 *tablespoons butter*	

Preparation

LIGHTLY dust the scallops with salt and pepper. Heat a sauté pan over medium heat, add 1 tablespoon of butter then sear scallops for approximately 3 minutes on each side until browned all over. Turn off heat. Mix brown sugar with brandy then add to scallops in pan. Caution! The brandy may flare with fire briefly, but this is normal. Once the sugar has caramelized slightly, add remaining 2 tablespoons of butter and stir. Remove to serving dish.

Serves 4

Wine Suggestion: Bennett Family Chardonnay

Turkey Melt Sandwich with Roasted Shallot Aioli

Bursting with flavor due to a zesty sandwich spread.

Ingredients

rye bread, sliced for sandwiches
Roasted Shallot Aioli (recipe follows)
sliced deli turkey (approximately 4
ounces per sandwich)
sliced mushrooms sautéed in butter

cooked bacon
sliced Fontina cheese
sliced tomato
sliced red onion
iceberg lettuce

Preparation

TOAST 2 slices of bread per sandwich and spread the Roasted Shallot Aioli on both pieces. In a skillet or surface of your choice, pile the turkey, mushrooms, and bacon and heat thoroughly. Place a slice of Fontina on top and allow to melt. Place the heated melt on 1 slice of bread then top with the raw vegetables to finish sandwich.

Wine Suggestion: Thomas Fogarty Gewurztraminer

For the Roasted Shallot Aioli

1 tablespoon butter
1 shallot, finely minced
1 tablespoon garlic, minced

1 teaspoon kosher salt
2 teaspoons granulated sugar
2 cups real mayonnaise

MELT butter in sauté pan over medium low heat. Add shallot, garlic, salt, and sugar. Lightly sauté until sugar seems to caramelize a bit and garlic becomes slightly soft and translucent. Be careful not to burn the garlic, as it will ruin the flavor of the aioli. Place mayonnaise in a small mixing bowl and add onion/garlic mixture from sauté pan. Scrape pan thoroughly with rubber spatula to remove all juices and seasonings. Mix and let stand for about 30 minutes to meld flavors.

Yield: about 2 cups

BRANDY DIJON FILET MIGNON

The staff at The Sardine Room often hear from diners "this is the best steak I've ever had."

Ingredients

2 ounces butter
4 8-ounce center cut filet mignons

Lawry's seasoning salt
Brandy Dijon Sauce (recipe follows)

Preparation

PREHEAT grill. Melt butter in small saucepan and skim off white impurities as they rise to top. Brush each filet with the clarified butter and season with Lawry's seasoning salt. Char-grill. Before turning steak, brush with additional butter and more Lawry's. Serve with Brandy Dijon Sauce.

Serves 4

Wine Suggestion: BR Cohn "Silver Label" Cabernet

For the Brandy Dijon Sauce

1 cup yellow onion, small dice
4 tablespoons unsalted butter
½ cup brandy
2 tablespoons Jim Beam whiskey
1 4-ounce can green peppercorns, drained
1 tablespoon chopped garlic

⅓ cup whole grain Dijon mustard
1 quart heavy cream
1 quart beef stock
2 tablespoons kosher salt
½ cup roux (approximately), equal parts butter and flour

IN medium stockpot begin lightly sautéing the onion with 2 ounces butter. Add the brandy and whiskey, and let simmer for 5 minutes. Add the remaining ingredients except the roux and bring to a boil. Add the roux and thicken.

Yield: about 2 quarts

MACADAMIA NUT CRUSTED FLORIDA GROUPER
with Vanilla Mango Sauce

We didn't realize how well-liked this dish was until we took it off the menu. Our guests strongly protested and we put it back on.

Ingredients

2 eggs
2 cups milk
2 cups Drake's Seasoning Flour, or a
   substitute
1 cup macadamia nuts, finely chopped

1 tablespoon Old Bay seasoning
2 pounds fresh grouper
2 ounces vegetable oil
   Vanilla Mango Sauce (recipe follows)

Preparation

PREHEAT oven to 400 degrees. Whisk together egg and milk in small mixing bowl. In another mixing bowl combine Drake's, chopped nuts, and Old Bay seasoning. Cut the grouper into 6 equal portions of approximately 5 to 6 ounces each. Dip each piece of fish into egg wash then dredge in nut mixture, making sure to lightly coat the entire piece of fish. Place a large frying pan over medium heat with the vegetable oil. When the oil is hot, place breaded fish portions in the pan, searing each side for about 2 minutes. Remove fish from the pan and place them on a baking sheet and bake in the oven for 12 to 15 minutes.

TO SERVE, place fish on plate and pour approximately ¼ cup sauce over each piece of fish.

Serves 6

Wine Suggestion: Altanuta Pinot Grigio

For Vanilla Mango Sauce

3 fresh mangoes (skinned, pitted and
   blended in a food processor yielding 2
   cups purée)

2 tablespoons vanilla extract
⅓ cup mango syrup
1 cup butter

IN A small stockpot or saucepan bring the mango purée, vanilla extract, and mango syrup to a simmer. Add butter and remove from heat. Stir until the butter is melted and blended consistently in the sauce.

Spring clean-up parade, Front Street, Traverse City, (1912).

Pennsylvania Central Airlines commercial airliner, Traverse City, (circa 1940).

Amical

amical

229 East Front Street
Traverse City, MI 49684
231-941-8888
www.amical.com

Lunch Monday through Saturday
11:00am – 4:00 pm
Dinner nightly 5:00pm – 10:00pm
Sunday Brunch 9:00am – 3:00pm

Amical

Chef / owner Dave Denison

For the wealth of fine dining restaurants dotting north-west lower Michigan over the past quarter century, Traverse City trudged through years without authentic, hand prepared food. That is, until the late 1990s when a French-inspired bakery/cafe with the playful name La Cuisine Amical transformed itself into a full-service bistro with an open kitchen reminiscent of something you might find on Paris' Left Bank. Now simply referred to as Amical, the city has been showering its appreciation ever since.

The adoration is most often directed toward Dave Denison, Amical's Executive Chef and co-owner (Don and Judy Phillips are partners). A chef/restaurateur in southern California for twenty years, Denison epitomizes the gracious host, frequently bouncing from behind the line to greet familiar patrons. It also helps that he is blessed with a fabulous kitchen staff including culinary school graduates Jon Eakes and Keil Moshier, the workhorses behind the seasonal menus. Recently, dishes like Lamb with Apricots & Almonds, Moroccan-Style Duck Breast, and Plantain-Crusted Salmon received most of the attention, but Denison's West Coast background assures Asian flavors and fresh seafood will always be available. First-time diners always pause to gawk at the French pastries, tarts, custards, and other heart-stoppers displayed steps inside the doorway.

In 1997, Amical introduced the monthly Cookbook Dinner Series featuring a one-week menu drawn from acclaimed cookbooks. Over the years, books authored by Thomas Keller, Cindy Pawlcyn, Mario Batali, Ming Tsai, and Marcus Samuelsson have been covered. The series has provided guests of Amical with a continuing array of ethnic menus throughout the winter and spring seasons.

Amical's wine list is bistro brief with perhaps seventy-five wines, but it represents a carefully chosen selection of predominantly French and North American gems. The dining room is managed by the ever-smiling and attentive Vicki Kaley who oversees a staff of servers, many of whom have been with Amical for years. They know how special this restaurant is and their devotion shows through to Amical's patrons.

Amical is located on Front Street in Traverse City's downtown district. For movie buffs, next door is the State Theater, now owned by the TC Film Festival Foundation and the main venue for the week-long festival held in August.

THAI CRAB CAKES

This recipe is a refreshing version of the traditional crab cake preparation. The zing comes from the peppers and lemon zest combined with fresh herbs. The cakes are great over a green salad.

Ingredients

2 cups cooked jasmine rice prepared
    with 2 tablespoons red lentils
1 pound crabmeat, canned claw meat
2 medium peppers, jalapeno or Serrano,
    chopped
1 tablespoon lemon zest
¼ cup fresh basil, chopped
3 tablespoons fresh mint leaves,
    chopped

1 lemon, juiced
2 teaspoons low-sodium soy sauce
1 teaspoon white pepper
2 large eggs beaten
¼ cup breadcrumbs
1 tablespoon olive oil

Preparation

COOK jasmine rice to package instructions. Add 2 tablespoons red lentils 10 minutes before rice is done. Chill rice and lentil mixture. Drain crabmeat and pick through for shells. In a large bowl gently combine the crabmeat, cooked rice and lentils, jalapenos, lemon zest, basil, and mint, then squeeze in the lemon juice. Stir in soy sauce, pepper, eggs, and bread crumbs, trying not to break up the crabmeat. Spoon 2 tablespoons onto parchment paper and press into a cake that is no more than 2 inches in diameter. Repeat with rest of mixture and chill. Preheat oven to 325 degrees. Heat olive oil in sauté pan and cook cakes until nicely browned on each side, approximately 1½ minutes per side. Add more olive oil as needed. Finish cooking cakes in oven for 5 minutes. Cakes may be prepared ahead and re-warmed in oven.

Yield: 16 two-ounce cakes

Wine Suggestion: Peninsula Cellars Pinot Grigio

Chicken Pot Pie

In the mid-nineties, comfort foods were beginning to come back into vogue. This comfort classic was added to our menu at the suggestion of partner Don Phillips, who was savoring a hot, golden-crusted entrée when we first opened. This dish has been featured on our menu from the very beginning. We like the light texture of the puff pastry versus a traditional savory pie dough topping.

Ingredients

4 ounces margarine
½ cup all-purpose flour
½ cup carrots, peeled and diced
½ cup celery, diced
1 small onion, diced
½ cup frozen peas
1 cup mushrooms, sliced
1 cup whole milk
1 cup heavy whipping cream
1 pound cooked potatoes, skinned and diced

2 cups cooked chicken breast, diced
1 tablespoon chicken base
1 tablespoon chervil
½ tablespoon dried basil
¼ tablespoon salt
¼ tablespoon pepper
2 tablespoons grated Parmesan
1 sheet puff pastry dough
1 egg white

Preparation

PREHEAT oven to 350 degrees. Melt margarine in small stockpot and sauté vegetables until onions are translucent. Add flour, stir and simmer for approximately 5 minutes to make a roux. Add milk, cream, potatoes, chicken, chicken base, spices, and Parmesan. Continue stirring until sauce thickens. Correct seasonings. Add more roux if mixture needs further thickening. Remove from stove. Pour mixture evenly into 6 individual 16-ounce ovenproof bowls. Or, one large casserole/baking dish can be used.

CUT out a round piece of puff pastry to cover. Brush pastry with eggwhite and bake at 350 degrees for 12 to 14 minutes, until pastry is golden brown and filling bubbles. (Larger casserole dish will take longer to cook.) Mixture can be made up to 3 days in advance.

Serves 6

Wine Suggestion: Belleruche Côte du Rhone

Raspberry Crème Brûlée

While just about every restaurant has a version of crème brûlée on their menu, our simple but elegant presentation is still one of the best. One of our local French patrons suggested early on to allow the crème brûlée to come to room temperature before caramelizing the sugar. A small touch, but definitely the best way to serve.

Ingredients

66-72 raspberries, depending on size
   3 cups heavy whipping cream
   8 large egg yolks
  ¼ cup sugar

  1 pinch salt
  1 teaspoon vanilla extract
12 tablespoons sugar, for caramelization
  6 sprigs fresh mint, for garnish

Preparation

PREHEAT oven to 350 degrees. Place 7 or 8 raspberries in the bottom of 6 different fluted ramekins. Bring the cream to a simmer in saucepan. In a separate bowl, whisk in the eggs, sugar, and salt. Then slowly add the hot cream, whisking all the while. Add vanilla extract. Divide mixture evenly between ramekins, set in a baking pan and place in oven. Pour preheated water into the baking pan halfway up the side of the ramekins. Bake for 30 to 35 minutes until set. Do not over bake.

REMOVE ramekins from pan to cool. Chill thoroughly. For service, sprinkle 2 tablespoons of sugar evenly over the top of each ramekin and caramelize sugar with a torch. Let set until hardened. Serve with a garnish of 4 to 5 fresh raspberries and a sprig of fresh mint.

Serves 6

Wine Suggestion: Late Harvest Riesling, or Ice Wine

Amical

157

Traverse City State Hospital, (circa 1900).

Mrs. Michigan publicity shoot in Traverse City with cherry cobbler, (circa 1960).

Trattoria Stella

Grand Traverse Commons
1200 West Eleventh Street
Traverse City, MI 49684
231-929-8989
www.stellatc.com

Lunch and Dinner
Monday – Thursday 11:30am – 9:00pm
Friday & Saturday 11:30am – 11:00pm
Sunday, dinner only 5:00pm – 9:00pm

Trattoria Stella

Executive Chef Myles Anton
Paul & Amanda Danielson, Owners

An asylum is an asylum is an asylum before taking a quiet respite – as if exorcising its demons – followed by the birth of an Italian restaurant instantly acclaimed as northern Michigan's best. In all seriousness, the Willow Lake State Hospital opened in 1885 and soon after acquired the name Northern Michigan Asylum before settling on the passive Traverse City State Hospital, which closed for good in 1989. Narrowly avoiding demolition, a full fifteen years passed before Paul and Amanda Danielson opened the doors to Trattoria Stella, the cornerstone business in the redevelopment of the former hospital's main 380,000 square foot Italianate-styled building. The ongoing project includes both office and residential space. Trattoria Stella occupies a portion of the garden level with exposed brick, open rafters, and classic arches bringing to mind the bistros and trattorias of Europe.

Local farmers, wineries, and artisans came to realize the happy marriage of their bounty with first-rate Italian cuisine. In fact, Stella buys from no less than forty northern Michigan suppliers and can't wait to include more. What this means is the herbs, arugula, beets, fingerling yams, Bibb lettuce, onions, pumpkins, squash, blueberries, strawberries, pears, maple syrup, cream, eggs, honey, sausage, trout, and rabbit, etc., add untold integrity to the food prepared by executive chef Myles Anton and his kitchen staff.

Anton's menus change every lunch and dinner. One day might bring grilled rainbow trout with sweet pea risotto and peppered mâche, and the next day, pork tenderloin with Calabrese sausage, butternut squash and maple sciroppo or sweet potato ravioli with seared parsnips, spiced nuts and brandy cream sauce. From the pasta to the gelato, everything served at Stella is made from scratch. Menus always include an enticing array of hot and cold antipasti, several pasta dishes, and four or five primary plates such as the aforementioned trout and pork presentations.

Amanda is responsible for the admirable Stella wine program. By the glass offerings number at least forty while the several hundred bottle main list includes rare varietals, Italian classics, and the best from the ever-improving local wine regions. As expected, *Wine Spectator* honors Stella with an *Award of Excellence*, year after year. A number of the waitstaff have earned Sommelier Certification status and, with Amanda's encouragement, more are studying for this challenge as well. The bar is thoroughly stocked with craft beers and fine liquors, including a few stellar grappas.

 Award of Excellence

AGNELLO CRUDO CON POMODORO (DUE PREPARAZIONE)

Appetizer: Lamb "Tartare" with Tomatoes Two Ways

Ingredients

1 pound ground lamb (the finest quality available, local if possible)	1st Tomato Accompaniment (recipe follows)
1 small red onion, minced extra fine	2nd Tomato Accompaniment (recipe follows)
4 tablespoons extra virgin olive oil	crostini
salt & pepper	

Preparation

TOSS lamb with minced onion, olive oil, and heavy amounts of salt & pepper. The trick here is to use enough salt & pepper. It will make or break the tartare.

Serve all items in separate piles on a board or platter with toasted bread. To add the extra touch, I sometimes melt a mildly stinky cheese (like Taleggio or Fontina Val D'Aosta) onto the crostini breads.

Serves 4

Wine Suggestion: Ucceliera, Rosso di Montalcino Rocca di Castagnoli, Chianti Classico
Even with the tomatoes to balance the fat in the lamb, the mere notion of raw red meat screams Sangiovese. In particular, a fine Chianti Classico would do nicely, but my favorite expression of this classic grape with this dish is Rosso di Montalcino.

For the 1st Tomato Accompaniment

2 vine ripe tomatoes	1 tablespoon minced garlic
½ cup extra virgin olive oil	salt & pepper

PREHEAT oven to 200 degrees. Slice the vine ripe tomatoes into thin disks. Toss in a bowl with olive oil, garlic, salt, and pepper. Spread out on a cookie pan with parchment paper. Slow roast for 2 hours at 200 degrees. Chill.

For the 2nd Tomato Accompaniment

½ cup sundried tomatoes (nice quality, reddish tinted & plump)	¼ cup olive oil
	salt & pepper

BUZZ sundried tomatoes & olive oil in a food processor until pasty. Season to taste.

ZUPPA DI PORCINI
Porcini Mushroom Soup with Cream

Porcini mushrooms are used extensively in Tuscan food. This is my play on a simple mushroom soup I had the extreme pleasure of sampling in Montacatini Alto, Italy (in the heart of Tuscany.) It is a hit every time it makes it onto the menu at Stella. Fresh porcinis are very hard to find in the U.S. even for chefs and restaurants, so I substitute the dried version. If by chance you do find fresh porcinis, don't under-utilize them in soups. Instead, highlight their freshness by simply grilling and serving with a salad or on a nice steak. Also, let's talk about garlic. Please do NOT use pre-minced garlic in water. The extra time to mince fresh makes all the difference in every recipe. It's another little secret we in restaurants rely on heavily.

Ingredients

1 large white onion, diced
½ pound dried porcini mushrooms
1 teaspoon dried thyme
1 teaspoon garlic, minced
⅛ pound butter

⅛ pound flour
1 quart mushroom stock (chicken stock or even water can be substituted)
½ cup heavy whipping cream
   salt & pepper

Preparation

SWEAT (sauté on low heat slowly) the onions, dried porcinis, thyme, garlic, and butter. Add the flour and mix. Add stock, and whisk. Bring to a low simmer. Simmer for 1 hour on low. Season to taste. Buzz the soup with a handheld food processor or mix in a blender until smooth. Add cream and season to taste again.

SERVE with chopped fresh chives, toasted crostini, or flatleaf parsley. Put a few drops of extra virgin olive oil into the bowl to finish, it adds a little extra richness and body.

Serves 4

Wine Suggestion: Parusso, Nebbiolo Langhe
Ferrando "Etichetta Bianca" Carema (Nebbiolo)
I suggest earthy aromatics found in Pinot Noirs, France or Oregon, or in Nebbiolo. There's need to spring for a pricey Barbaresco or Barolo; try a Nebbiolo Langhe or something from Carema.

Costoletta de Maiale con Mela e Maple Sciroppa
Pork Cutlets with Apples & Maple Syrup

I believe very strongly in using local produce, meats, and food products as frequently as possible. I developed this fall recipe to showcase Traverse City's best eating apple, the prized Honeycrisp (courtesy of Bardenhagen Farms on Leelanau Peninsula). It turned into a "hat trick" dish by pairing the apples with local pork (from Halpin Farms of Kaleva) and local butternut squash (from Edmonson Farms on the famed Old Mission Peninsula). Throw in local maple syrup (Majszak Farm) and the entire dish literally came from Stella's back yard. Honeycrisps work best, but substitute any good tasting apple.

Ingredients

1 large butternut squash	olive oil
½ cup honey (Sleeping Bear Farms, Leelanau Peninsula)	2 links Calabrese sausage (a spicy Italian reddish sausage), sliced thin
½ cup brown sugar	2 Honeycrisp apples, cut in French fry-like sticks
¼ pound butter	
salt & pepper	½ cup maple syrup
2 pork tenderloins, cleaned (from your local reputable butcher)	½ cup pork or chicken stock
	⅛ pound butter

Preparation

PREHEAT oven to 300 degrees. Quarter butternut squash. Scoop out the seeds and discard. Place squash in a roasting pan and top with honey, brown sugar, butter and a pinch of salt and pepper. Pour ½-inch of water in bottom of the pan. Roast covered in foil for 2 hours in 300-degree oven until tender. Keep warm until service.

RAISE oven temperature to 400 degrees. Cut each tenderloin into 2 pieces. Season with salt and pepper. Sear in a smoking hot pan with olive oil until brown on all sides. Transfer to a baking pan and finish in 400-degree oven for 5-8 minutes until desired doneness (medium rare to medium is my preference). Let stand for 5 minutes.

MEANWHILE, sear Calabrese sausage & apples in the initial tenderloin pan until sausage is 90% cooked. Add maple syrup, stock, and butter, bring to a boil…this is your sauce!

PLACE tenderloin on squash and pour sauce over both.

Serves 4

Wine Suggetion: Vestini Campagnano "Le Ortole" Pallagrello Bianco
Caggiano "Macchia dei Goti" Taurasi, Aglianico
If you like rustic and peppery, then try a Taurasi or Aglianico del Vulture—both red. A white wine option, if you can find it, is Pallagrello Bianco from Campagna—delicious!

Tonno alla Liguriana
Tuna in the Style of Liguria

Liguria is the thin coastal strip of land in Italy made famous by the "five villages" of Cinque Terre. As it is the Italian Riviera, seafood abounds, but also equally famous is the area's basil pesto. This is my take on a traditional preparation highlighting both the seafood and the pesto. The green beans and potatoes are a classic pairing with tuna (think of the French and their Niçoise). As with all wine pairings, grapes from the region work best with the food from that region. It just so happens that a lot of Vermintino is produced in this area. The clear brightness of the wine shines in unison with the crisp basil and garlic.

Ingredients

¼ pound green beans (thin haricot vert types work best)
1 large Idaho potato, peeled & cubed
½ teaspoon olive oil
Trenette Pasta (recipe follows)
Basil Pesto (recipe follows)

¼ pound baby spinach
4 5-ounce ahi tuna steaks (from a reputable fishmonger)
pinch cracked black pepper
salt
extra virgin olive oil

Preparation

BLANCH green beans in boiling salted water for 30 seconds. Shock in ice water to stop cooking. Strain. Blanch potatoes in boiling salted water for 15-18 minutes until fork tender. Shock in ice water to stop cooking. Strain. In a deep sauté pan, add ½ teaspoon olive oil and sear potatoes until golden brown. (Should have a hash brown appearance).

REDUCE heat to medium-low and add cooked Trenette Pasta to potatoes. Add ¼ cup water and Basil Pesto. Stir until warm. Add green beans, spinach. Take it to the plates.

DUST tuna steaks with cracked black pepper and salt. Sear in a smoking hot pan with olive oil until cooked to your liking. Serve on top of pasta and tell the story of Liguria's most famous dish.

Serves 4

Wine Suggestion: Bisson "Marea" Cinque Terre (Bosco, Vermentino and Albarola)
Vermentino is the classic grape here and will work well with this dish. With a little searching, you may find blends of indigenous white grape varieties from Cinque Terre that can be delicious and quite food friendly. Stay away from the sweet ones though.

For the Trenette Pasta

6 eggs
¼ cup semolina flour
¾ cup all-purpose flour

1 tablespoon extra virgin olive oil
pinch salt & pepper

MIX all ingredients in a mixer with a dough hook until stiff and incorporated. Form into a dough ball. Wrap in plastic wrap and chill in refrigerator for 2 hours.

ROLL out into thinnest setting on a pasta roller. Trenette pasta is classically the width of a fettuccine noodle with a jagged saw-like edge on one side. Achieve this by cutting one side with a knife and the other with a ravioli cutter. Cook in salted boiling water until al dente. Shock in ice water to stop cooking. Strain. (If making fresh pasta is too much, simply substitute a nice fresh store-bought fettuccine noodle.)

For the Basil Pesto

¼ pound fresh basil leaves
⅛ pound baby spinach
2 cloves garlic

1 tablespoon toasted pine nuts
¾ cup olive oil
salt & pepper

BUZZ all ingredients in a food processor. Season to taste. As a side note: I like my basil pesto oily and bright green. The spinach gives the green. I also leave out Parmesan cheese, which some find reprehensible, but I feel it muddles the pesto. All that said, if you have a pesto recipe you like better, by all means, go for it.

PANNA COTTA CON FRAGOLA E VANIGLIA
Panna Cotta with Strawberries and Vanilla

Ingredients

2 vanilla beans
⅓ cup granulated sugar
3 cups, plus 2 tablespoons heavy
    whipping cream

½ tablespoon powdered gelatin
Strawberry Sauce (recipe follows)

Preparation

SPLIT 1 vanilla bean and scrape the seeds out. (Reserve scrapings for sauce). Blend ⅓ cup of sugar and vanilla bean pod in food processor until mixed.

CUT the other vanilla bean lengthwise and scrape into pot. Add the bean pod to pot also. Add 3 cups heavy cream and vanilla sugar mixture to pot. Bring to a boil. Remove from heat. Cover with plastic wrap. Let stand for 10 minutes.

IN A separate bowl, add 2 tablespoons cream. Sprinkle the gelatin on top. Let stand for 10 minutes for gelatin to bloom.

BRING vanilla cream back up to a boil, whisk in gelatin cream mixture. Let boil together for 1 minute. Strain.

SPRAY 6 ceramic bowls with nonstick pan spray; divide mixture evenly between the bowls. Refrigerate for 3 hours until firm.

UNMOLD panna cotta from bowls onto plates. A spatula or knife may be needed to loosen the edges. Finish with Strawberry Sauce.

Serves 6

Wine Suggestions: Badia Coltibuono Vin Santo del Chianti Classico
Maculan "Dindarello" Moscato
Accompanying the dessert, you may enjoy Moscato d'Asti or Vin Santo, the latter being richer. Then, finish the whole meal off with a shot of espresso and a nip of good Jacopo Poli Grappa.

For the Strawberry Sauce

2 tablespoons corn starch
8 tablespoons water
5 cups fresh strawberries, sliced ¼ inch
    thick

vanilla bean scrapings from above
½ cup water
½ cup sugar
½ fresh lemon, juiced

COMBINE cornstarch and water in bowl and mix well. Combine strawberries and vanilla bean scrapings with the ½ cup of water and sugar in a sauce pot. Bring to boil and add cornstarch mixture. Return to a boil. Remove from heat. Add lemon juice. Transfer to a container and chill until cool.

North
Centennial Inn

NORTH
FINE FOOD, WINE & SPIRITS
A CENTENNIAL INN ★ 1893

149 E. Harbor Highway
Maple City, MI 49664
231-228-5060
www.northci.com

Open 7 days, Jul. – Mid-Sept.
Wed. –Sun., Mid-Sept. – Dec.
Friday – Sunday, Jan. – Mid-April
Wed. – Sun., Mid-Apr. – Mid-Jun.
Tues. – Sun., Mid-Jun. – Jul.

North Centennial Inn

Chef / co-owner Greg Murphy
Nick and Livia Vanden Belt, Co-Owners

For centuries, travelers around the world have utilized the hospitality of roadside inns to secure overnight lodging and meals, earning them the distinction of being one of history's oldest industries. We can also assume they nurtured along the evolution of food and cooking as more than simply filling the belly. The exchange of money has a way of inspiring innovation and competition. Word travels fast in the form of restaurant reviews when carried along by discerning travelers.

Country inns, and the more recent phenomenon of bed and breakfasts, abound in Michigan's abundant rural areas. Since the 1890s, Leelanau County has been blessed with a stately two-story inn on Little Traverse Lake. But in recent times, its stellar reputation stemmed from the quality of the food they put in guests' bellies. Formerly the Leelanau Country Inn, the building was purchased and refurbished in 2005 as a restaurant intent on national attention. Word has it North Centennial Inn is well on its way.

Chef/owner Greg Murphy and his partners Nick and Livia Vanden Belt sought a contemporary feel for the interior of the restaurant. The walls and dining room carpet are sand-colored and large windows assure "lightness" in both senses of the word. Wood floors and darker tones carry through the lobby into a modern bar setting of particular warmth. The wrap-around enclosed porch assures no one will lose sight of the building's country inn beginnings.

Murphy's background includes twelve years as Executive Chef at Le Becasse, a very fine French restaurant not far away on Glen Lake. With appetizers like Sweet Pea Napoleon, Seafood Crepe, and Country Pâte, we can see that the cooking of France still heavily influences Murphy. But others dishes including Boursin and Basil Won Ton Ravioli, and Shiitake Gnocchi tossed with artichoke hearts announce his newfound culinary freedom.

Gallic elegance however, is seen everywhere in his creations. He serves basil-chicken mousseline, for instance, over chicken breast in a potato crust, and uses the technique again in a roasted duck breast dish where he also stuffs quail with white truffle & chicken mousseline before finishing with wild mushroom sauce. White truffles make another appearance in a demi glace served over elk chops. Also deserving of mention on the list of entrées are yellow fin tuna and lobster served with a mango-ginger vinaigrette, and Pheasant Wellington: pheasant breast stuffed with confit of duck leg, shiitake mushrooms and dried cherries, wrapped in puff pastry, baked, and served with green peppercorn-cognac sauce.

Murphy is also a regular at wine tastings and trade shows put on by Michigan wine distributors, a good indication of the careful thought put into North's excellent cellar of wine.

ROASTED POTATO & SHIITAKE MUSHROOM SOUP

Ingredients

1 small onion	½ teaspoon green peppercorns
3 pounds large Idaho or russet potatoes	12 ounces shiitake mushroom caps
4 ounces Parmesan cheese, shredded	2 cups heavy cream, divided
(for Parmesan crisps)	1 tablespoon green onion, chopped
1 quart chicken broth	

Preparation

PREHEAT oven to 350 degrees. Wash onion and potatoes. Do not peel. Bake in oven for 90 minutes, until vegetables are cooked through. Cool for 30 minutes or so.

WHILE the potatoes are baking, place a sheet of parchment paper on a baking sheet and place 8 separate scoops of shredded Parmesan onto parchment like mounds of cookie dough. Place in 350-degree oven for 15 minutes after removing potatoes.

PEEL onion and potatoes once they are cool. Chop the onion and 2 pounds of the potatoes. Place in soup pot with chicken broth and green peppercorns. Bring to a boil and simmer for 10 minutes. Purée with hand blender or in food processor until smooth. Add shiitake mushrooms and 1½ cups of the cream. Bring back to simmer and cook for 15 minutes. Adjust seasonings if needed. Place remaining cream and potatoes in a saucepot. Bring to a boil and mash together with a potato masher. Season to taste with salt and pepper.

PLACE large spoonful (⅛ of potato and cream mixture) in a large soup bowl. Ladle 8 ounces soup over potato mixture. Garnish with Parmesan crisp and chopped green onions.

Serves 8

Wine Suggestion: Susana Balbo Torrontes

CHICKEN STRUDEL WITH MUSTARD SAUCE

Ingredients

8 5-ounce chicken breasts
4 ounces baby spinach
1 roasted red bell pepper, fresh or
    canned, sliced into 8 strips

8 ounces French feta cheese
1 package phyllo dough
½ cup melted butter
    Mustard Sauce (recipe follows)

Preparation

PREHEAT oven to 375 degrees. Place chicken between 2 plastic freezer bags and pound to an even thickness of approximately 3/8 inch. Trim chicken to a rectangular dimension of 5 by 6 inches. Place spinach over entire breast. At one end, place a slice of red bell pepper and 1 ounce of feta. Starting with the pepper/cheese end, roll the breast and filling as tightly as possible. Set aside and repeat with remaining chicken breasts.

REMOVE phyllo from package. (It is important to work quickly with phyllo, as it will dry out and crumble rather quickly. It is a good idea to keep a damp paper towel over the exposed phyllo when not being used.) Lay out 2 layers of phyllo and brush with melted butter. Place chicken roulade at one end of the phyllo sheets and roll but only one-third of the way and then tuck in one side. Roll one-third more and tuck in the other side. Butter the remaining end and complete rolling. Also, butter the top to seal the dough and prevent drying.

BAKE for 25 minutes. Allow strudels to rest 5 minutes before slicing into thirds with a serrated knife and serving atop a bed of Mustard Sauce.

Serves 8

Wine Suggestion: Napema Sauvignon Blanc, Argentina

For the Mustard Sauce

2 cups heavy cream
¼ cup Dijon mustard
¼ cup stone ground mustard

1 tablespoon garlic, chopped
¼ teaspoon white pepper

PLACE all ingredients in a saucepot and bring to a boil over medium heat, stirring frequently to prevent burning. Done. (Incredibly simple, this sauce is very versatile, working well with chicken, beef, pork, and seafood.)

Pheasant Wellington

Ingredients

3 pheasants
mirepoix – ½ cup each, leeks, carrots,
and celery, rough cut
1 pound wild mushrooms
1 tablespoon shallots, chopped
½ teaspoon salt

½ cup dry white wine
1 tablespoon cornstarch
6 ounces foie gras
6-inch x 6-inch sheets puff pastry
1 tablespoon milk
1 egg yolk

Preparation

ONE day ahead of service, break down pheasants and refrigerate breasts overnight. Place all bones, legs, and wings in slow cooker, add mirepoix, and water. Cover pot and simmer for 2 hours. Remove legs and wings. Remove meat from legs and wings and refrigerate until next day. Place leg and wing bones back in pot, cover, and simmer overnight.

ON day of service, strain broth from slow cooker and reduce to 2 cups in a saucepan over medium heat. Discard bones. Sauté mushrooms and shallots; add ½ teaspoon salt, white wine, and ½ cup broth and bring to a boil. Reduce until mushrooms are dry. Place in refrigerator to cool.

HEAT remaining 1½ cups of broth and thicken with cornstarch. Return to boil and set aside, keeping sauce warm for service.

PREHEAT oven to 400 degrees. Place 6" X 6" sheet of pastry on cutting board. Place pheasant breast on top, then 1 ounce of foie gras, leg meat and mushrooms. Wrap pastry around mixture and brush with egg wash (equal parts milk and egg yolk). Bake at 400 degrees until brown, about 25 minutes. Serve with sauce and fresh vegetables.

Serves 6

Wine Suggestion: Grgich Hills Chardonnay

CRÈME BRÛLÉE

Ingredients

9 egg yolks
1 cup powdered sugar
2 cups heavy cream
2 cups milk

1 vanilla bean, split lengthwise
brown sugar for topping, pushed
through sieve or strainer

Preparation

PREHEAT oven to 300 degrees. In a mixing bowl, combine the egg yolks and powdered sugar and set aside. Scald the cream, milk and vanilla bean. Remove the vanilla bean and scrape out the seeds. Return the seeds to the cream/milk mixture. Pour milk mixture into egg yolks and sugar and stir until blended.

POUR mixture into 8-ounce ramekins and bake on a sheet tray at 300 degrees until firm in the middle, approximately 50 minutes. Cool and refrigerate for at least 2 hours before serving.

JUST before serving, sprinkle top with an even coat of brown sugar and caramelize under a broiler or with a blow torch. Note: this recipe does not employ the use of a water bath in cooking. Use one if desired. Additional cooking time will be necessary.

Serves 6

Wine Suggestion: Inniskillin Ice Wine

The

Riverside Inn

The Riverside Inn

302 River Street
Leland, MI 49654
231-256-9971
www.theriverside-inn.com

Summer Schedule
Dinner Nightly 5:00pm – 9:00pm
Sunday Brunch 10:00am – 2:00pm
Spring and Fall Hours Are Limited
Call Ahead

The Riverside Inn

Executive Chef / co-owner Tom Sawyer
Barb & Kate Vilter, Co-Owners

Best known for the Sleeping Bear Dunes National Lakeshore, the exquisite Leelanau Peninsula is home to many charming communities perched along the shore of Lake Michigan. Foremost among them is the village of Leland, unrivaled for its beauty, history, and eclectic shopping. Food and wine lovers throughout the Midwest also know Leland lays claim to one of Michigan's best kept secrets: The Riverside Inn, an impeccably fine restaurant owned by the mother-daughter team of Barb and Kate Vilter, and operated by Kate and her husband, Chef Tom Sawyer.

The Riverside Inn is gifted in so many ways one scarcely knows where to begin. We could talk about the Leland River meandering past, offering an idyllic bank replete with shade from huge oaks and willows. Or the majestic building itself, a hundred-year-old dance hall remodeled back in the 1920s to include a second floor of guest rooms, with an enclosed porch—now serving as the main dining room—overlooking the river. Let's not forget the outdoor patio, a beautiful rectangular lobby bar of marble and wood, and oak floors with a perfectly pitched creak. Indeed, you'd be hard pressed to improve the ambiance.

A sense of tradition and authenticity are trademarks of Chef Sawyer's menus. The subtle variations he'll make on classic dishes stem from his desire to use locally raised produce, meats, cheeses, and other food items. Michigan morel mushrooms, whitefish, dried cherries and blueberries, maple syrup, all make appearances from Sunday brunch through the dinner hour and Michigan-raised ostrich happens to be a mainstay entrée over the past few years. Sawyer's Key West background leads to spirited dishes like whitefish with lime and cilantro aioli then topped with a plantain crust and broiled. Halibut brushed with soy-ginger glaze served with a tangy slaw of bok choy, carrots, and cabbage showcase Tom's personal interest in Asian cooking. But generally you can count on more traditional-minded fare with flair, like a beautiful tower of Black Angus beef tenderloins served with grilled onions and blue cheese whip, or Pekin duck breast accompanied with porcini and black truffle polenta cake.

Kate Vilter's passion is wine. She's far along the path to achieve her Master Sommelier certification and the inn's wine list is a stellar example of how to overcome the intimidation factor, with a list representing many small producers without name recognition. Yes, you'll find big-hitter Burgundy, Bordeaux, and California Cabernet but what makes this list remarkable is Kate's desire to offer wonderful wines at reasonable prices.

Award of Excellence

POTATO GNOCCHI
with a Tuscan Vegetable Béchamel

Sous chef Chris Hoffman writes, "This is an adaptation of a dish I encountered while working at Ristorante Belvedere in San Gervasio, Italy. Making gnocchi requires one special tool, a potato ricer, which should be available at any kitchen store. A gnocchi paddle is also helpful, but not necessary since they are difficult to locate and the back of a fork works just fine.

Ingredients

4　large russet or Idaho baking potatoes
2　eggs
¼　cup Parmigiano Reggiano, or other good Parmesan
⅛　teaspoon nutmeg
⅛　teaspoon white pepper

¼　teaspoon salt
2　cups all purpose flour
　butter or olive oil
　Tuscan Vegetable Béchamel (recipe follows)

Preparation

PRE-HEAT oven to 425 degrees. Wrap potatoes with aluminum foil and bake until just done, about 70 minutes. The potato should be cooked completely through, but not to the point where it is mushy. Remove from oven and discard aluminum foil. Allow potato to cool to the point it can be handled easily. Remove skin with small knife or peeler and push potato through potato ricer and into bowl. Add eggs, cheese, nutmeg, pepper, and salt to the potato and gently mix together with a fork. Add flour and begin to combine with fork. When mixture begins to become one mass, place onto floured surface and knead until the dough is uniform, with no streaks of flour or egg. It is important not to over knead. As soon as it is all incorporated, stop and roll into a log about 3 inches in diameter and 6 inches long.

CUT log into approximately 1-inch thick discs and roll each disc into a ¾-inch diameter rod, dusting lightly with flour as you go. Cut the long rope of gnocchi dough into pieces 1 inch long. Roll gnocchi along gnocchi paddle or back of fork, and drop gnocchi into a 6-quart pot of boiling water and cook until the gnocchi aggressively float. Remove with slotted spoon and plunge into bowl of ice water. Remove the gnocchi to a paper towel and repeat with remaining discs of dough.

TO SERVE, heat butter or olive oil in large sauté pan, add gnocchi and toss constantly until gnocchi is warm through and slightly golden. Add Tuscan Vegetable Béchamel to pan, toss to coat, and serve.

Serves 4

Wine Suggestion: This is a versatile dish when it comes to wine pairings. A light bodied Pinot Noir would work, such as Campion Pinot Noir from Edna Valley. But truly, this deserves a rich white wine. You can easily do a Chardonnay, but if you want to go Italian, Fiano di Avalino is rich enough to stand up to the sauce, but also has lovely acidity to balance the cheese.

For the Tuscan Vegetable Béchamel

1 fennel bulb, stalks and core removed	1 tablespoon Italian seasoning
1 leek, white part only	1 tablespoon all purpose flour
1 celery stalk	1 cup dry white wine
1 peeled carrot	1 cup whole milk
2 tomatoes	¾ cup grated Parmigiano Reggiano
2 tablespoons butter	salt & white pepper to taste

WASH all vegetables and rough chop. Heat butter in 2-quart saucepan and add all vegetables, except tomatoes. Cook over medium-low heat until vegetables are translucent, about 10 minutes. Add tomato and Italian seasoning; cook an additional 5 minutes stirring frequently to avoid scorching the bottom of pan. Sprinkle flour over vegetables and stir to incorporate. Cook 1 minute, add wine, increase heat to medium-high and cook 5 minutes. Reduce heat to low and add milk slowly, stirring constantly. Gently bring sauce to simmer. Allow sauce to simmer 15 min, then purée with either a stick blender in the pan, or remove sauce and purée in batches in blender. Push sauce through fine mesh sieve using a ladle. Discard solids and return sauce to pan over low heat. Add cheese, salt, and white pepper to taste. Ladle sauce over hot gnocchi and toss.

OSTRICH FILLET WITH MOREL MUSHROOM SAUCE

This dish is a long-standing favorite at the Inn. Ostrich has about one-fourth the fat of beef and a flavor profile very similar. Because ostrich is so lean, this dish really does need to be served at rare or medium rare. Serve with Rustic Yukon Gold Mashed Potatoes for a perfect meal.

Ingredients

4   tablespoons butter
½   cup whole dried morels
½   cups dried forest mushroom mix, crushed slightly (or ¾ cup mixed fresh mushrooms)
2   tablespoons diced fresh shallot
2   cloves garlic minced
1   tablespoon fresh thyme, or 1 teaspoon dried
1   teaspoon ground pink peppercorn
1   teaspoon ground peppercorn mélange
2   tablespoons minced fresh flat leaf parsley

pinch   salt
½   cup Pinot Noir
½   cup Port
4   cups homemade or high quality chicken stock
1   cup reduced beef stock or demi-glace roux or cornstarch
3   pounds ostrich inside strip or tenderloin, cut into 6-ounce portions
2   tablespoons clarified butter

Preparation

OVER low heat, add the 4 tablespoons butter, mushrooms, and herbs and sweat, stirring occasionally for 10 to 15 minutes. Add wine and turn heat to high simmering until liquid is reduced by 75%. Add both stocks and simmer over low heat for 45 minutes. Add roux or cornstarch slowly to reach desired thickness.

PRE-HEAT oven to 500 degrees. Season ostrich fillets with salt and pepper. Heat a medium sauté pan with the clarified butter until butter is smoking. Flash sear the ostrich fillets on all sides (do not overcrowd the pan – use two pans if you don't have enough space). Place the sauté pans in the oven (if your pans are not ovenproof, move the fillets to a baking sheet). Bake at 500 degrees for 6 minutes, remove and rest for 5 minutes for rare to medium rare. Slice against the grain and fan slices over the prepared morel sauce. Serve with Yukon Gold mashed potatoes and vegetables of your choice.

Serves 6

Wine Suggestion: This dish is lovely with sturdier Pinot Noirs and balanced Syrahs (not over-the-top huge). A personal favorite with this dish would be Joseph Phelps Le Mistral, a California Rhone blend.

RUSTIC YUKON GOLD MASHED POTATOES
with Roasted Garlic, Shallot, and Fresh Herbs

Ingredients

8-10 Yukon Gold potatoes washed, but not
      peeled
   5 tablespoons Roasted Garlic and
      Shallots (recipe follows)
  ½   cup heavy cream
  ¼   cup butter

2 teaspoons ground peppercorn mélange
1 tablespoon salt
1 tablespoon minced fresh thyme
1 tablespoon minced fresh flat leaf
   parsley

Preparation

BOIL potatoes in a large stockpot until fork tender, approximately 30 minutes. Drain water and add all ingredients to the warm pot. Mash until semi-smooth. Check seasoning and adjust to taste.

Serves 8 – 10

For the Roasted Shallot & Garlic

6 shallots, peeled
2 heads garlic, peeled
2 tablespoons olive oil

PRE-HEAT oven to 400. Arrange peeled shallot and garlic on sheet pan and coat with olive oil. Bake for 25 to 35 minutes or until light brown. Remove and cool. Using food processor, grind shallot and garlic together into a fine paste.

Caramel Apple Spice Cake

Ingredients

8 *Granny Smith apples*
1 *cup sugar*
1½ *cups flour, sifted*
½ *teaspoon baking powder*
2 *pinches salt*
¼ *teaspoon ground cloves*
½ *teaspoon allspice*
¼ *teaspoon cinnamon*
¼ *teaspoon nutmeg*

¼ *teaspoon ground ginger*
⅛ *teaspoon white pepper*
4 *large eggs*
¼ *cup vegetable oil*
1 *tablespoon molasses*
Frosting (recipe follows)
freshly whipped cream
caramel sauce

Preparation

PRE-HEAT oven to 350. Grate apples and then squeeze as much juice out of the apples with your hands as possible. Put sugar in saucepan and cook over medium-high heat to brown. Be careful not to burn the sugar (look for a dark golden color). Add the grated and squeezed apples and stir until well blended with the caramelized sugar. Set aside to cool.

SIFT all dry ingredients together into one bowl. In a second bowl, mix the eggs, vegetable oil, and molasses. Add cooled apples and blend in dry ingredients. Stir thoroughly and place in two 9-inch cake pans. Bake in 350-degree oven for 30 to 40 minutes. Cool. Once cakes are thoroughly cooled, place a layer of frosting on one, and place the second cake on top. Frost completely. Serve with freshly whipped cream and caramel sauce.

Wine Suggestion: This cake is rather sweet, so you want a dessert wine that isn't overwhelmingly sweet and unctuous. Look for a Late Harvest Riesling or Gewürztraminer that still has some nice acidity. Leelanau County's Black Star Farms makes a fantastic Riesling and Shady Lane's Gewürztraminer is another great find.

For the Frosting

¼ *pound butter*
¾ *cup packed light brown sugar*

3 *cups powdered sugar*
4 *tablespoons buttermilk*

PLACE all ingredients in a mixing bowl and cream until just about doubled.

Loading potatoes, Bower's Harbor dock, Grand Traverse Bay, (circa 1900)

Lulu's Bistro

213 North Bridge Street
Bellaire, MI 49615
231-533-5252

Lunch
Tuesday – Saturday 11:00am – 2:30pm
Dinner
Tuesday – Saturday 5:00pm – 9:00pm
Sunday 4:00 – 8:00pm

Lulu's Bistro

Chef / owner Michael Peterson

Such an improbable number of top quality res-taurants dot the northern Michigan landscape, one might be tempted to toss al dente gnocchi at a map to help decide where to dine that night. Prospective restaurateurs on the other hand, might successfully use the method when choosing a fitting town to set up shop. For diners, perhaps the luckiest throw would land on Bellaire, home to ultra-chic Lulu's Bistro—where New American cuisine is pushed to a level that would be welcomed anywhere on the globe. Northern Michigander's know how tough it is to get Detroit's media to lift their gaze up north, so a recent article in *Hour Detroit* touting Lulu's, "Bold, sleek, upscale and casual dining with astonishingly good contemporary American food, and a wide-ranging wine list," is doubly notewor-thy.

Chef/owner Michael Peterson, a Culinary Institute of America graduate and Traverse City native came to Lulu's by way of the Black Bass Hotel in Lumberville, PA, and Alden's acclaimed (now closed) Spencer Creek Landing. Bespectacled and good-naturedly intense, Peterson opened Lulu's in 2000 after noticing a void of casual fine dining restaurants in the region. (Remember, Tapawingo and the Rowe Inn are about twenty-five miles away.) He counted on support from the multitude of summer residents inhabiting cottages around the area but also knew Bellaire, with Shanty Creek Resort just a couple miles down the road, possessed a viable year-round population for just the right restaurant. Not one to be contained, Peterson's Sunday Fondue Nights were embraced immediately and the bar at Lulu's offers the perfect after-work venue for a quick appetizer and glass of wine. Additions to the menu are posted in casual longhand on a chalkboard in the dining room.

Casual, contemporary American cuisine by Peterson's definition means appetizers such as guacamole and whitefish pâté served without fuss. Other recent appetizers included Smoked Baby Back Ribs with Creole Slaw, and decadent Lump Crab Baked in Sherry Cream with Cheddar Cheese. Entrées on any given night might range from Roasted Striped Bass with White Bean and Eggplant Caponata, Parmesan Crusted Walleye, or everyone's favorite, Braised Short Ribs served with Brie Mashed Potatoes.

Lulu's encourages creative menu ordering and table sharing. This is a restaurant commit-ted to making diners comfortable.

Lulu's wine list has New World verve prioritizing great food wines like Riesling, Sauvignon Blanc, and French Chardonnay. The reds also tend towards leaner, structured styles. Overall, Lulu's regulars count on a big-city experience in one of northern Michigan's hipper towns. First-time diners rarely remain that way. Lulu's will keep them coming back time after time.

Aged Goat Cheese, Roasted Beet and Hydro Watercress Salad

with Currant Tomatoes, Daikon Radish and White Truffle Vinaigrette

Ingredients

½   cup Champagne vinegar
 1   tablespoon lemon juice
 2   teaspoons white truffle oil
½   cup olive oil
     salt & white pepper
12   ounces golden beets, roasted & peeled

 2   bunches watercress
10   ounces aged goat cheese, preferably Bucheron
 1   cup currant tomatoes
½   cup daikon radish, julienned

Preparation

WHIP together the vinegar, lemon juice, truffle oil. Slowly add the olive oil while vigorously whipping to create an emulsion. Season with salt and pepper.

THINLY slice the beets and lay them on your serving plate. Toss watercress with the vinaigrette and place in the middle of the plate. Slice the goat cheese and arrange around the pile of watercress. Garnish with currant tomatoes and daikon radish. Spoon a little vinaigrette over the daikon radish.

Serves 6

Wine Suggestion: Buehler Russian River Chardonnay, California
The light aromatic flavor of this Chardonnay pairs up nicely with the sharpness of the goat cheese and the daikon radish; and its earthiness pairs well with the truffle oil and the watercress.

BAKED JUMBO LUMP CRAB
with Sharp Cheddar and Sherry Cream

Ingredients

16 ounces jumbo lump crab, fresh or pasteurized
8 slices of good quality sharp white cheddar

12 ounces heavy cream
1 tablespoon sherry
salt & pepper

Preparation

PREHEAT oven to 475 degrees. Place crab in 4 small baking dishes or ramekins. Place 2 slices of cheddar over the top. Reduce heavy cream by half, and then add the sherry and salt and pepper to taste. Pour 1½ ounces of the sherry cream over the cheddar and bake for 6-8 minutes, then flash in the broiler until golden brown. Serve with crusty bread.

Serves 4

Wine Suggestion: Caymus Conundrum, Blend, California
This blend of grapes is able to be rich and creamy matching cheddar and sherry cream, but unlike many California Chardonnays it is not so oaky as to cover the delicate and sweet flavors of the crab.

SEARED SEA SCALLOPS

with Short Rib Potato Hash, Parsnip Purée, Roasted Brussels Sprouts and Fines Herbes
Caper Lemon Aioli

Ingredients

24-30 medium Brussels sprouts
   1 tablespoon olive oil
  12 large sea scallops (dry)
   1 tablespoon canola oil
    Short Rib Potato Hash (recipe follows)

Parsnip Purée (recipe follows)
Fines Herbes Caper Lemon Aioli
(recipe follows)
salt & pepper

Preparation

PREHEAT oven to 350 degrees. Cut ends off Brussels sprouts. Sauté in pan with olive oil until caramelized and finish cooking the Brussels sprouts in the oven until tender, about 10 to 15 minutes. Pull out and season with salt and pepper, keep warm.

SEAR scallops in hot sauté pan with a little canola oil until both sides are caramelized. Pull scallops out of the pan and set aside to rest, the scallops should be medium to medium rare.

TO SERVE, put Short Rib Hash in center of the plate and put a dollop of Parsnip Purée on top. Place scallops on top of the purée and put Brussels sprouts around scallops. Spoon the Fines Herbes Caper Lemon Aioli over the scallops.

Serves 6

Wine Suggestion: Giesen Sauvignon Blanc, New Zealand
Giesen's herbal notes pair perfectly with the fines herbes in the aioli while the citrus flavor and acids match with the capers and cut through the richness of the scallops and creamy aioli.

For the Short Rib Hash

8-10 ounces short rib meat, small dice
  2 cups Yukon potatoes, medium dice
  1 large Vidalia onion, small dice

SWEAT the onions in sauté pan until translucent. In the same pan, on medium high heat add potatoes and cook until they start to caramelize. Add short rib meat and salt and pepper to taste. Set aside.

For the Parsnip Purée

2 pounds parsnips, peeled, roughly
  chopped
½ cup heavy cream

COOK parsnips in water until soft. Strain and purée in Robo coupe or blender, add cream at the end. Salt and pepper to taste. Keep warm.

For the Fines Herbes Caper Lemon Aioli

2 egg yolks
2 cups olive oil
1 tablespoon lemon zest
1 tablespoon lemon juice

2 tablespoons capers, roughly chopped
¼ cup fines herbes blend, (chives, parsley, tarragon and chervil)

IN Robo Coupe or blender, add egg yolk and slowly add to the running machine the olive oil until emulsified. Halfway through, add the lemon zest and lemon juice then the rest of the olive oil and capers. Add the fines herbes blend and season with salt and white pepper.

Tapawingo

Tapawingo

9502 Lake Street **Dinner nightly from end of June**
Ellsworth, MI 49729 **through Labor Day**
231-588-7971 **Lunch Tuesday – Saturday during**
www.tapawingo.net **high season**
Call for times during slower seasons

Tapawingo

Executive Chef Jeremy Kittelson
Pete Peterson, Chef / Owner

A little understood quirk about innovators is why they so often choose to work in relative seclusion. As if their particular road less traveled also need be off the path beaten by peers or competitors. One such Michigan visionary, a former car designer turned chef, practices his trade in the remote village of Ellsworth in a restaurant he quizzically named Tapawingo. Ultra-fine diners and professional chefs around the country refer to it in hushed tones of reverence, and shower owner Pete Peterson with the type of praise usually limited to acclaimed musicians or authors. Indeed, the mystique surrounding Tapawingo is difficult to overstate.

Much has been made about Peterson's art and industrial design background and successful career as an automobile designer in Detroit. The decision to pursue food over Ford came in 1977 and subsequently resulted in an apprenticeship at the Rowe Inn (also featured in this book) before he opened Tapawingo in 1984. Success was immediate and soon after a stream of national media lead by *The New York Times*, *Gourmet*, *Saveur*, and others started posting regular reports from Ellsworth. Over the years, both *Zagat* and *Gourmet* named Tapawingo as Michigan's best.

The executive chef position under Peterson is coveted and Tapawingo has always been blessed with superb talent. The list includes Stuart Brioza, named one of *Food & Wine* magazine's "Ten Best New Chefs" in 2003 for his three years of work at Tapawingo, and a hard act to follow, to be sure.

The executive chef position is currently held by Jeremy Kittelson, formerly of Blackbird in Chicago. Intensely meticulous, Kittelson continues the tradition of serving some of America's most beautifully prepared and presented contemporary, regional cuisine. Dishes like Sautéed Skatewing sing with the accompanying flavors of ruby red grapefruit, parsnips, Brussels sprouts, candied ginger, and pancetta; Marcona Almond Crusted Veal Sweetbreads partner with stuffed Medjol date, ham hock, ricotta, spinach, cranberry beans, Picholine olives, and chile de arbol sauce; and Butternut Squash and Coconut Soup is served with shrimp satay, caramelized squash, and triple curry, on a recent menu. Note the seamless marriage of midwestern regional ingredients with the exotic.

Tapawingo offers a three-course menu—First Course, Principal Dish, and Dessert—including an Amuse Bouche. Executive Chef Kittelson and Sommelier Lee McCoy also conspire on a nightly Tasting Menu featuring as many as eight individual dishes with wine. The wine list is lengthy and complete with a *Best of Award of Excellence* from the *Wine Spectator*.

 Best of Award of Excellence

Chestnut Soup

A satisfying hot soup best served in chestnut season. A soup that many people have never tasted.

Ingredients

¼ cup leeks, small dice
¼ cup celery root, small dice
¼ cup shallot, small dice
 8 ounces butter, divided
½ pound chestnuts, peeled and chopped

1 tablespoon sugar
3 cups chicken stock
1 cup heavy cream
2 tablespoons sherry wine
   salt, pepper and Tabasco

Preparation

IN A saucepot over medium-low heat, sweat the leeks, celery root and shallot in 4 ounces of the butter. Add the chestnuts and sugar and lightly caramelize for about 5 to 6 minutes. Season as needed. Add chicken stock and simmer for about 20 minutes. Purée in a blender and put back into a saucepot. Add cream and simmer for about 10 minutes. Purée again in a blender, adding the wine and remaining butter. Season to taste and pass through a chinois. Serve immediately.

Serves 4

Wine Suggestion: Madeira – The nuttiness of the wine complements the soup.

CHEESE BEIGNETS

Small cheese puffs, quickly fried – they are the perfect warm hors d'oeuvres.

Ingredients

1 cup water
½ stick unsalted butter, cut into 1-tablespoon pieces
½ teaspoon salt
1 cup all-purpose flour
4 large eggs

1 cup Parmigiano-Reggiano, finely grated
½ cup Gruyere, finely grated
¼ teaspoon black pepper
4 cups peanut or vegetable oil for deep-frying

Preparation

PUT oven rack in middle position and preheat oven to 200 degrees. Cut parchment into 10 strips: 12 inches by 3 inches. Bring water, butter, and salt to a boil in a 3-quart heavy saucepan over high heat, then reduce heat to moderate. Add flour all at once and cook, stirring vigorously with a wooden spoon, until mixture pulls away from side of pan, about 2 minutes. Remove saucepan from heat and cool mixture slightly, about 3 minutes. Then add egg 1 at a time, beating well after each addition (with the addition of each egg, batter will initially appear to separate but will then become smooth). Stir in cheeses and pepper.

LINE a large baking sheet with a double layer of paper towels. Heat 2 inches oil in a wide 3- to 4-quart heavy pot over moderate heat until it registers 335 degrees on thermometer. While oil is heating, spoon 5 rounded teaspoons of batter onto each of 2 strips of parchment. Holding strips with your fingers at one end and tongs at the other, lower both strips, one at a time, into hot oil and remove parchment as soon as beignets release. Fry beignets, turning occasionally, until puffed and golden brown, 4 to 5 minutes. Transfer beignets with a slotted spoon to a lined baking sheet to drain and transfer sheet, uncovered, to oven to keep warm. Make more beignets with remaining batter in same manner, transferring to sheet as fried. (Return oil to 335 degrees between batches.) Season beignets with salt and pepper before serving.

BATTER can be made 24 hours ahead and chilled, covered. Chilled beignets will need to be fried 7 to 8 minutes per batch.

Wine Suggestion: Champagne

Yukon Gold Potato Soup

with Grilled Diver Scallops, Pickled Chanterelles, Chives, and Crème Fraîche

A rich, silky, and golden soup that everyone likes.

Ingredients

¼ cup butter
1 onion, diced
1 leak, diced
1 stalk celery, diced
8 Yukon gold potatoes, diced
4 quarts water
¼ cup white truffle oil

4 diver scallops, cleaned
2 teaspoons extra virgin olive oil
  Pickled Chanterelles (recipe follows)
1 cup crème fraîche, for garnish
2 tablespoons fresh chives, chopped, for
  garnish

Preparation

IN A stockpot, add the butter and melt over low heat. Add diced vegetables, cover and cook until the vegetables begin to soften. Add the water and bring mixture to a boil. Reduce to a simmer and cook for about 20 minutes or until vegetables are very soft. Allow the soup to cool slightly and begin adding the soup into a blender. Be careful blending hot mixtures—the top can fly off and you could find yourself covered in hot soup! Blend the soup until it is nice and smooth. Season the soup to taste with truffle oil, salt and pepper.

PRE-HEAT a grill. Lightly coat the scallops in olive oil and place on the grill. Grill the scallops for about 1 minute on each side, or until medium rare.

IN 4 warm bowls, ladle in 1 cup of soup. Lay the sliced scallop and a few pieces of Pickled Chanterelles into the soup and top with 1 tablespoon of crème fraîche. Sprinkle 1 tablespoon of minced chives over each bowl. Serve immediately.

Serves 4

Wine suggestion: White Burgundy – To match the richness of the soup.

For the Pickled Chanterelles

2 cups cleaned chanterelle mushrooms
1 quart water
1 cup rice wine vinegar

¼ cup sugar
¼ cup kosher salt
  sachet of spices

IN A saucepot, combine the water, vinegar, sugar, salt, and sachet and bring to a boil. Put the chanterelles in a non-reactive container and pour the pickling liquid over them. Cover and let the mixture cool to room temperature. Reserve.

ROASTED CERVENA VENISON LOIN
with Parsnips, Braised Red Cabbage, and a Huckleberry Gastrique

A lean cut of meat, simply roasted and complemented by a fruity, somewhat acidic huckleberry reduction.

Ingredients

2 *pounds cleaned, venison strip loin*
¼ *cup thyme leaves, picked*
¼ *cup extra virgin olive oil*
1 *tablespoon cracked black pepper*
   grapeseed oil

Braised Red Cabbage (recipe follows)
Parsnips with Truffle Butter (recipe follows)
Huckleberry Gastrique (recipe follows)
fresh huckleberries, for garnish

Preparation

PRE-HEAT oven to 350 degrees. Rub venison with the thyme, extra virgin olive oil, and black pepper. In a large sauté pan on high heat, add some grapeseed oil and sear venison loin on all sides. Place the venison loin in the oven for about 10 minutes or until medium rare. Remove from oven and allow meat to rest at least 10 minutes before slicing.

PLACE Braised Red Cabbage on a plate and place the Parsnips with Truffle Butter on top. Slice the venison into 8 slices and place on top. Spoon some of the Huckleberry Gastrique over the dish and garnish with fresh huckleberries. Serve immediately.

Serves 4

Wine Suggestion: Shiraz - Venison is lean, so a wine with lots of tannin is not desirable. The fruit of the wine should pick up the flavor of the huckleberry gastrique.

For the Parsnips with Truffle Butter

¼ *cup butter*
1 *tablespoon white truffle oil*
2 *tablespoons truffles, chopped*
1 *tablespoon chives, minced*

1 *quart milk*
2 *pounds parsnips, peeled and sliced into 1-inch by ¼-inch pieces*

ALLOW the butter to stand at room temperature. When the butter is tempered add truffle oil, chopped truffles, and minced chives. Mix thoroughly. In a saucepot, bring the milk to a simmer and add parsnips. Poach parsnips for about 20 minutes or until tender. Remove parsnips, toss them with the truffle butter, and adjust with salt and pepper. Serve immediately.

For the Braised Red Cabbage

2 pounds red cabbage, sliced	¼ cup balsamic vinegar
1 red onion, julienne	1 apple, peeled and diced
1 cup bacon, diced	1 bay leaf
1 cup red wine	2 teaspoons sugar
1 cup water	2 tablespoons butter
¼ cup red wine vinegar	

COMBINE the cabbage, onions, and bacon in a large pot and simmer until the cabbage is wilted. Add the water, wine, vinegars, apple, bay leaf, sugar and salt. Bring the cabbage to a simmer and cook for about 30 minutes or until the cabbage is very tender. Serve immediately.

For the Huckleberry Gastrique

2 cups red wine	2 cups huckleberries
1 cup red wine vinegar	1 juniper berry, crushed
¼ cup honey	1 sprig fresh thyme
2 shallots, thinly sliced	1 teaspoon cold butter
2 cups veal stock	

IN A heavy medium saucepan, combine red wine, red wine vinegar, honey, and shallots and bring to a boil over moderately low heat. Cook until the mixture has reduced to 1 cup. Strain the mixture into a small saucepan and add veal stock, huckleberries, juniper berry, and thyme. Bring to a boil and simmer until the sauce has reduced to ⅔ cup. Whisk in a teaspoon of cold butter and season to taste with salt and pepper. Reserve.

CARAMEL APPLE WITH CREAM CHEESE ICE CREAM

A great winter dessert when other fresh fruits are sparse. You can also purchase puff pastry and/or high quality ice cream from your grocer, instead of making these items.

Ingredients

8 *firm baking apples*
3 *cups sugar*
½ *cup water*
1 *vanilla bean, split & scraped*
1 *tablespoon salt*
1 *cup butter*

2 *tart eating apples.*
Puff Pastry (recipe follows)
Cream Cheese Ice Cream (recipe follows)
fresh mint and toasted pecans, for garnish

Preparation

PEEL, core and halve the baking apples. Combine sugar, water, vanilla, and salt in a wide saucepan. Let cook over medium heat until light golden brown. Whisk in butter. Add apple halves in one layer to saucepan and cook over low heat until a cake tester enters apples without resistance. Remove apples with a slotted spoon and set aside, keeping warm. Remove pot from heat, reserving poaching liquid.

MAKE an apple soup with the tart eating apples. Peel and core apples. Purée apples and poaching liquid until smooth and then strain. Heat apple soup over low heat until warm.

To serve, ladle warm soup into a bowl. Place a Puff Pastry square in bowl. Put a warm apple on one side of pastry. Place a scoop of Cream Cheese Ice Cream on the other side. Garnish with mint and toasted pecans.

Serves 8

Wine Suggestion: Trocken Beerenauslese Riesling – A can't miss with Riesling.

For the Puff Pastry

1½ *cups cold butter*
1 *teaspoon white vinegar*
3 *cups all-purpose flour*

2 *teaspoons salt*
1 *cup cold water*
¼ *cup soft butter*

PREHEAT oven at 450 degrees. Pound cold butter into a ¾-inch x 6-inch x 6-inch block between 2 sheets of plastic wrap. Store in cooler. Mix all remaining ingredients in mixer with a dough hook, just until mixed. Form dough into a ball. Score the top of the ball in an X with a serrated knife. Wrap in plastic. Let dough rest in the cooler for 2 hours. Roll dough on a floured surface into a 10-inch x 10-inch square. Place butter block into dough. Fold excess dough around butter and seal edges. Roll dough and butter into a 10-inch x 24-inch rectangle. Bring the short edges into the middle. Fold dough in half lengthwise. Let dough rest in cooler.

Repeat the previous three steps five more times, letting the dough rest for a few minutes in between folds. Roll dough out on a floured surface to ⅛-inch thickness. Bake at 450 degrees in between two sheet pans until golden brown. Cut into 1-inch x 3-inch rectangles.

For the Cream Cheese Ice Cream

1 quart half & half	pinch salt
1 cup sugar	1 cup cream cheese, cubed
10 yolks	

BRING half & half to a simmer. Whisk sugar, yolks, and salt together. Whisk 1 cup of hot half & half into yolk mixture. Whisk yolk mixture back into half & half. Cook mixture over medium heat while whisking for 1 minute. Strain into a bowl set in a larger bowl of ice. Whisk in cream cheese until smooth. Stir mixture occasionally until cold. Process in an ice cream machine.

CHEWY SALTED CARAMELS

A little crunchy sea salt emboldens the caramel flavor.

Ingredients

2½ cups sugar	½ vanilla bean, scraped
¼ cup corn syrup	2 cups cream
1¼ cups butter	⅛ teaspoon baking soda
1 teaspoon salt	

Preparation

PLACE sugar and corn syrup in a wide saucepan. Cook over medium heat until golden brown, stirring minimally. Whisk in butter, salt and vanilla bean pulp until completely absorbed. Warm cream and baking soda until slightly warm and whisk into caramel mixture. Cook caramel over medium heat, stirring constantly to 248 degrees. Remove from heat. Stir 30 more seconds and pour into greased mold. Cut when cool.

Wine Suggestion: Champagne

White Pine lumbering, northern Michigan, (circa 1870).

White Pine lumbering with oxen, (circa 1870).

Rowe Inn

THE ROWE
Michigan's Country Inn

6303 East Jordan Road   Seven days a week, open at 6:00pm
Ellsworth, MI 49729
866-432-5873
231-588-7351
www.roweinn.com

Rowe Inn

Executive Chef Scott Lyons
Wes Westhoven, Owner

I n rural areas throughout the United States, much is made about character, as in, "he's a real character," to describe an especially quirky, or complicated individual. The words are often accompanied by a wry grin because the phrase is double-loaded with mischievous entendre. Michigan's list of culinary "characters" includes a handful of chefs and restaurateurs featured in this book, foremost among them, Wes Westhoven, owner of the legendary Rowe Inn in Ellsworth, though "real character" doesn't begin to tell the story.

In many minds, Westhoven deserves credit for establishing northern Michigan's fine-dining reputation. In 1972, his formula for restaurant success was straight out of the pages of a French aristocrat: 1) find a suitable building in a charming rural village, 2) stock the cellars full of carefully selected wine, 3) employ a talented chef, and 4) host guests with infectious good cheer.

Some might grumble that Westhoven has had astounding luck in the chefs that have passed through his kitchen, including Tapawingo's Pete Peterson, and Jim Milliman of Hanna in Traverse City, but the Rowe has never missed a beat and is still acclaimed across the Midwest.

Rowe diners count on impeccably prepared French-country fare, founded on local and regional ingredients. Chef Scott Lyons' current list of appetizers includes several hearty dishes like Grilled Venison Sausage, and Pork, Dried Cherry and Walnut Terrine, along with such sophisticates as Sea Scallops with Apples and Cider Brown Butter, Escargot, Mussels Provencal. Entrées of special note range from Duck with Cherry Balsamic Glaze, to Char Grilled Beef Tenderloin with Peppercorn Crusted Chèvre Medallion, and Veal Scaloppini served with Blue Cream.

Locally harvested morel mushrooms are another Rowe favorite and always figure into a dish or two, as well as special morel dinners every spring. First-time diners (are there any left?) must make a point to wander down to see the peerless wine cellar stocked overflowing with 16,000 bottles. New world wines do compete for space but primarily we're talking prestigiousEuropean appellations and wineries.

MOREL MUSHROOM AND WILD RICE BISQUE

This is our most requested soup.

Ingredients

6   strips bacon, chopped
1   cup onion, diced
1   cup carrot, diced
1   cup celery, diced
2   tablespoons garlic, minced
½   cup flour
12 cups chicken stock, preferably
    homemade

1   teaspoon thyme
1   cup wild rice
3   ounces morels, sautéed in butter
3   cups heavy cream
2   tablespoons parsley, minced
    salt & pepper

Preparation

SAUTÉ the bacon until crisp and reserve bacon, leaving grease in pan. Add the vegetables and garlic to the bacon grease and sauté until crisp yet tender. Add the flour and continue stirring and cooking for 3 minutes, then add chicken stock, thyme, and wild rice. Bring to a boil then reduce heat. Simmer covered until rice is tender, about 40 minutes. Add sautéed morels, heavy cream, parsley, and reserved bacon and heat through. Salt and pepper to taste.

Serves 8

Wine suggestion: Rombauer Chardonnay, Napa Valley

Pork, Duck, Dried Cherry and Mixed Nut Terrine

A mixed-fruit chutney would go great with this.

Ingredients

1½ cups leeks, diced	½ cup walnuts
2 tablespoons garlic, minced	½ cup pine nuts
2 tablespoons olive oil	½ cup pistachios
1 cup dry sherry	1 cup dried cherries
1½ tablespoons ground fennel seed	3 tablespoons fresh sage, chopped
2 eggs	1 tablespoon Herbs de Provence
1 pound ground pork	1 tablespoon kosher salt
1 pound ground duck	2 tablespoons ground black pepper
½ cup almonds	¾ pound bacon strips

Preparation

PREHEAT oven to 300 degrees. In a medium saucepan cook diced leeks and garlic in 2 tablespoons olive oil until they are soft. Add sherry and fennel seed, continuing to cook until the liquid is cooked off. Set aside to cool.

IN A large bowl quickly whisk the eggs then combine with ground meat, leek mixture, nuts, dried cherries, herbs, salt, and black pepper. Line two terrine pans with bacon and fill to the top with the terrine mixture. Fold ends of bacon strips over the mixture, place pans in a shallow pan and fill half way with water. Cook in a 300-degree oven for 1 hour and 30 minutes or until internal temperature is 165 degrees.

Serves 16

Wine Suggestion: Laetitia Pinot Noir, Arroyo Grande Valley

APRICOT GINGER SAUCE

Serve this sauce with your choice of grilled pork tenderloin or perhaps, roasted duck breast.
You can't go wrong.

Ingredients

3 cups onion, chopped
4 tablespoons olive oil
½ cup red wine vinegar
36 ounces apricot preserves
4 tablespoons Dijon mustard

1 teaspoon powdered ginger
1 teaspoon powdered cloves
2 teaspoons fresh ginger, chopped
4 cups demi-glace

Preparation

SAUTÉ onion slowly in olive oil until soft, and then add remaining ingredients except the
demi-glace. Cook together for 15 – 20 minutes and add demi-glace cooking for an additional
10 minutes. Remove from heat and let cool. Purée mixture in a food processor until smooth.
This recipe makes several cups of sauce. Don't hesitate to cut the recipe in half or more.

Wine Suggestion: Brys Estate Merlot, Old Mission Peninsula

MOREL AND LEEK PIEROGI

Probably the best appetizer we make.

Ingredients

4 cups leeks, chopped
4 cups morel mushrooms
3 cups crimini mushrooms
2 tablespoons unsalted butter, divided
2 teaspoons fresh sage, chopped
2 cups all-purpose flour

1½ cups cake flour
4 eggs, and 1 additional egg whisked
  briefly for egg wash
1½ teaspoons salt
⅓ cup water
⅓ cup sour cream

Preparation

PREPARE filling by sautéing leeks, morels, and crimini in 1 tablespoon of the butter. Season with sage, salt, and pepper.

STIR together all-purpose and cake flour in a large bowl. Make a well in the flour and add 4 eggs, salt, water, and sour cream then stir together with a fork without touching flour. Slowly incorporate the flour until a soft dough forms. Transfer dough to a lightly-floured work surface and knead until smooth and elastic, adding only as much additional flour as needed to keep dough from sticking, about 8 minutes. Cover and let rest at least 30 minutes. On a well-floured surface, divide the dough in half. Roll out each piece to ⅛ inch thick. Use a 3- or 4-inch round cutter to cut dough into circles. Place 1 tablespoon of the mushroom filling in middle of dough, wet the edges with egg wash, fold over, and crimp the edge with a fork.

TO COOK, place pierogies in a pot of boiling water for about 6 – 8 minutes, or until they start to float. Remove from water and sauté in remaining tablespoon butter until golden brown.

Serves 4 (about 20 pierogies)

Wine Suggestion: G. Raphet Chambolle Musigny

Latitude°
Restaurant

LATITUDE°

45°21'56.67"N

795 Front Street
Bay Harbor, MI 49770
231-439-2750
www.latituderestaurant.com

May through September
Open seven days a week for lunch and
dinner
October through May
Open seven days a week for dinner,
Thursday through Saturday for lunch

Latitude°

Executive Chef Rich Travis
Larry & Toni Wisne, Owners

Generally, traveling to and from a top-tier restaurant is limited to transport of the four-wheeled variety, be it car, cab, or limo. Helicopters offer speed but parking is a hassle and jumpy pilots can sabotage a stomach from enjoying the best of meals. Boats provide an option, but too often the restaurants situated on waterways rely heavily on deep fryers, and rarely approach greatness. In rare circumstances, the privileged few with yachts can walk down their gangways and, in a few steps, be seated at a restaurant of genuine acclaim. Latitude at Bay Harbor offers just such an opportunity. Yachters sitting dockside are shocked to realize the water beneath them is seventy-five feet deep. Even the grandest of the grand—think Forbes, Ellison, Turner, etc.—can tie up their mega-yachts here.

Situated on five miles of Lake Michigan shoreline between Charlevoix and Petoskey, Bay Harbor offers luxury unlike anywhere else in northern Michigan. Aside from the afore-mentioned marina, other features include an Olympic-caliber equestrian facility, 27-hole championship golf course designed by Arthur Hills, conference center, and first class hotel. Some of the Midwest's most spectacular homes line the beach on a spit of land separating the deep-water marina (actually an old cement plant quarry) from Little Traverse Bay. The Village at Bay Harbor adjoins the marina and includes boutiques, resort-style shopping, and restaurants. One needs to see Bay Harbor to fathom just how unique a setting it is.

To find Latitude's rightful place among Michigan's top restaurants, we only need to know that Executive Chef Rich Travis worked under Master Chef Milos Chelka in Detroit, and then spent eight years at incomparable Tapawingo in Ellsworth. Fussy and energetic, Travis continually changes his menus to reflect the best that's available in seasonal produce and cutting-edge American cuisine. A recent Latitude appetizer and first-course menu ranged from several preparations of sushi, to four enticing brick oven flatbread pizzas, Maryland Crab Cakes with Lobster Tartar Sauce, and Korean Barbecue Beef Short Ribs.

More Asian influences crept into Travis's entrée choices including Hunan Barbecue Duck (barbeque breast, Hunan glazed duck leg, crispy spring rolls, sweet-chili sauce, grilled pine-apple) and Wok-Seared Jumbo Sea Scallops (coconut curry broth, Asian vegetables, shiitake mushrooms, soba noodles). Other entrées calling for attention on a winter menu: Slowly Braised Leg of Lamb "Off the Bone" (house baked sourdough-rosemary bread bowl, natural braising sauce, crimini mushrooms, gremolata) and a Chef's Special of Cedar Planked Salmon (warm Yukon potato salad with leeks & baby spinach, bacon vinaigrette).

Like Tribute—another restaurant owned by Epoch Restaurant Group—Latitude cellars a collection of wine to meet any taste and budget. The list includes over 300 labels chosen by General Manager David Waskiewicz.

 Award of Excellence

WARM ASPARAGUS SALAD
with Saffron Vinaigrette

This is my adaptation of the asparagus salad served in First Class on the fateful night the Titanic sank. This salad would make a great entrée course by topping it with pan-seared dry pack sea scallops or grilled chicken breast.

Ingredients

2 pounds asparagus, steamed until just tender
½ cup olive oil
pinch saffron
2 tablespoons tarragon vinegar
2 teaspoons Dijon mustard

⅛ teaspoon freshly ground black pepper
⅛ teaspoon kosher salt
1 teaspoon shallot, minced
2 tablespoons parsley, chopped, divided
6 ounces fresh chèvre (goat cheese), crumbled

Preparation

HEAT the olive oil and saffron in a small saucepan just until the oil becomes warm, about a minute. Transfer the oil to a small bowl. Whisk in the vinegar, Dijon, seasonings, shallots, and half of the parsley. Sprinkle the chèvre over a platter of steamed asparagus, drizzle with some of the vinaigrette, then sprinkle with the remaining parsley. Serve immediately, passing the remaining vinaigrette in a sauceboat.

Serves 6

Wine Suggestion: Peter Franus Sauvignon Blanc, Carneros Valley

MOREL MUSHROOM BURGERS
with Apple-Jicama Slaw

Ingredients

1 pound morel mushrooms	3 tablespoons parsley, chopped
1 pound crimini mushrooms, thinly sliced	3–6 tablespoons Japanese bread crumbs
4 tablespoons olive oil	3 tablespoons butter
salt & pepper	5 tender-crusted burger buns
½ teaspoon nutmeg	¾ cup roasted garlic mayonnaise
1 tablespoon roasted garlic	2 tablespoons basil pesto
2 tablespoons cream cheese	2–3 cups arugula
2 tablespoons Asiago cheese	5 grilled onion slices
1½ tablespoons Dijon mustard	bread & butter pickles
	Apple-Jicama Slaw (recipe follows)

Preparation

WASH morels by immersing in salted water briefly. Do not soak. Agitate & drain. Cut stems off and chop up. Check insides of caps for insects and debris. Finely chop ¼ of the morels and thinly slice the remaining mushrooms. Heat olive oil in a very large sauté pan until hot and almost brown. Add all the mushrooms, spreading them out as thinly as possible, and cook for about 5 minutes, until golden brown. Season to taste with salt, pepper and nutmeg. Transfer the mushrooms to a bowl. Chill uncovered.

WHEN the mushrooms are cool, add roasted garlic, cream cheese, Asiago, mustard, parsley, and 3 tablespoons of the breadcrumbs, and mix well. Add more crumbs if needed to hold the mixture together. Portion out into 5 patties.

HEAT butter over medium-high heat in a non-stick skillet or on a griddle. When hot and before it begins to brown, season the patties with salt and pepper, add to the pan, and gently sauté until golden brown on the first side. Turn the patties and cook on the other side until brown and hot through.

SPREAD the buns with the mayonnaise and pesto. Place the arugula and onions on the bottoms, followed by the mushroom burgers, and then the tops. Serve with the pickles and Apple-Jicama Slaw.

Serves 5

Wine suggestion: Kotare Pinot Noir, Marlborough Valley

For the Apple-Jicama Slaw

¼ cup rice wine vinegar
1¼ teaspoons cumin seeds, toasted and
　ground
　salt & pepper
¾ cup olive oil

2 jalapenos, seeded and minced
2 scallions, cut on the diagonal
2 cups McIntosh apples, battonne-cut
2 cups jicama, peeled and battonne-cut

COMBINE the vinegar and cumin and season with salt and pepper to taste in a bowl, whisking until the salt has dissolved. Gradually whisk in the oil, and continue to whisk until fully emulsified. Stir in the jalapenos and scallions. Prepare the apples and jicama and toss with the vinaigrette.

MORELS STUFFED WITH HAM DUXELLE

Ingredients

25 whole morel mushrooms
2 tablespoons butter
½ cup onion, fine dice
1 teaspoon garlic, minced
12 ounces ham, fine dice

½ cup sherry wine
¼ cup flour
½ cup heavy cream
½ cup parsley, chopped
　salt & pepper

Preparation

PREHEAT oven to 400 degrees. Wash morels by immersing in salted water briefly. Do not soak. Agitate & drain. Cut stems off and chop up. Check insides of caps for insects and debris. Melt butter over medium heat in a large skillet and add onion and garlic, cooing until onion is translucent, about 8 minutes. Add ham and chopped stems and cook over brisk heat until mushrooms are tender. Add sherry and reduce slightly. Add flour and cook until absorbed. Add cream and mix until smooth. Remove from the heat, cool, fold in parsley. Adjust seasonings with salt and pepper. Pipe mixture into morels, place in oven and bake until warmed through.

Yield: 25 stuffed morels

Wine Suggestion: Vieux Telegraph, Chateauneuf-du-Pape

MORELS STUFFED WITH PHEASANT MOUSSE

Ingredients

24 morel mushrooms, medium size
1 pound pheasant breast, boneless,
   skinless (chicken may be substituted)
3 tablespoons shallots, fine dice
2 egg whites
2 cups heavy cream, divided
2 tablespoons Cognac

pinch nutmeg
pinch cayenne pepper
1 tablespoon parsley, chopped
1 tablespoon chives, chopped
1 cup chicken broth
   salt & pepper

Preparation

WASH morels by immersing in salted water briefly. Do not soak. Agitate & drain. Cut stems off and chop up. Check insides of caps for insects and debris.

CUT the pheasant into small pieces and mix with the shallots and egg whites. Chill well. Purée the pheasant mixture to a completely smooth paste in a food processor. Remove to a stainless steel mixing bowl. Place the mixing bowl over a bowl of ice. Add 1 cup of the cream a few drops at a time, whipping with a whisk so that the mixture emulsifies. The consistency should remain about the same through the entire process. After incorporating the cream, add Cognac, nutmeg, cayenne, parsley, and chives. Season lightly with salt and pepper. To check seasoning, drop a spoonful into a little simmering broth and cook. Taste and adjust the seasoning.

PREHEAT oven to 350 degrees. Place half of the mousse into a piping bag fitted with a piping tube that will easily fit into the bottom of a morel. Fill a morel with the mousse and pipe a small amount at the end to create a morel stem with the mousse. Continue with the remaining morels. Once they are all filled place them in a large casserole dish that has been generously buttered. Bring the chicken broth to a boil, pour into the casserole; cover with aluminum foil and place in oven for 20 minutes or until the mousse is cooked through.

TRANSFER the morels to a platter and keep warm. Pour the cooking liquid into a saucepan and reduce to about ½ cup. Add the remaining cream and cook until the liquid coats the back of a spoon. Adjust the seasoning with salt and pepper. Pour the sauce over the morels and serve.

Yield: 24 stuffed morels

Wine suggestion: Keenan Cabernet Sauvignon, Napa Valley

Chandler's

CHANDLER'S
A RESTAURANT

215½ Howard Street
Petoskey, MI 49770
231-347-2981

Lunch daily 11:00am – 4:00pm
Dinner
Monday – Thursday 5:00pm – 9:00pm
Friday – Sunday 5:00pm – 11:00pm
Breakfast
Saturday – Sunday 9:00am – 4:00pm

Chandler's

Executive Chef Peter Hamm
Chef de Cuisine Andrew Adams
Chandler Symon III, Owner

Petoskey offers northern Michigan's best resort town experience. Big enough to shoulder a vibrant downtown yet charming and contained in a ruff-hewn, upscale Western ski town way. Of course, the imposing presence of Lake Michigan just a couple hundred yards down the slope is a ready reminder of why visitors flock here from around the country.

Chandler's is tucked underneath Symons General Store in the downtown Gaslight District. The Symons family owns both (in addition to a wildlife gallery) and the restaurant name derives from a father, son, grandson line of Petoskey natives. Chandler III launched the restaurant in 1999 as a "natural progression" of the General Store's deli and wine shop business but didn't quite anticipate (or dream, we imagine) just how fine his creation would be.

Recently, the credit belongs to Executive Chef Peter Hamm and Chef de Cuisine Andrew Adams who share duties equally. A culinary school grad and veteran of several Grand Rapids restaurants, Hamm also worked in Scotland before accepting the sous chef position at the bay Harbor Yacht Club. At Chandler's he provides the steady influence while his enthusiastic partner, a Harbor Springs native, draws from his experience in the kitchens of Bradley Ogden and Charlie Trotter. That alone, shold tell you what to expect at Chandler's.

As it turns out, Ogden and Adams are still tight and when they speak the mentor stresses "fresh is best" like a mantra. So Adams and Hamm with significant input from Chandler, spend a great deal of time searching out the nation's best suppliers of exotic seafood, allowing them to fully explore the heights of New American and Global Cuisine. They also count on deliveries each morning from no less than ten local farmers, pushing them to experiment with heirloom varieties of herbs and vegetables. Such attention to ingredients is a sure sign that Chandler's is not about gimmicks. From dishes like Broiled Gulf Oysters to Baked Goat Cheese Salad, flavors are bright and pure. We find innovation in unexpected sushi and tartare preparations, as well as the way entrées are paired with one of several risottos that appear from time to time.

Wine lovers need only to remember that Chandler's shares space with one of northern Michigan's best wine shops. In addition to a lengthy and well-rounded list, diners are encouraged to wander the shelves for a bottle to be uncorked at their table. Otherwise, over twenty wines are available by the glass, all of them familiar to the knowledgeable waitstaff. In midsummer and winter alike, an A List of locals and tourists frequents the long wood bar. Drink of choice: martinis or Champagne.

GRILLED ROMAINE SALAD
with Charred Tomato Vinaigrette

Ingredients

4 tablespoons olive oil
4 romaine hearts
1 cup feta cheese

1 cup assorted nuts: almonds, pecans, walnuts, etc.
Dressing (recipe follows)

Preparation

PREHEAT grill. Brush romaine hearts with olive oil and char on grill until blackened all over, but not excessively so. Assemble grilled leaves on plate and drizzle with Dressing. Garnish with feta cheese and assorted nuts.

Serves 4

Wine Suggestion: Stevenson Barrie "Shea Vineyard" Pinot Noir, Willamette, OR

For the Dressing

6 tomatoes
1 lime, juiced
½ red onion
1 bunch cilantro, rough chopped, stems removed

2 tablespoons srirachi
Salt & pepper
1 cup olive oil
½ cup white wine or Champagne vinegar
3 tablespoons stone ground mustard

ON hot grill, char tomatoes until black. In food processor, pulse tomatoes, lime juice, red onion, cilantro, and srirachi until smooth. In separate mixing bowl, whisk mustard and vinegar together, then slowly drizzle olive oil in while continuing to whisk. Combine with tomato mixture and store in refrigerator.

LEMON PARMESAN GNOCCHI

Ingredients

1 quart water
⅓ pound butter
  zest of 1 lemon
1 teaspoon nutmeg
  salt & pepper

1 quart flour
2 cups grated Parmesan
12 egg yolks
  olive oil

Preparation

BRING water, butter, lemon zest, and spices to a simmer in saucepan. Add flour and Parmesan to wet mixture and cook 2 minutes stirring. Take off heat and add egg yolks one at a time until incorporated. Let cool then put in pastry bag.

BRING a pot of salted water to boil. Pipe mixture into water in 1-inch lengths, using scissors to cut. Remove when floating, approximately 1 minute. Put into ice bath and rinse. Sauté in olive oil until golden.

Serves 4

Wine Suggestion: Cakebread Cellars Sauvignon Blanc

Chandler's interior

HONEY MANCHEGO POTATO CROQUETTE

Serve this with a favorite pan-seared fish dish as a starch.

Ingredients

4 large Yukon potatoes
1 cup Manchego cheese, grated
½ cup premium honey
   salt & pepper
2 cups panko breadcrumbs
3 eggs

½ cup water
½ cup milk
1 cup flour
   olive oil
   butter

Preparation

BAKE potatoes in 350-degree oven until fully cooked. Scrape innards of potato into mixing bowl and fold in grated cheese and honey. Season to taste. Using an ice cream scoop, portion mix into 8 disks on a baking sheet and set in refrigerator to set up.

PLACE breadcrumbs in 1 of 3 separate bowls. Whisk eggs, water, and milk in another. Place flour in third. Remove potato disks from refrigerator and dust them with flour on both sides. Proceed to dip them in the egg wash and finally roll them in the breadcrumbs.

HEAT olive oil and butter and sauté approximately 1 minute (until browned) on each side, and finish in 350-degree oven, approximately 8 minutes. Serve with browned butter from pan.

Serves 4

Wine Suggestion: Mayacamas Vineyards Chardonnay, Mt. Veeder

CLASSIC STEAK TARTARE

Ingredients

1 pound beef tenderloin	¼ cup ketchup
2 shallots	2 tablespoons olive oil
6 cloves garlic	1 tablespoon sriracha
8 cornichons	½ tablespoon Worcestershire
1 red onion, rough chopped	1 tablespoon parsley
6 anchovy fillets	1 tablespoon chives
1 tablespoon capers	1 teaspoon salt
½ teaspoon cayenne	1 teaspoon pepper
2 tablespoons mustard	1 egg yolk

Preparation

DICE beef in small pieces with knife until consistency is almost like ground beef. In small food processor combine shallot, garlic, cornichons, red onion, anchovies, and capers till chopped fine. Remove mixture from processor into bowl and mix well with cayenne, mustard, ketchup, olive oil, sriracha, and Worcestershire. Chop parsley and chives well and add to mixture. Add the beef and mix well with wooden spoon season with salt and pepper. Shape into round mold, or scoop with a large spoon, and place on serving plate. Pile on top. Serve with crackers, crostini, French fries, etc., and shaved Parmesan.

Serves 4

Wine Suggestion: Folie A Deux Cabernet Sauvignon, St. Helena

The New York Restaurant

101 State Street
Harbor Springs, MI 49740
231–526–1904
www.thenewyork.com

Open daily at 5:00pm.

The New York Restaurant

Chef / Owner Matt Bugera

Michigan is so disproportionably endowed with beauty and diversity as to make one question the randomness of nature. Every year, millions of tourists head north from their midwestern homes with unique travel plans, each of them asking this bountiful state to deliver on a promise of expectation. The choices are endless: solitude in a still grove of white pines, waves to body surf, wild huckleberries or cherries or deer or salmon or grouse for the table, (fill in your own preference here), and for our purposes, high on the list for many is a world-class meal at a particular restaurant.

The New York Restaurant in Harbor Springs sits on the corner of State and Bay Streets, a location just a few steps from both the harbor and some of northern Michigan's most upscale boutiques and galleries. Four brothers from the Big Apple state built the New York Hotel on the site in 1904. Bowling alleys, theaters, dance halls, and various shops all competed for space in the building over the next seventy-plus years until the ground floor was refurbished to its present configuration. Much of the original hotel charm remains.

Chef /owner Matt Bugera nurtured The New York into dining prominence by serving wonderfully eclectic "all-inclusive" food. Unusual for a restaurant of this quality is the extensive list of entrée offerings - as many as twenty including the nightly additions to the menu. Such breadth allows Bugera to feature comfort food alongside ultra contemporary dishes. Indeed, no one will feel out of place here.

From the top, a few recent appetizers begin with Smoked Whitefish Chowder served New England style using locally smoked fish, Roasted Garlic and Peppers with Warm Goat Cheese and Foccacia, Duck & Wild Mushroom Egg Roll with Spicy Plum Dipping Sauce, and Smoked Whitefish Ravioli finished with Herbs, Tomato Horseradish Cream.

Salad offerings include Bugera's take on classics like Caesar, Cobb, Baby Spinach with Bacon, and a Roasted Beet Salad with Red Onion, Goat Cheese, Spiced Pecans, dressed with Petoskey's own American Spoon Foods Cherry Vinaigrette.

Highlights from the aforementioned lengthy list of entrées include these seafood preparations: Prawns in Chili Sauce, Scampi Riva (gulf shrimp sautéed with Kalamata olives, spinach, tomato, and garlic, tossed with spinach and egg linguini, and glazed with balsamic vinegar), and local whitefish simply served broiled with lemon dill sauce.

Diners looking for heartier fare will decide between Colorado Lamb Shank, Tuscan Rib Eye, Veal Delmonico Steaks, Double Cut Pork Rib Chop with Dried Cherry Chutney, or Shaking Beef (sliced tenderloin stir fried with French beans, red onion, garlic, and spicy red chile), to name just a few.

Sommelier Bill Miller manages the dining room and wine list with great skill. A bar-side chalkboard always includes additions to his list and several wine-by-the-glass features.

 Award of Excellence

WORLD FAMOUS, AWARD WINNING WHITE BEAN AND LOBSTER CHILI WITH ANCHO CHILE CREAM

Ingredients

4 large onions, chopped
1 tablespoon olive oil
4 15-ounce cans crushed plum tomatoes
5 pounds Great Northern beans, soaked overnight in water
2 quarts water
8 ounces clam base
2 pounds lobster meat, cooked

oregano
cumin
chili powder
thyme
1 each, red, yellow, and green peppers, diced
1 4-ounce can ancho chiles, puréed
16 ounces sour cream

Preparation

SAUTÉ onions in olive oil until transparent, and add tomatoes. Drain the soaked beans and add to mixture along with the water. Simmer until beans are cooked. Add clam base, lobster, seasonings, and peppers. Adjust seasoning.

MIX puréed ancho chili with sour cream and spoon into soup before serving.

Serves 8

Wine Suggestion: Casa Castillo Jumilla

Chicken Breast with Crab Stuffing, Roasted Pepper Aioli, and Corn and Potato Risotto

Ingredients

6 chicken breasts, boneless, skin on
½ each red, yellow, and green pepper, diced finely
1 bunch green onions, sliced thin
½ cup Dijon mustard
1 tablespoon Worcestershire sauce
3 large eggs
1 pound jumbo lump crabmeat, drained and picked for shells
1 cup breadcrumbs

1 teaspoon garlic, chopped
½ teaspoon Tabasco
1 teaspoon oregano
1 tablespoon parsley, chopped
salt & pepper
Corn and Potato Risotto (recipe follows)
½ cup demi glace, heated through
Roasted Red Pepper Aioli (recipe follows)

Preparation

PREHEAT oven to 400 degrees. Combine all ingredients except chicken in a large bowl until wet. Cut a pocket in each chicken breast starting at the thick end. Be sure to cut evenly and go the length of the breast. Using a spoon or a large pastry bag without the tip, begin stuffing each breast with the stuffing. Butter or oil chicken breast and bake for 20-30 minutes or until done.

WHEN ready to serve, slice the chicken breasts. Spoon the Corn and Potato Risotto onto center of plate. Ring the risotto with demi glace and shingle the sliced chicken on top. Drizzle with Roasted Red Pepper Aioli.

Serves 6

Wine suggestion: Chateau La Roque, Pic Saint Loup

For the Corn and Potato Risotto

1 cup onion, diced
1 tablespoon butter
3 cups russet potatoes, peeled and cubed

½ cup white wine
1 cup fresh or frozen corn
1 cup heavy cream
salt & pepper

SAUTÉ onion in butter, over medium heat, but do not brown. Add diced potato and white wine. Reduce by half. Add the corn and cream and simmer till potatoes are cooked and the cream thickens, approximately 20 minutes. Season with salt and pepper to taste.

For the Roasted Red Pepper Aioli

> ¼ cup mayonnaise
> ¼ cup roasted red pepper purée
> ½ teaspoon garlic, minced

COMBINE ingredients and refrigerate until ready to use.

ROAST PORK OR VEAL LOIN
with Dried Cherry and Wild Rice Stuffing

Ingredients

1 center cut veal or pork loin (Have your butcher butterfly the loin)	salt & pepper
1 cup breakfast sausage	¼ cup shallots or onion, minced
1 cup cooked wild rice	rosemary
½ cup dried cherries	thyme
	parsley

Preparation

PREHEAT oven to 400 degrees. Pound butterflied loin between plastic wrap till even. Combine the rest of the ingredients in a bowl. Place the filling down the center of the loin in a tube shape. Fold the meat over the stuffing and tie with butchers twine. Roast in oven for 45 minutes. When done, remove the meat and let it rest. Make a pan gravy with the fat and juice left in the roasting pan.

Serves 4

Wine Suggestion: Emilo Morro, Ribera del Duero

Northern Michigan Asylum baseball team, (circa 1900).

Grand Hotel

Mackinac Island, MI 49757   May through October
906-847-3331   Nightly 6:30pm – 8:45pm
www.grandhotel.com

The Grand Hotel

Executive Chef Hans Burtscher

Hard to argue about the pedigree of a restaurant that has served five U.S. presidents, dozens of state governors, senators, celebrities including Mark Twain, and more captains of industry over the past 120 years than all but a handful of dining rooms anywhere. It also doesn't hurt to provide diners with the opportunity to sip Champagne and stroll along the largest porch in the world before dinner. Mind you, a 660-foot porch overlooking extensive gardens and the Straits of Mackinac, not to forget the mighty bridge. No, there's nothing quite like the Grand experience. You would not be the first to swoon slightly under a heady trance of history and unparalleled elegance.

Mackinac Island is one of those mystical, in-between places; valued for its strategic position—the French, British, Native Americans, and newly formed United States all fought to control the passageway between Lake Huron and Lake Michigan, as well as the lucrative fur trade. But the in-between-ness also extends to the place in time the island seeks to retain. No motorized vehicles are allowed, horse and carriage are the preferred mode of travel, and centuries of history exude from the architecture. The imposing walls of Fort Mackinac, built by the British in 1780 on the island's bluffs also add to the enchantment.

A stay at The Grand Hotel includes breakfast and a prix fixe five-course dinner in the main dining room. Non-hotel guests are certainly welcome, though everyone is required to sport evening attire: coat and tie for men, dresses or pantsuits for women. The stately dining room deserves such respect, as does the elegant food prepared by Executive Chef Hans Burtscher and his kitchen staff of 100.

After training in Austria, Burtscher spent time honing his skills in Spain and Switzerland, before joining the hotel in 1983. Named Executive Chef in 1991, he has received numerous awards, though none better than an invitation to cook for The James Beard Foundation in 2004. His European background is revealed in richly prepared dishes such as Filet of Amberjack with Lobster Risotto and Shellfish Broth, Sautéed Chicken Breast with Crabmeat and Apple-Nut Stuffing and Yellow Tomato Fondue, and Prime Aged Beef Tenderloin Medallions with Shrimp Sauté and Bordelaise Sauce. Burtscher winters in Georgia and we can spot the southern influence in his Grilled Breast of Duck and Duck Confit on Black Truffle Grits with Collard Greens. A recent appetizer menu featured Lamb Carpaccio, Arugula, Pine Nuts with Horseradish Oil, as well as Smoked Mackinac Whitefish on Buckwheat Pancakes with Coriander Jicama Slaw.

A choice of similarly decadent soups, salads, and stunning desserts are served with each meal. And yes, there is a collection of wine in the cellar befitting the Hotel's grand setting. Burtscher also serves as Vice President of Food and Beverage, so count on many European favorites. Following dinner, guests are encouraged to visit The Parlor for demitasse and music performed by the Grand Hotel Orchestra.

ROQUEFORT AND BRIE CHEESE PRALINE
with Radish Sprouts and Balsamic Syrup

Ingredients

⅓ cup pecans, chopped
⅓ cup walnuts, chopped
4 ounces Roquefort cheese
14 ounces Brie cheese
4 ounces cream cheese
1 tablespoon gin
1 tablespoon white balsamic

2 tablespoons chives
salt & pepper
cherry brioche, toasted and precut
radish sprouts, for garnish
roasted baby beets, for garnish
Balsamic Syrup (recipe follows)

Preparation

PREHEAT oven to 350 degrees. Toast pecans and walnuts in oven until golden brown. Let cool. Combine the cheeses, gin, white balsamic, and chives in a bowl and whip until smooth. Scoop out 12-14 small, equal amounts of mixture and place on a baking sheet covered in saran wrap. Place in cooler to firm. Once chilled, roll the balls in the nut mixture and coat them evenly.

TO SERVE, place on precut and toasted cherry brioche. Garnish with radish sprouts, oven-roasted baby beets, and drizzle with Balsamic Syrup.

Yield: 12 – 14 pralines

Wine Suggestion: Sauterne or Tokai.

For the Balsamic Syrup

2 cups balsamic vinegar
⅓ cup honey
1 tablespoon thyme, finely chopped

POUR vinegar, honey, and thyme into a sauté pan, bring to a boil, then reduce heat and simmer until reduced by ¾ or until a syrup-like consistency. Strain through fine sieve.

ROASTED VEGETABLE SALAD

One of our signature salads at the Grand Hotel.

Ingredients

2 yellow beets
1 zucchini, diced
1 yellow squash, diced
1 small eggplant, diced
24 pearl onions
12 asparagus spears, diced
1 yellow pepper, diced

1 red pepper, diced
2 fresh artichokes, cleaned and diced
1 tablespoon rosemary, chopped
1 tablespoon thyme
1 cup olive oil
24 cherry tomatoes, cut in half
    Grand Hotel Dressing (recipe follows)

Preparation

PREHEAT oven to 360 degrees. Roast the beets in oven for about 1 hour and then peel and dice.

RAISE oven temperature to 450 degrees. Toss the diced vegetables, except the cherry tomatoes, with the herbs and olive oil and roast them at 450 degrees for about 10 minutes. Let cool and combine with beets, cherry tomatoes, and dressing.

Serves 8

For the Grand Hotel Dressing

½ cup balsamic vinegar
2 tablespoons soy sauce
½ cup extra virgin olive oil
¼ cup water
1 tablespoon Dijon mustard
1 tablespoon honey

1 teaspoon ground celery seed
1 lime, juice of
3 cloves garlic, minced
½ cup scallions, diced
   salt & pepper

BLEND the first 8 items together, then whisk in garlic, scallions, salt and pepper.

TARTARE OF BUFFALO TENDERLOIN
on Pumpkin Seed Crostini with Caramelized Pearl Onions

Ingredients

1 pound buffalo tenderloin
2 tablespoons shallots, minced
1 tablespoon anchovies, minced
2 tablespoons capers
2 tablespoons sour pickles, minced
2 tablespoons Italian parsley, chopped
2 tablespoons ketchup
2 tablespoons Dijon mustard
1 tablespoon Tabasco

1 tablespoon Cognac
2 teaspoons garlic, minced
2 teaspoons paprika
2 teaspoons olive oil
2 egg yolks
   Salt & Pepper
   Pumpkin Seed Crostini (recipe follows)
   Caramelized Pearl Onions (recipe follows)

Preparation

REMOVE all silver skin and fat from the tenderloin. Dice the meat finely, using a knife. Add the remaining ingredients and mix together thoroughly, adjust seasonings if needed. Serve on top of Pumpkin Seed Crostini topped with Caramelized Pearl Onions.

Yield: about 30 buffalo crostini

Wine Suggestion: Louis Jadot Beaujolais Villages, or a Valpolicella Classico to your liking. Try Allegrini.

For the Pumpkin Seed Crostini

1 slender French baguette
1 cup pumpkin seed oil

2 tablespoons chives, finely diced

PREHEAT oven to 350 degrees. Slice the bread into ½-inch rounds. Place the rounds in a single layer on a baking sheet and set aside. Combine oil and chives in a small bowl. With a pastry brush, brush half the oil mixture onto the bread rounds. Bake in the middle rack of the oven for 4 to 5 minutes. Turn the slices over; brush with the remaining chive-oil mixture, and bake another 5 minutes, or until golden. Allow the crostini to cool.

For the Caramelized Pearl Onions

1 teaspoon pumpkinseed oil
1 cup pearl onions, finely diced
1 tablespoon sugar

   salt & pepper
1 tablespoon thyme, chopped
1 tablespoon balsamic vinegar

SAUTÉ the onion and sugar in pumpkinseed oil over medium-low heat for 30 minutes. Add thyme and season with salt and pepper. When the onions are completely caramelized, add balsamic vinegar and cook for 2 more minutes.

Buffalo Tenderloin

with Blackberry Sauce, Wild Mushroom Salad, and Wild Rice with Pecans and Basil

The buffalo meat we are using at the Grand Hotel has been farm raised in Cheboygan, Michigan.

Ingredients

12 ounces buffalo tenderloin, cut into 2-
    ounce medallions
    olive oil
    salt and pepper

Wild Mushroom Salad (recipe follows)
Wild Rice with Pecans and Basil
(recipe follows)
Blackberry Sauce (recipe follows)

Preparation

PLACE a sauté pan coated with olive oil over medium-high heat. Sear the seasoned buffalo medallions until medium rare, or desired temperature.

TO SERVE, place a portion of the Wild Mushroom Salad on the upper left third of each plate. Place a portion of the Wild Rice with Pecans and Basil on the upper right third. Place 3 buffalo medallions, overlapping, in a circle leaning up against the lower edges of the salad and rice. Drizzle the Blackberry Sauce over the medallions.

Serves 2

Wine suggestion: Bandol from Provence. Too often overlooked in this country.

For the Wild Mushroom Salad

2 tablespoons butter
1 shallot, diced
1 clove garlic, minced
⅓ cup shiitake mushrooms
⅓ cup crimini mushrooms
⅓ cup morel mushrooms

1 teaspoon curry
2 tablespoons fresh herbs, chopped
    salt & pepper
⅓ cup hazelnut oil
⅓ cup olive oil
⅓ cup rice vinegar

IN A skillet, melt butter and sauté shallot and garlic, then add the wild mushrooms, curry, herbs, salt and pepper. Next add the oils and rice vinegar into the skillet and remove from heat. Pour the mixture into a bowl to infuse. Keep warm for service.

For the Wild Rice with Pecans and Basil

1 teaspoon butter
1 cup wild rice, cooked
1 shallot, diced

2 tablespoons pecans
1 tablespoon basil, chopped
    salt & pepper

HEAT sauté pan, add butter, shallots, wild rice, basil, pecans and seasonings. Heat through and hold for service.

For the Blackberry Sauce

1 tablespoon olive oil	1 cup meat stock
2 shallots, diced	3 tablespoons blackberry jam
2 tablespoons pickled ginger, diced	2 tablespoons thyme
1 tablespoon tomato paste	⅓ cup fresh blackberries
2 tablespoons soy sauce	

IN A saucepan, heat the olive oil and add shallots and ginger, sautéing for 1 minute. Then add the tomato paste, soy sauce, meat stock, blackberry jam, and thyme and reduce by half. Strain and adjust seasonings. Add fresh blackberries and set aside.

Green Olive and Cucumber Granita

Ingredients

4 large English cucumbers, seeded and peeled	¼ cup water
½ cup superfine sugar	¼ cup aquavit
¼ cup green olive juice	1 tablespoon lime juice
	salt

Preparation

COARSELY chop the cucumber to measure about 5 cups, then purée with remaining ingredients until smooth. Freeze, stirring and crushing lumps with a fork every hour until frozen.

Serves 8

MACKINAC WHITEFISH BISQUE
with Smoked Trout and Fennel Ragoût

Ingredients

1 tablespoon butter	2 tablespoons fresh thyme, chopped
½ cup onions, diced	1 tablespoon ginger, chopped
½ cup celery root, diced	1 Idaho potato, peeled and diced
½ cup carrots, diced	salt & white pepper
1 tablespoon garlic, minced	2 cups heavy cream
1½ pounds whitefish, cubed	1 cup crème fraîche
½ cup white wine	Smoked Trout and Fennel Ragout
6 cups fish stock or vegetable stock	(recipe follows)
1 cup coconut milk	salmon caviar, for garnish
2 tablespoons lemongrass, fine dice	

Preparation

MELT butter in saucepan on low heat. Add onions, celery root, carrots, and garlic and sauté for approximately 4 to 5 minutes. Add whitefish and sauté for additional 3 minutes. Add white wine, fish stock, coconut milk, lemongrass, thyme, ginger, potatoes, and seasonings and bring to a simmer. Let reduce by half. Remove saucepan from heat, cool slightly and transfer ingredients to a blender container and purée until smooth. Transfer ingredients back into the saucepan and return to a simmer. Stir in heavy cream and adjust seasonings if needed. JUST before serving soup add crème fraîche, Smoked Trout and Fennel Ragoût, and then top with salmon caviar.

Serves 8

Wine suggestion: Gruner Veltliner from Austria

For the Smoked Trout and Fennel Ragoût

1 tablespoon olive oil	1 tablespoon garlic, minced
⅓ cup smoked trout, diced	salt & pepper
⅓ cup cooked fennel, diced	½ cup Pernod
⅓ cup tomato, diced	1 tablespoon chives, chopped

HEAT olive oil in sauté pan on medium heat. Add trout, fennel, tomatoes, garlic, and salt and pepper and sauté for 2-3 minutes. Then add Pernod and chives, sauté 1 more minute. Remove from heat.

Bayside Dining

at Drummond Island Resort

Bayside Dining

33494 South Maxton Road,
Drummond Island, MI 49726
800-999-6343
www.drummondisland.com

Friday & Saturdays 6:00pm – 9:00pm
End of January thru second week of
March
Friday & Saturdays 6:00pm – 9:00pm
May thru June
7 days a week 6:00pm – 9:00pm July
thru September
Friday & Saturdays 6:00pm – 9:00pm
until end of October
Open for Valentines Day, Mothers
Day, and New Years Eve.

Bayside Dining
at Drummond Island Resort and Conference Center

Executive Chef Nathaniel Mileski

Island food comes in nearly as many forms as there are islands. Generally, one can count on tropical fare – fresh seafood, bright, citrus, spicy flavors prepared over fire, though not always. What happens to food on an island surrounded by the frigid waters of Lake Huron's North Channel, a stone's skip from Canada? What can a diner expect there?

Fabulous food, as it turns out, prepared by a Culinary Institute of America-trained chef intent on competing with the best restaurants in the state. The restaurant we're referring to anchors the Drummond Island Resort, once home to pizza baron Tom Monaghan's twenty million dollar private estate complete with an airstrip and one of Michigan's best golf courses. Drummond is the world's third largest freshwater island. Located off the eastern tip of the U.P., it boasts 160 miles of shoreline with 87,000 acres of public land.

A Michigander and Northern Michigan University grad, Chef Nathan Mileski rode his CIA degree into a five-year stint at Minnesota's acclaimed Lafayette Country Club, then under the direction of Master Chef Kevin Walker. The island cuisine Mileski prepares at Bayside Dining easily ranges from International to American with ample attention paid to the fresh local fish and wild game of the upper Midwest. Venison Ragoût with Drunken Pappardelle Pasta, Wild Mushroom and Italian Sausage Stuffed Quail, and the cross-cultural Salmon Saltimbocca with Artichoke, Leek, and Saffron Risotto, all appeared on a recent menu. Start your evening with an app of Creamy Crab, Shrimp, and Spinach Baked Green Shell Mussels followed by a Chardonnay Poached Apple and Spinach Salad and any of the above-named entrées and a memorable night is guaranteed. Off-season, Mileski loves running themed wine dinners and cooking classes allowing guests to work alongside him in the creation of that night's dinner.

The modestly priced wine list is full of food-friendly selections including Alsatian Pinot Gris and Pinot Blanc, northern Italian Arneis, and California Sauvignon Blanc from St. Supery, Cakebread Cellars and Ferrari Carano. The list of reds is predominantly Californian. Expect to find bottles from Ridge, Markham, Cinnabar, Sanford, David Bruce, and Cline.

Midsummer diners should schedule reservations to coincide with 10:00pm sunsets, an often-forgotten bonus in latitudes that far north of the 45th parallel.

Wild Mushroom Crostini with Leek Hay

This is a simple and elegant dish inspired by the northern woods of the Upper Peninsula. This pleases both the strongest of lumberjacks and ladies alike with its earthy taste and presentation.

Ingredients

1 tablespoon garlic
1 tablespoon shallot
1 tablespoon olive oil
1 pound wild mushrooms (your choice)
1 tablespoon Dijon mustard
½ cup red wine

1 quart veal demi-glace
salt & pepper
1 French baguette
olive oil or clarified butter
Leek Hay (recipe follows)
truffle oil (optional)

Preparation

HEAT olive oil in sauté pan, add garlic and shallots and cook over medium heat until slightly browned, approximately 5 minutes. Add mushrooms and cook down until almost no liquid is left in pan. Add mustard and red wine. Reduce for 6 to 8 minutes longer. Add demi-glace, season to taste with salt and pepper, and continue reducing until thickened.

PREHEAT oven to 350 degrees. Cut bread into half-inch thick rounds, season with salt and pepper, brush with olive oil or clarified butter, then bake until slightly golden and crisp.

TO SERVE, spoon mushroom mixture over slice of crostini. Garnish the very top with Leek Hay. If desired, drizzle truffle oil over crostini before serving.

Wine suggestion: Ravenswood Zinfandel

For Leek Hay

2 leeks, julienned
1 tablespoon olive oil
kosher salt

HEAT olive oil over medium-low heat (275 degrees). Place leeks in pan and fry until golden brown. Drain on paper towel. Season with kosher salt.

HALIBUT BAYSIDE
with Lemon Butter Sauce and Roasted Garlic Whipped Yukons

This was a special the first summer I arrived at the resort. A guest liked it so much she thought it should be more than a special one-time offering and she was willing to bet all her husband's elk meat from his yearly hunt that if I placed the halibut on the menu full time it would outsell all our other entrées combined. If I lost, I had to buy them dinner the following year. She won, and five years later it still outsells all other entrées almost two to one. She still collects every year on our original bet.

Ingredients

8 6- to 8-ounce halibut fillets
2½ tablespoons grapeseed oil, divided
1 pound shiitake mushrooms, halved
1 pound crimini mushrooms, quartered
1 pound asparagus, cut into 2-inch
    lengths

1 pint grape tomatoes, halved
8 ounces pancetta, diced
    Garlic Whipped Yukon Potatoes
    (recipe follows)
    Lemon Butter Sauce (recipe follows)

Preparation

PREHEAT oven to 350 degrees. Season halibut with salt and pepper. Heat sauté pan over medium-high heat, add 2 tablespoons of the grapeseed oil, and sear halibut until lightly golden. Flip and sear other side. Place on baking sheet and place in oven. Bake for 10 to 15 minutes.

HEAT remaining half tablespoon of grapeseed oil in another sauté pan over medium heat. Sauté mushrooms and asparagus for approximately 10 minutes until mushrooms juices have almost reduced and asparagus is still slightly crisp. Add tomatoes and pancetta and continue cooking for 2 or 3 minutes until heated through.

TO SERVE, place a scoop of Roasted Garlic Whipped Yukons in center of plate. Place one halibut fillet over potatoes. Spoon mushroom and asparagus sauté around fish and potatoes. Cover with Lemon Butter Sauce.

Serves 8

Wine suggestion: Cakebread Sauvignon Blanc

For the Roasted Garlic Whipped Yukons

1 pound Yukon Gold potatoes, scrubbed
4 tablespoons roasted garlic, mashed
½ cup heavy cream

4 ounces unsalted butter
    salt & pepper

BOIL potatoes whole in large pot. Place in mixing bowl and add garlic, heavy cream, and butter. Mix on medium to low speed until smooth. Season with salt and pepper.

For Lemon Butter Sauce

4 shallots, roughly diced	8 whole black peppercorns
2 lemons, juiced and zested	2 cups heavy cream
2 cups dry white wine	1 pound unsalted butter
2 sprigs of thyme	salt and pepper to taste

PLACE shallots, lemon juice, lemon zest, white wine, thyme, and peppercorns in stainless pot and bring to slow simmer. Reduce until half the wine is gone. Add heavy cream and reduce by half. Carefully whisk in butter, 2 ounces at a time, until sauce is combined. Strain and season with salt and pepper.

SPINACH SALAD WITH MAPLE SHERRY VINAIGRETTE

This salad returns every fall thru early spring by request of our guests. One of the key ingredients holds an extra special place in their hearts and mine; for the maple syrup is harvested and made right here on Drummond Island.

Ingredients

8 ounces pancetta or bacon
8 ounces walnuts
8 ounces Gorgonzola cheese

2 pounds spinach
    Maple Sherry Vinaigrette (recipe
    follows)

Preparation

SAUTÉ pancetta or bacon until crisp, cool on paper towel, and then chop coarsely. Toast walnuts in sauté pan over medium heat stirring constantly, for approximately 5 minutes. Cool completely. Crumble gorgonzola. Toss all ingredients in bowl with Maple Sherry Vinaigrette.

For the Maple Sherry Vinaigrette

2¼ cups maple syrup
  1 cup sherry vinegar

3½ cups olive oil blend
    salt & white pepper, fresh ground

WHISK all ingredients together and reserve.

Serves 8

Wine suggestion: Vero Drouhin, Pinot Noir, Bourgogne, France

Capers
Restaurant
at The Landmark Inn

Capers
RESTAURANT

230 N. Front Street
Marquette, MI 49855
906-228-2580
888-752-6362
www.thelandmarkinn.com

Summer Hours 5:30pm – 10:00pm
Winter Hours
Sunday – Thursday 5:00pm – 9:00pm
Friday & Saturday 5:00pm – 10:00pm

Capers Restaurant
at The Landmark Inn

Executive Chef Tim Reinbold
Bruce and Christine Pesola, Co-owners

Much like the massive lake it faces, one word may best describe the seventy-five year history of Marquette's premier hotel: tumultuous. Nothing came easy; not the original financing, not the unfortunate groundbreaking just months before the stock market crash of October 1929, and certainly not the refurbishment required in 1995 when present owners Bruce and Christine Pesola purchased the six-story shamble all but overtaken by birds and nature. But six million two hundred thousand dollars later, The Landmark Inn towers proud and beautiful over this city of twenty-thousand people, named recently as "One of America's ten most livable cities."

Everything in the hotel was refurbished or replaced to its original luster. Along with spectacular views of Lake Superior, many of the rooms come with Jacuzzis and fireplaces. Guests might even luck into sleeping in the same bed as Mick Jagger or Louis Armstrong, two famous guests. One element of the hotel was improved far beyond its former reputation: the hotel's fine dining reputation. Marquette has never known a restaurant like Caper's at The Landmark Inn.

As the restaurant name suggests, Executive Chef Tim Reinbold has implemented a menu based on the robust flavors of Spain, Portugal, Italy, and Morocco. So ingredients like goat cheese, kalamata olives, calamari, tapenade, hummus, marinated mushrooms, and artichokes, make appearances; most of them served tapas style. A few hot tapas selections include Pork Empanadas (shredded pork and spiced apples mixed with fresh herbs folded in pastry and served with wild mushroom dipping sauce), Cioppino (hearty Italian seafood stew combined with a zesty tomato base and fresh vegetables), and tempting Garlic Shrimp (shrimp slowly poached in garlic oil and served with rustic rosemary bread.)

Reinbold's entrées draw more from contemporary American cuisine than Europe, but they are no less compelling. Duet of Oven Roasted Quail (stuffed with apples and Maryland blue crab topped with sweet basil pesto), compete with Seared Hawaiian Ahi Tuna (with gingered pineapple and jalapeno salsa on coconut risotto), and other dishes like Oven Roasted Rack of New Zealand Lamb (with forest mushroom ragout and fried leeks). Angus beef lovers will also be tempted by NY strip, filet mignon, and rib-eye, as well as veal shank.

The Caper's wine list is carefully constructed to complement the eclectic menu. Guests will certainly want to catch the elevator (or maybe the staircase after a particularly hearty meal) up to the Northstar Lounge on the hotel's top floor for a nightcap. It's the highest perch in Marquette and a perfect place to watch a November gale approach.

Capers Restaurant

BRIE IN PASTRY WITH DRIED CHERRIES

This appetizer is perfect for a cold winter day. The creamy texture of the baked cheese combined with the sweet taste of Michigan dried cherries is enough to keep you warm all day.

Ingredients

1   *sheet puff pastry, defrosted*
8   *ounces dried cherries*
4   *¼-pound wedges Brie*

1   *tablespoon olive oil*
1   *egg*

Preparation

PREHEAT oven to 400 degrees. Cut the puff pastry in half lengthwise, and then cut each half sheet in half widthwise, leaving you with 4 rectangular pieces of puff pastry. In the center of each sheet, place 2 ounces dried cherries. Place a wedge of Brie on each pile of cherries. Fold the sides of the pastry around the Brie, folding sides in first and then the rear. Oil a baking tray with olive oil. Place encased Brie wedges on tray. Whisk egg briefly and brush the top of wedges with the egg wash. Bake for approximately 15 minutes.

Serves 4

Wine Suggestion: Seven Deadly Zins, blend of 7 Zinfandel grapes

Polenta with Ratatouille

Ingredients

1 cup corn meal
2 tablespoons salt
¾ cup milk
1 tablespoon unsalted butter
¼ cup Parmesan
¼ cup olive oil
2 cups water
1 teaspoon olive oil
1 onion, diced

1 small eggplant, peeled, diced
6 tomatoes, diced
2 zucchini, halved and sliced
1 green pepper, julienned
1 tablespoon garlic, minced
2 cups tomato juice
salt & pepper
grated Parmesan, for garnish

Preparation

BRING the water to a boil and add the salt and corn meal. Turn burner down to medium heat and simmer until thickened. Add the milk and let thicken again. Be sure to stir the polenta to keep it from burning. When polenta has thickened with the milk, add the butter and the Parmesan and allow to melt into the polenta while stirring. Continue stirring and drizzle in olive oil. Keep warm.

FOR the ratatouille, warm a saucepan and heat one teaspoon of olive oil. Sauté onion and eggplant for 2 minutes, then add rest of vegetables and sauté until al dente. Add garlic and tomato juice. Simmer for 15 minutes and season to taste with salt and pepper.

TO SERVE, place a mound of polenta in middle of serving plate and ladle vegetables over the top. Skim out sauce and pour over polenta. Garnish with grated Parmesan.

Serves 4

Wine Suggestion: Treana White—a very full bodied and complex Marsanne/Viognier blend

Prosciutto Wrapped Salmon with Caper Sauce

With salmon being one of the area's most popular fish dishes, it was a necessity to include it on my menu. The prosciutto wrapping and the light caper sauce is the perfect Mediterranean influence to this fish.

Ingredients

8 ounces salmon fillet, cut in half
  lengthwise
1 deli slice prosciutto
2 wooden skewers soaked in water
1 ounce olive oil

2 ounces capers
1 tablespoon flour
¼ cup Chardonnay
1 ounce butter

Preparation

SKIN side to skin side, place the thickest end of each fillet against the thickest part of the other fillet, and then roll the thin end of the fillets clockwise into the thicker end. Cut the prosciutto lengthwise into 2 long strips and wrap the pieces around the salmon. Secure with the skewers all the way through the fish and prosciutto, so that they make an X if looking down from the top. Broil the salmon for 15 minutes until the flesh feels firm to the touch.

WHILE the salmon is cooking prepare the caper sauce. Warm a sauté pan with olive oil. Toss capers in flour until coated and add to sauté pan. Cook capers until flour starts to brown. Deglaze with Chardonnay and let wine reduce by ¼. Turn off heat and swirl in butter. Season to taste.

Serves 1

Wine Suggestion: The Creator, Cabernet/Syrah blend, Oregon

SEARED TUNA WITH SPICY MANGO PURÉE

Ingredients

2 carrots, peeled
2 leeks, cleaned, trimmed of green tops
½ cup olive oil
½ cup white balsamic vinegar
2 cloves garlic, minced
1 teaspoon salt

1 teaspoon pepper
6 ounces ripe mango, diced
½ cup fresh orange juice
1½ teaspoons crushed red pepper
16 ounces tuna, cut in 4-ounce portions
   salt & pepper

Preparation

CUT carrot and leek into ribbons ½ inch across, 3 inches long, and 1/8 inch thick. Whisk together olive oil, vinegar, garlic, salt, and pepper and cover vegetables in marinade for 2 hours or as long as overnight.

PLACE mango, orange juice, and crushed pepper in food processor and purée. Reserve.

Season tuna with salt and pepper. Heat a small amount of olive oil in sauté pan until smoking and sear tuna on each side.

TO SERVE, pile marinated vegetables on individual serving plates, place a piece of seared tuna on vegetables, and spoon mango purée on top.

Serves 4

Wine Suggestion: Sanford Pinot Noir

North Shore Pub 'n Grill

2131 Jasberg Street   Monday – Thursday 4:00pm – 9:00pm
Hancock, MI 49930   Friday & Saturday 4:00pm – 10:00pm
906-482-4678   Closed Sundays

North Shore Pub 'n Grill

Todd & Kerry Auger, Roger & Amy Hyrkas, and Mark Wiitanen, Owners

Only the sturdiest of individuals are willing to turn misfortune into opportunity and that is exactly the stock of people behind a restaurant thought by many to be the best in Michigan's Upper Peninsula. On a stormy night late in the winter of 2002, fire destroyed a small restaurant employing three talented men, leaving them jobless. Without missing a beat, the idea was born to create the North Shore Pub 'n Grill utilizing their combined sixty years of restaurant experience pooled with the business acumen of two of their wives. The following months included more setbacks but eventually they secured ownership of Hancock's former Eagles Club and the deft hands of chefs went to work with crowbars and hammers to refurbish the building. Doors opened on New Year's Eve and Hancock found itself on the culinary map.

Todd Auger, Roger Hyrkas, and Mark Wiitanen each draw on experience from restaurants around the country including The Snuggery in Chicago, Port Tack in Las Vegas, and Tampa, FL where Auger lived after graduating from a culinary school in Minnesota. He also spent time at Houghton's acclaimed Steamer's Grill. A National Guardsman, Wiitanen relies on the pluck he earned recently serving a yearlong stint in Iraq.

Their culinary backgrounds reveal themselves in North Shore's contemporary menu, featuring an array of wild game, top grades of beef, seafood, local lake trout and whitefish, and creative homemade pasta dishes all served with great attention paid to presentation.

The beverage selection includes several Belgian ales, as well as domestic and imported wines that match well with a wide array of dishes. North Shore seats over one hundred guests in the dining room with an additional twenty or so seats in the pub. Recently, they were asked to manage Spica and The Thirsty Fish, situated on the seventh floor of the nearby Best Western. Isn't it a wonder what great happenings can rise out of the ashes of a little misfortune.

North Shore Pub 'n Grill

Seared Ahi Tuna

VENISON MEDALLIONS
with Thimbleberry Port Wine Demi-Glace

Here in the very most north woods of Michigan, whitetail deer and thimbleberries can be found in abundance. The two combine to make a classic north-woods style game dinner.

Ingredients

2 pounds venison loin
  kosher salt & black pepper

Thimbleberry Port Wine Demi-Glaze
(recipe follows)

Preparation

CLEAN and trim venison loin and cut into 2 - 3 ounce medallions. Charbroil to medium rare and season with kosher salt and black pepper. Serve immediately with sauce ladled on or aside tenderloin, or served in a ramekin on the plate.

Serves 4

Beverage Suggestion: Stimson Merlot or Cabernet Sauvignon - Or serve with Chimay Grande Reserve or any strong, dark Belgian ale.

For the Port Wine Demi-Glace

1 tablespoon fresh garlic, minced
1 tablespoon shallot, minced
1 tablespoon fresh rosemary, chopped
2 tablespoons olive oil
pinch salt & pepper

1 cup Port wine
1 cup Pinot Noir wine
1 cup demi-glace
3 tablespoons thimbleberry jam
3 tablespoons black raspberry preserves

SAUTÉ fresh garlic, shallots, and rosemary in olive oil, with a pinch of salt and pepper for 1 – 2 minutes. Add Port and Pinot Noir. Cook off alcohol for 2 – 3 minutes. Add demi-glace, thimbleberry jam and raspberry preserves. Bring to a boil and reduce until sauce becomes thick enough to coat spoon. Reserve.

SEARED AHI TUNA
with Wasabi Cream Sauce & Chili Oil

Ingredients

2 4-ounce pieces of sashimi grade ahi
  tuna
  olive oil
  Cajun Seasoning (recipe follows)

Cole Slaw (recipe follows)
Wasabi Cream Sauce (recipe follows)
Chili Oil (recipe follows)

Preparation

COAT ahi with olive oil, and then roll in Cajun Seasoning. Sear in a cast iron skillet for 1 to 2 minutes on each side, until rare to medium rare.

SLICE cooked ahi into thin pieces and arrange around a mound of Cole Slaw on a small plate. Spoon small dollops of Wasabi Cream Sauce around the ahi, finish with Chili Oil, and impress your friends.

Serves 2

Wine Suggestion: Pinot Grigio or Chardonnay
Beer Suggestion: Belgian Wit Hoegarden or Blauche De Champlay

For the Cajun Seasoning

¼ cup kosher salt
⅓ cup garlic, minced
⅔ cup paprika
⅓ cup black pepper

3 tablespoons cayenne pepper
⅓ cup thyme
⅓ cup oregano
3 tablespoons rosemary

MIX thoroughly in bowl. Extra may be reserved in airtight container for other uses.

For the Wasabi Cream

¼ cup wasabi
1 teaspoon water

½ cup sour cream

STIR water into wasabi until incorporated. Mix with sour cream.

For the Cole Slaw

3 cups cabbage, shredded
⅓ cup mayonnaise
⅛ cup white vinegar
¼ cup granulated sugar

1½ teaspoons celery seed
1½ teaspoons sour cream
  salt & pepper

PLACE all ingredients in a large bowl and mix thoroughly. Keep chilled for service

For the Chili Oil

1½   cups olive oil
⅛   cup chili powder

ADD chili powder to olive oil. Heat oil to 140 degrees for 10 minutes, then cool overnight. Strain chili powder out next day through cheese cloth.

RUBBED RIB EYE

Ingredients

4 12-ounce lean, trimmed rib eyes of
beef

Emeril's Chipotle Marinade
Dry Rub (recipe follows)

Preparation

COAT each rib eye with a thin layer of Emeril's Chipotle Marinade, then rub with a generous amount of Dry Rub. Char-broil on high heat to medium rare. It is important to sear the rub, as searing causes the sugars to caramelize and gives the meat a sweet, spicy, smoky flavor. Serve with wild rice.

Serves 4

Beverage Suggestion: Serve with a Vienna style lager, such as Negra Modelo, Dos Equis, or Michigan's own Bell's Amber Ale

For the Dry Rub

4 tablespoons paprika
2 tablespoons smoked hickory salt
2 tablespoons brown sugar
4 tablespoons granulated sugar

4 tablespoons chili powder
4 tablespoons cumin
3 tablespoons ground black pepper
1½ teaspoons cayenne pepper

MIX all ingredients together in bowl and reserve.

WILD BOAR SCALOPPINI
with Wild Mushroom Demi-Glace

Ingredients

2 pounds wild boar tenderloin
2 cups seasoned flour
   olive oil

Wild Mushroom Demi-glace (recipe follows)

Preparation

TRIM boar tenderloin of silver skin, cut into 2 – 3 ounce pieces, and then gently pound tenderloin to ⅛-inch thickness. Dredge boar in seasoned flour and sauté in hot olive oil for 1 to 2 minutes on each side. Remove from pan and keep warm. (Reserve juices in pan for sauce.)

Serves 4

Beverage Suggestion: Penfolds Shiraz 28, or consider serving with Unibroue Trois Pistoles, a strong Belgian Dark Ale.

For the Wild Mushroom Demi-Glace

2 tablespoons olive oil
1 teaspoon fresh garlic, minced
1 teaspoon shallots, minced
8 ounces shiitake mushrooms, sliced
1 teaspoon fresh thyme, minced
1 teaspoon fresh dill, minced
1 teaspoon fresh sage, minced

1 teaspoon fresh basil, minced
½ cup sweet Marsala
½ cup brandy
8 ounces demi-glace
8 tablespoons Boursin cheese
   salt & pepper

IN same pan in which boar was cooked, add olive oil and sauté garlic, shallots, mushrooms, and herbs for 1 minute. Deglaze pan with Marsala and brandy. Cook off alcohol, add demi-glace and Boursin cheese. Whisk until smooth and adjust seasonings. Serve over boar tenderloin.

GLOSSARY

amuse bouche French, meaning "to amuse the mouth", this is usually a small bit of food before the meal to waken the taste buds.

brioche A French pastry bread made rich with butter and eggs that is used not only for desserts, but also in many meat and cheese dishes.

chiffonade Similar to julienne, the process of cutting lettuce, endive, or herbs into thin even strips.

chinois A very fine mesh cone-shaped metal sieve used for pureeing or straining. Often a spoon or pestle is used to press the food through it.

concassé; concassee A French term for chopping or pounding, often applied to tomatoes or herb mixtures.

corn salad Also called mâche, lamb's lettuce, and loblollie, this is a small plant that is used in salads in the spring and autumn when the leaves are the most tender.

crème fraîche A thick, velvety cream that is slightly tangy and can be boiled without curdling. Can be purchased in gourmet markets, or made at home by adding buttermilk to heavy cream.

demi-glace A rich brown sauce (usually meat stock) combined with Madeira or sherry and slowly cooked until it's reduced by at least half, to a thick glaze.

fines herbes A combination of very finely chopped herbs used in cooking. Usually contains chervil, chives, parsley, and tarragon.

gastrique A mixture of vinegar and sugar that is reduced until almost evaporated. Usually used in sauces made with fruit.

konbu; kombu Also called kelp, konbu is a dark brown to grayish black seaweed used in Japanese cooking. It is sun-dried and folded into sheets.

Merguez A spicy sausage used in North African cooking. Made with lamb or beef, it derives its distinctive red coloring from the red chile paste in its ingredients.

mirepoix; mirepois A mixture of diced carrots, onion, celery, and herbs that is sautéed in butter.

nappe A term indicating the thickness of a liquid, usually described as thick enough to coat the back of a spoon.

piment d'Espelette A long red pepper native to Mexico, that was imported originally by Columbus to Spain. It is used extensively in Basque cooking. It is milder than cayenne, with a fruity finish.

quinoa A grain used in South American cooking. It compares to couscous because of its light flavor that blends well with other flavors.

sansho The dried and ground pod of the prickly ash tree, it is used to counter fatty tastes. It is similar to the Chinese spice, Szechuan pepper.

togarashi A 7-spice blend used in Japanese cooking. It usually contains ginger, seaweed, black and yellow sesame seeds, Japanese pepper, red chile pepper, and roasted orange peel.

umami The fifth taste sense, not discovered until the 1980s. The other 4 are sweet, sour, salty, and bitter. Umami is found in glutamate, and is a savory taste that is naturally found in meat, fish, vegetables, and dairy products.

CULINARY SOURCES

This list is provided for your convenience. While many of the suggested suppliers have been recommended, not all suppliers have been individually checked out. We do not endorse any particular vendor or supplier.
Visit www.absolutemichigan.com for additional contacts.

CHERRY REPUBLIC
Over 100 cherry products.
6026 South Lake Street
Glen Arbor, MI 49636
Phone: 800-206-6949
www.cherryrepublic.com

GRAND TRAVERSE PIE COMPANY
Amazing pies, baked goods, and more.
525 West Front Street
Traverse City, MI 49684
Phone: 231-922-7437
www.gtpie.com

FOOD FOR THOUGHT
Organic & wild harvested gourmet products.
10704 Oviatt Road
Honor, MI 49640
Phone: 888-935-2748
www.foodforthought.net

ZINGERMAN'S
Offering full-flavored traditionally made olive oils, vinegars, breads, cheeses and pastries.
422 Detroit Street
Ann Arbor, MI 48104
Phone: 888-636-8162
www.zingermans.com

GROCER'S DAUGHTER CHOCOLATES
High quality herb and fruit infused chocolate.
12020 S. Leelanau Highway
Empire, MI 49630
Phone: 231-326-3030
www.grocersdaughter.com

MAPLE CREEK FARM
Certified organic produce.
11841 Speaker Road
Yale, MI 48097
Phone: 810-387-4365
www.maplecreekfarm.com

TRAVERSE BAY FARMS
Tart cherry juice concentrate, cherry capsules, dried tart cherries.
Bellaire, MI 49615
Phone: 877-746-7477
www.traversebayfarms.com

STEVE-N-SONS GRASSFIELDS CHEESE
Raw milk cheeses, all-natural pastured chickens, turkeys, eggs, and steaks.
14238 60th Avenue
Coopersville, MI 49404
Phone: 616-997-8251
www.grassfieldscheese.com

LEELANAU CHEESE
Award-winning traditional European style cheeses from raw, fresh, local cow's milk.
10844 East Revold Road
Suttons Bay, MI 49682
Phone: 231-271-2600
www.blackstarfarms.com/creamery

ANDRULIS FARMERS CHEESE
Old world recipe Baltic-style cheeses.
4295 East Millerton Road
Fountain, MI 49410
Phone: 877-6-CHEESE
www.andrulischeese.com

SLEEPING BEAR FARMS
Gourmet honey products.
971 S. Pioneer Road
Beulah, MI 49617
Phone: 888-912-0017
www.sleepingbearfarms.com

Anna Bach Chocolates
Wide variety of chocolates, marzipan, kringles and coffeecakes from Danish recipes.
102 West Ludington Avenue
Ludington, MI 49431
Phone: 231-843-9288
www.annabachchocolates.com

Moonlight Mile Herb Farm
Native herbs, guinea fowl, heritage breed chickens.
10144 Tanksley Court
Willis, MI 48191
Phone: 734-461-6296
www.moonlightmileherbs.com

Renaissance Acres Organic Herbs
Highest quality organic herbs.
4450 Valentine Road
Whitmore Lake, MI 48189-9691
Phone: 734-449-8336
www.provide.net

American Spoon Foods
Gourmet jams, jellies, preserves, salsas, condiments, and gift baskets.
1668 Clarion Avenue
Petoskey, MI 49770-0566
Phone: 231-347-9030
www.spoon.com

Alden's Mill House
Custom blend seasonings and spices.
Alden, MI 49612
Phone: 800-226-5481
www.aldenmillhouse.com

Alexander & Hornung
Ham, sausage, deli meats, and sausages.
20643 Stephens Road
St. Clair Shores, MI 48080
Phone: 586-771-9880
www.alexanderhornung.com

Billy Bones BBQ
BBQ sauces, chili mixes, dry rubs, & hot sauces.
751 Saginaw Road
Sanford, MI 48657
Phone: 989-687-7880
www.billybonesbbq.com

Earthy Delights
Fresh specialty foods and ingredients to professional chefs and the home gourmet.
1161 E. Clark Road, Suite 260
DeWitt, MI 48820
Phone: 800-367-4709
www.earthy.com

Great Lakes Buffalo Company
100% natural buffalo products.
2690 Riggsville Road
Cheboygan, MI 49721
Phone: 231-290-4444
www.greatlakesbuffalo.com

Sprik Farms Buffalo Store
Natural buffalo steaks, ribs, & more.
4111 8 Mile Road NW
Grand Rapids, MI 49544
Phone: 888-465-2711
www.sprikfarms.com

Hanover's Michigan Mints
High quality chocolate using Michigan mint.
401 S. Oakland Street
St. Johns, Michigan 48879
Phone: 989-224-0475
www.michiganmints.com

Cook's Sugarbush
Honey, maple syrup & other natural sweeteners.
297 Gumwood Road
Niles, MI 49120
1-866-45-MAPLE
www.cookssugarbush.com

PHOTO COPYRIGHTS/CREDITS

Front Cover, left to right: ©Rattlesnake; ©Denise Busley; ©The Dining Room at Clearbrook; ©The 1913 Room; ©Grand Hotel; ©Courtesy Archives of Michigan; ©Courtesy Archives of Michigan; ©Rugby Grille; ©Denise Busley; ©Brian Confer; ©Courtesy Archives of Michigan; ©Coach Insignia
Back Cover, left to right: ©Michael Buck; ©John Robert Williams; ©The Dining Room at Clearbrook; ©Rattlesnake; ©San Chez Bistro; ©Brian Confer

i: ©Courtesy Archives of Michigan; iii: ©Tracy Johnson; iv: ©Tracy Johnson; v: ©Tracy Johnson; vi: ©Tracy Johnson; vii: ©Tracy Johnson; viii: ©Tracy Johnson; ix: ©Tracy Johnson; ivx: ©Courtesy Archives of Michigan; x: ©Courtesy Archives of Michigan; xiv: ©Courtesy Archives of Michigan; 1-4: ©Coach Insignia; 7: ©Coach Insignia; 8,9: ©Giovanni's; 12: ©Courtesy Archives of Michigan; 13, 14, 21: ©Rattlesnake; 23, 24: ©Seldom Blues; 29, 30, 34: ©The Lark; 36: ©Courtesy Archives of Michigan; 37, 38, 40: ©Tribute; 44: ©Courtesy Archives of Michigan; 45: ©Denise Busley; 46: © Bacco Risorante; 52: ©Courtesy Archives of Michigan; 53, 54: ©Rugby Grille; 61, 62, 65, 66: ©Big Rock Chophouse; 67: © Cherry Blossom; 73, 74: ©Les Ward; 79: ©Denise Busley; 80: ©Restaurant Villegas; 87: ©Denise Busley; 88: ©The Farm; 94: ©Courtesy Archives of Michigan; 95: ©Christine LePottier; 96, 103: ©Mark Thomas; 104: ©Courtesy Archives of Michigan; 105, 106, 109: ©Michael Olsen; 111-113: ©Michael Buck; 117, 118, 122: © Butch's Dry Dock; 123-125, 129, 131: ©The Dining Room at Clearbrook; 133, 134: ©The 1913 Room; 139, 140, 142: ©San Chez; 145, 146, 148: ©The Sardine Room; 152: ©Grand Traverse Pioneer & Historical Society; 153, 154, 157: ©John Robert Williams; 158: ©Grand Traverse Pioneer & Historical Society; 159, 160, 165: ©Trattoria Stella; 167, 168, 172: ©North; 173, 174, 176: ©Riverside Inn; 180: ©Grand Traverse Pioneer & Historical Society; 181, 182, 184, 186-189, 193: ©Brian Confer; 196: ©Grand Traverse Pioneer & Historical Society; 197: ©Denise Busley; 198: ©Rowe Inn; 203-204: ©Latitude°; 209, 210, 212: ©Chandler's; 215-217: ©The New York Restaurant; 220: ©Grand Traverse Pioneer & Historical Society; 221, 222: ©Grand Hotel; 229, 230, 233, 234: ©Bayside Dining; 235-237, 240: ©Capers Restaurant; 241, 242: ©North Shore;

ABOUT THE PUBLISHERS

Chuck and Blanche started Wilderness Adventures Press, Inc. in 1993, publishing outdoor and sporting books. Along with hunting and fishing, they love fine dining, good wines, and traveling. They have always been able to "sniff out" the most outstanding and interesting restaurants in any city they visit.

On weekends, they experiment in the kitchen, cooking a variety of fish and meats, as well as preparing the harvest from their time in the field. This love of cooking has resulted in a large library of cookbooks, and has inspired them to create a series of cookbooks based on their love of travel and fine dining.

Chuck and Blanche make their home in Gallatin Gateway, Montana, along with their four German wirehaired pointers.

INDEX

Symbols

THE 1913 ROOM 133–138

A

Aged Goat Cheese, Roasted Beet and Hydro Watercress Salad 183
Agnello Crudo con Pomodoro 161
AMICAL 153–157
Ancho Chile Cream 217
APPETIZERS
   Agnello Crudo con Pomodoro 161
   Baked Jumbo Lump Crab 184
   Brie In Pastry with Dried Cherries 237
   Broiled Artichoke Stuffed 107
   Cajun Steak Bites 63
   Cheese Beignets 190
   Classic Steak Tartare 214
   Enoki Bacon 69
   Figs, Bleu Cheese, and Walnuts in Phyllo Canapés 125
   Foie Gras and Monkfish Liver Torchon 39
   Gulf Shrimp 31
   Lobster Barigoule 43
   Lobster Corn Dog 3
   Mezze Café Hummus 142
   Morel and Leek Pierogi 202
   Morels Stuffed with Ham Duxelle 207
   Morels Stuffed with Pheasant Mousse 208
   Moroccan Scallops 97
   Pork, Duck, Dried Cherry and Mixed Nut Terrine 200
   Roasted Artichoke 89
   Roquefort and Brie Cheese Praline 223
   Sakura Roll 70
   Shiitake Hakata 69
   Shrimp Fondue 119
   Tartare of Buffalo Tenderloin 225
   Thai Chicken Salad on Crostini 127
   Thai Crab Cakes 155
   Wild Mushroom Crostini 231
Apple-Jicama Slaw 207
Apple Cider Gastrique 138
Apricot Ginger Sauce 201
AZ Bronzed Salmon 28
AZ Sauce 28
AZ Vegetables 28

B

Baba Ghanoush 141
BACCO RISTORANTE 45–51
Baked Jumbo Lump Crab 184
Baked Michigan Navy Beans 83
Balsamic Syrup 223
Barley Risotto 114
Basic Tomato Sauce 48
Basil Pesto 165
Bayside Dining 229–234
BEEF & VEAL
   Beef Short Ribs 66
   Big Rock Chili 65
   Braised Wagyu Beef Short Rib 59
   Brandy Dijon Filet Mignon 150
   Cajun Steak Bites 63
   Classic Steak Tartare 214
   Cocoa and Coffee Crusted Filet of Prime Cab Beef 18
   Costoletta di Vitello Valdostana 50
   Fiery Grilled Beef Salad 93
   Grilled Beef Tenderloin 121
   Manzo Di Braciole 10
   Osso Bucco 116
   Pan Seared Veal Medallions 26
   Peppered Flank Steak 132
   Roast Pork or Veal Loin 219
   Rubbed Ribeye 245
   Short Rib Hash 185
Beef Short Ribs 66
Beurre Blanc 58
Beurre Blanc Sauce 91
Big Rock Chili 65
Big Rock Chophouse 61–66
BISTRO ON THE BOULEVARD 111–116
Blackberry Sauce 227
Blue-B-Que Bass 25
Blue-B-Que Sauce 25
Blueberry, Peach, and Watercress Salad 126
Braised Kale 138
Braised Red Cabbage 193
Braised Wagyu Beef Short Rib 59
Brandy Buttered Sea Scallops 148
Brandy Dijon Filet Mignon 150
Brandy Dijon Sauce 150
Brie In Pastry with Dried Cherries 237
Brioche Bread Pudding 138
Broiled Artichoke Stuffed 107

Broiled Loup de Mer 109
Buffalo Tenderloin 226
BUTCH'S DRY DOCK 117–122
Buttermilk Panna Cotta 51

C

Cabernet Sauce 19
Cajun Seasoning 244
Cajun Steak Bites 63
CAPERS RESTAURANT 235–240
Caramel Apple 194
Caramel Apple Spice Cake 179
Caramelized Pearl Onions 225
Carrot Ginger Reduction 56
Celeriac Cream with Maple Popcorn 135
Cèpe Cream 102
CHANDLER'S 209–214
Charred Tomato Vinaigrette 211
Cheese Beignets 190
CHERRY BLOSSOM 67–72
Cherrywood Smoked Trout 76
Chestnut Soup 189
Chewy Salted Caramels 195
Chicken Breast with Crab Stuffing 218
Chicken Pot Pie 156
Chicken Strudel 170
Chili Mélange 101
Chili Oil 245
Chive Oil 26
Chocolate Pâté with Praline and Raspberries 78
Citrus Powder 55
Citrus Roasted Black Cod 55
Classic Steak Tartare 214
Coach Crab Cake 4
COACH INSIGNIA 1–5
Cocoa-Coffee Spice Blend 19
Coconut Curry Ahi Tuna 5
Cole Slaw 244
Corn and Potato Risotto 218
Costoletta di Vitello Valdostana 50
Cranberry Sauce 34
Cream Cheese Ice Cream 195
Crème Brûlée 172
Crème Fraîche 98
Crispy Fried Red Onions 27

D

DESSERTS
    Buttermilk Panna Cotta 51
    Caramel Apple 194
    Caramel Apple Spice Cake 179

Chewy Salted Caramels 195
Chocolate Pâté with Praline and Raspberries 78
Cream Cheese Ice Cream 195
Crème Brûlée 172
Flourless Chocolate Cake 122
Frozen Grand Marnier Soufflé 35
Ginger White Chocolate Ice Cream 21
Mango Vanilla Gelée 51
Panna Cotta con Fragola e Vaniglia 166
Raspberry Crème Brûlée 157
Spice Crusted Pineapple Steak 20
Sugared Mint Leaves 103
Tapioca Pudding 31
Dijon Tarragon Vinaigrette 126
THE DINING ROOM 123–132
DRESSINGS, MARINADES, & RUBS
    Balsamic Syrup 223
    Cajun Seasoning 244
    Charred Tomato Vinaigrette 211
    Chili Mélange 101
    Citrus Powder 55
    Cocoa-Coffee Spice Blend 19
    Dijon Tarragon Vinaigrette 126
    Dry Rub 245
    Grand Hotel Dressing 224
    Hot Bacon Vinaigrette 129
    Maple Sherry Vinaigrette 234
    Moroccan Spice 97
    Mussel Dust 143
    Pastrami Spice Blend 17
    Pear Nectar Vinaigrette 136
    Pecan Vinaigrette 147
    Saffron Vinaigrette 205
    Salad Dressing 93
    Smoked Trout Brine 76
    Spice Mix 63
    White Truffle Vinaigrette 183
    Yuzu Vinaigrette 42
Dry Rub 245
Duck Breast 110

E

THE EARLE UPTOWN 105–110
Enoki Bacon 69
EVE 95–103

F

Fall Vegetable Salad 60
THE FARM 87–93
Fiery Grilled Beef Salad 93
Fig Purée 39

Fines Herbes Caper Lemon Aioli 186
Fire Roasted Mussels 143
FISH, SEAFOOD
  AZ Bronzed Salmon 28
  Baked Jumbo Lump Crab 184
  Blue-B-Que Bass 25
  Brandy Buttered Sea Scallops 148
  Broiled Loup de Mer 109
  Cherrywood Smoked Trout 76
  Chicken Breast with Crab Stuffing 218
  Citrus Roasted Black Cod 55
  Coach Crab Cake 4
  Coconut Curry Ahi Tuna 5
  Fire Roasted Mussels 143
  Great Lakes Whitefish Meatballs 84
  Grilled Yellow Fin Tuna 77
  Gulf Shrimp 31
  Halibut Bayside 232
  Java Chili Rubbed Salmon 120
  Kamo Nabe 72
  Lake Michigan Salmon En Croute 91
  Lobster Barigoule 43
  Lobster Corn Dog 3
  Lump Maine Crab Meat Crépinette 55
  Macadamia Nut Crusted Florida Grouper 151
  Mackinac Whitefish Bisque 228
  Monkfish Liver 40
  Moroccan Scallops 97
  My Paella of Aspen Hills Rabbit and Michigan
      White Shrimp 86
  Olindo's Special 11
  Paella 144
  Pan-seared Sea Scallops 130
  Pan Seared Whitefish 92
  Pastrami Scented Wild Alaskan Salmon 16
  Prosciutto Wrapped Salmon with Caper Sauce 239
  Sakura Roll 70
  Sauté of Dover Sole A La Meunière 57
  Scallop, Fluke and Tuna Sashimi 42
  Seared Ahi Tuna 244
  Seared Salmon 64
  Seared Sea Scallops 108, 185
  Seared Tuna with Spicy Mango Purée 240
  Shrimp Fondue 119
  Smoked Trout and Fennel Ragoût 228
  Spaghetti al Salmone 49
  Sunomono Combination 71
  Thai Crab Cakes 155
  Tonno alla Liguriana 164
  White Bean and Lobster Chili 217

  Yukon Gold Potato Soup 191
FIVE LAKES GRILL 73–78
Five Onion Tart 19
Flourless Chocolate Cake 122
Foie Gras 39
Foie Gras and Monkfish Liver Torchon 39
Fondue of Bartlett Pear 59
FOWL
  Chicken Breast with Crab Stuffing 218
  Chicken Pot Pie 156
  Chicken Strudel 170
  Duck Breast 110
  Foie Gras 39
  Morels Stuffed with Pheasant Mousse 208
  Ostrich Fillet 177
  Paella 144
  Pork, Duck, Dried Cherry & Mixed Nut Terrine 200
  Roasted Breast of Pheasant 137
  Roast Goose 33
  Thai Chicken Salad on Crostini 127
  Turkey Melt Sandwich 149
Framboise Accents 35
Frozen Grand Marnier Soufflé 35

G

GAME
  Buffalo Tenderloin 226
  Duck Breast 110
  Michigan Rabbit Braised in Cèpe Cream 100
  Morels Stuffed with Pheasant Mousse 208
  My Paella of Aspen Hills Rabbit and Michigan
      White Shrimp 86
  Ostrich Fillet 177
  Pheasant Wellington 171
  Pork, Duck, Dried Cherry and Mixed Nut Terrine
      200
  Roasted Breast of Pheasant 137
  Roasted Cervena Venison Loin 192
  Tartare of Buffalo Tenderloin 225
  Venison Medallions 243
  Wild Boar Scaloppini 246
Ginger White Chocolate Ice Cream 21
GIOVANNI'S 7–11
Giovanni's Risotto 9
Glazed Carrots 33
Grainy Mustard Beurre Blanc Sauce 89
GRAND HOTEL 221–228
Grand Hotel Dressing 224
Great Lakes Whitefish Meatballs 84
Green Olive and Cucumber Granita 227

Grilled Beef Tenderloin 121
Grilled Romaine Salad 211
Grilled Vegetable Terrine 75
Grilled Yellow Fin Tuna 77
Gulf Shrimp 31

H

Halibut Bayside 232
Haricot Vert Almandine 57
Harissa Sauce 143
Honey Glazed Carrots 56
Honey Manchego Potato Croquette 213
Honey Sauce 40
Hot Bacon Vinaigrette 129
Huckleberry Gastrique 193

J

Java Chili Rubbed Salmon 120

L

Lake Michigan Salmon En Croute 91
LAMB
  Agnello Crudo con Pomodoro 161
  Roasted Loin of Lamb 115
THE LARK 29–35
LATITUDE° RESTAURANT 203–208
Leek Hay 231
Lemon Butter Sauce 233
Lemon Parmesan Gnocchi 212
Lemon Verbena Beurre Blanc 32
Lime Tequila Glaze 31
Lobster Barigoule 43
Lobster Corn Dog 3
LULU'S BISTRO 181–186
Lump Maine Crab Meat Crépinette 55

M

Macadamia Nut Crusted Florida Grouper 151
Mackinac Whitefish Bisque 228
Mango Vanilla Gelée 51
Manzo Di Braciole 10
Maple Popcorn 135
Maple Sherry Vinaigrette 234
Melanzane alla Parmigiana 48
Mezze Café Hummus 142
Michigan Corn Pudding 99
Michigan Facts xiv
Michigan Rabbit Braised in Cèpe Cream 100
Michigan Wild Ramp Quiche 81
Monkfish Liver 40
Morel and Leek Pierogi 202

Morel Mushroom and Wild Rice Bisque 199
Morel Mushroom Burgers 206
Morel Mushroom Sauce 177
Morels Stuffed with Ham Duxelle 207
Morels Stuffed with Pheasant Mousse 208
Moroccan Scallops 97
Moroccan Seasoned Flour 98
Moroccan Spice 97
Mushroom Ragoût 64

N

NORTH 167–172
NORTH SHORE PUB 'N GRILL 241–246

O

Olindo's Special 11
Osso Bucco 116
Ostrich Fillet 177

P

Paella 144
Pan-seared Sea Scallops 130
Panna Cotta con Fragola e Vaniglia 166
Pan Seared Veal Medallions 26
Pan Seared Whitefish 92
Parsley Oil 17
Parsnip Purée 185
Parsnips with Truffle Butter 192
PASTA
  Great Lakes Whitefish Meatballs 84
  Lake Michigan Salmon En Croute 91
  Lemon Parmesan Gnocchi 212
  Morel and Leek Pierogi 202
  Olindo's Special 11
  Pastrami Scented Wild Alaskan Salmon 16
  Potato Gnocchi 175
  Simple Tomato Sauce & Pasta 85
  Spaghetti al Salmone 49
  Tonno alla Liguriana 164
  Trenette Pasta 165
Pastrami Scented Wild Alaskan Salmon 16
Pastrami Spice Blend 17
PASTRY & BREAD
  Cheese Beignets 190
  Chicken Pot Pie 156
  Chicken Strudel 170
  Figs, Bleu Cheese, & Walnuts in Phyllo Canapés 125
  Lemon Parmesan Gnocchi 212
  Morel and Leek Pierogi 202
  Pâté Brisée 81
  Polenta Biscuits 102

Potato Gnocchi 175
Puff Pastry 194
Pumpkin Seed Crostini 225
Vegetable Strudel 90
Warm Tomato Torte 128
Wild Mushroom Crostini 231
Pâté Brisée 81
Pear Nectar Vinaigrette 136
Pecan Vinaigrette 147
Peppered Flank Steak 132
Pesto 10
Pheasant Wellington 171
Pickled Chanterelles 191
Pinot Noir Sauce 17
Pistou Gruyère Alfredo 119
Polenta Biscuits 102
Polenta with Ratatouille 238
PORK
    Costoletta de Maiale con Mela e Maple Sciroppa
        163
    Paella 144
    Pork, Duck, Dried Cherry & Mixed Nut Terrine 200
    Roast Pork or Veal Loin 219
Port Wine Demi-Glace 243
Potato Gnocchi 175
Prosciutto Crème Sauce 27
Prosciutto Wrapped Salmon with Caper Sauce 239
Puff Pastry 194
Pumpkin Seed Crostini 225

Q

Quick Tomato Bisque 113

R

Raspberry Crème Brûlée 157
RATTLESNAKE CLUB 13–21
Red Cabbage 60
RESTAURANT VILLEGAS 79–86
RICE, GRAINS, & BEANS
    Baked Michigan Navy Beans 83
    Barley Risotto 114
    Giovanni's Risotto 9
    My Paella of Aspen Hills Rabbit and Michigan
        White Shrimp 86
    Paella 144
    Polenta with Ratatouille 238
    Sushi Rice 70
    Three-Pepper Quinoa 130
    Tomato Risotto 27
    Zuppa di Farro 47

THE RIVERSIDE INN 173–179
Roasted Artichoke 89
Roasted Breast of Pheasant 137
Roasted Cervena Venison Loin 192
Roasted Cipollini Onions 17
Roasted Farmer's Market Carrots 101
Roasted Fingerling Potatoes 57
Roasted Garlic Purée 82
Roasted Garlic Whipped Yukons 232
Roasted Loin of Lamb 115
Roasted Potato & Shiitake Mushroom Soup 169
Roasted Red Pepper Aioli 219
Roasted Red Skin Hash 25
Roasted Shallot Aioli 149
Roasted Vegetable Salad 224
Roast Goose 33
Roast Pork or Veal Loin 219
Roast Yellow and Red Beet Salad 15
Roquefort and Brie Cheese Praline 223
ROWE INN 197–202
Rubbed Ribeye 245
RUGBY GRILLE 53–60
Rustic Yukon Gold Mashed Potatoes 178

S

Saffron Aioli 77
Saffron Vinaigrette 205
Sakura Roll 70
Salad Dressing 93
Salad of Frisée and Belgian Endive 136
SALADS
    Aged Goat Cheese, Roasted Beet and Hydro Wa-
        tercress Salad 183
    Apple-Jicama Slaw 207
    Blueberry, Peach, and Watercress Salad 126
    Cole Slaw 244
    Fall Vegetable Salad 60
    Fiery Grilled Beef Salad 93
    Grilled Romaine Salad 211
    Mixed Greens with Apples, Pecans, and Gorgon-
        zola 147
    Roasted Vegetable Salad 224
    Roast Yellow and Red Beet Salad 15
    Salad of Frisée and Belgian Endive 136
    Scallop, Fluke and Tuna Sashimi 42
    Spinach Salad 234
    Thai Chicken Salad on Crostini 127
    Warm Asparagus Salad 205
    Warm Tomato Torte 128
    Wild Mushroom Salad 226

Wilted Spinach & Apple Salad 129
SAN CHEZ BISTRO 139–144
THE SARDINE ROOM 145–151
SAUCES & SALSAS
    Ancho Chile Cream 217
    Apple Cider Gastrique 138
    Apricot Ginger Sauce 201
    AZ Sauce 28
    Basic Tomato Sauce 48
    Basil Pesto 165
    Beurre Blanc 58
    Beurre Blanc Sauce 91
    Blackberry Sauce 227
    Blue-B-Que Sauce 25
    Brandy Dijon Sauce 150
    Cabernet Sauce 19
    Carrot Ginger Reduction 56
    Cèpe Cream 102
    Chili Oil 245
    Chive Oil 26
    Cranberry Sauce 34
    Crème Fraîche 98
    Fig Purée 39
    Fines Herbes Caper Lemon Aioli 186
    Framboise Accents 35
    Grainy Mustard Beurre Blanc Sauce 89
    Harissa Sauce 143
    Honey Sauce 40
    Huckleberry Gastrique 193
    Lemon Butter Sauce 233
    Lemon Verbena Beurre Blanc 32
    Lime Tequila Glaze 31
    Mango Vanilla Gelée 51
    Morel Mushroom Sauce 177
    Moroccan Seasoned Flour 98
    Mustard Sauce 170
    Parsley Oil 17
    Parsnip Purée 185
    Pesto 10
    Pinot Noir Sauce 17
    Pistou Gruyère Alfredo 119
    Port Wine Demi-Glace 243
    Prosciutto Crème Sauce 27
    Roasted Garlic Purée 82
    Roasted Red Pepper Aioli 219
    Roasted Shallot Aioli 149
    Saffron Aioli 77
    Simple Tomato Sauce & Pasta 85
    Strawberry Sauce 166
    Tomato Buerre Blanc 77

Tuscan Vegetable Béchamel 176
Vanilla Mango Sauce 151
Vegetable Demi-glaze 90
Vinegar Sauce 71
Wasabi Cream 244
White Truffle Roasted Tomato Sauce 121
Wild Mushroom Demi-Glace 246
    Yellow Beet Purée 131
Sauté of Dover Sole A La Meunière 57
Scallop, Fluke and Tuna Sashimi 42
Seared Ahi Tuna 244
Seared Salmon 64
Seared Sea Scallops 108, 185
Seared Tuna with Spicy Mango Purée 240
SELDOM BLUES 23–28
Shiitake Hakata 69
Short Rib Hash 185
Shrimp Fondue 119
SIDE DISHES
    AZ Vegetables 28
    Baba Ghanoush 141
    Barley Risotto 114
    Braised Kale 138
    Braised Red Cabbage 193
    Brioche Bread Pudding 138
    Caramelized Pearl Onions 225
    Chestnuts 34
    Corn and Potato Risotto 218
    Crispy Fried Red Onions 27
    Fig Purée 39
    Five Onion Tart 19
    Fondue of Bartlett Pear 59
    Glazed Carrots 33
    Grilled Vegetable Terrine 75
    Haricot Vert Almandine 57
    Honey Glazed Carrots 56
    Honey Manchego Potato Croquette 213
    Leek Hay 231
    Lemon Parmesan Gnocchi 212
    Melanzane alla Parmigiana 48
    Michigan Corn Pudding 99
    Michigan Wild Ramp Quiche 81
    Mushroom Ragoût 64
    Parsnips with Truffle Butter 192
    Pickled Chanterelles 191
    Polenta with Ratatouille 238
    Potato Gnocchi 175
    Red Cabbage 60
    Roasted Cipollini Onions 17
    Roasted Farmer's Market Carrots 101

Roasted Fingerling Potatoes 57
Roasted Garlic Whipped Yukons 232
Roasted Red Skin Hash 25
Rustic Yukon Gold Mashed Potatoes 178
Shiitake Hakata 69
Short Rib Hash 185
Smoked Trout and Fennel Ragoût 228
Stuffing 33
Sweet Fennel Flan 32
Sweet Potato Gratin 132
Tapioca Pudding 31
Three-Pepper Quinoa 130
Vanilla Poached Pears 136
Vegetable Strudel 90
Simple Tomato Sauce & Pasta 85
Smoked Trout and Fennel Ragoût 228
Smoked Trout Brine 76
SOUPS
  Big Rock Chili 65
  Celeriac Cream with Maple Popcorn 135
  Chestnut Soup 189
  Kamo Nabe 72
  Mackinac Whitefish Bisque 228
  Morel Mushroom and Wild Rice Bisque 199
  Quick Tomato Bisque 113
  Roasted Potato & Shiitake Mushroom Soup 169
  Watermelon Soup 41
  White Bean and Lobster Chili 217
  Yukon Gold Potato Soup 191
  Zuppa di Farro 47
  Zuppa di Porcini 162
Spaghetti al Salmone 49
Spice Crusted Pineapple Steak 20
Spice Mix 63
Spinach Salad 234
Strawberry Sauce 166
Sugared Mint Leaves 103
Sunomono Combination 71
Sweet Fennel Flan 32
Sweet Potato Gratin 132

T

TAPAWINGO 187–195
Tapioca Pudding 31
Tartare of Buffalo Tenderloin 225
Thai Chicken Salad on Crostini 127
Thai Crab Cakes 155
THE NEW YORK RESTAURANT 215–219

Three-Pepper Quinoa 130
Tomato Buerre Blanc 77
Tomato Risotto 27
Tonno alla Liguriana 164
TRATTORIA STELLA 159–166
Trenette Pasta 165
TRIBUTE 37–43
Turkey Melt Sandwich 149
Tuscan Vegetable Béchamel 176

V

Vanilla Mango Sauce 151
Vanilla Poached Pears 136
Vegetable Demi-glaze 90
Vegetable Strudel 90
Venison Medallions 243
Vinegar Sauce 71

W

Warm Asparagus Salad 205
Warm Tomato Torte 128
Wasabi Cream 244
Watermelon Soup 41
White Bean and Lobster Chili 217
White Truffle Roasted Tomato Sauce 121
White Truffle Vinaigrette 183
Wild Boar Scaloppini 246
Wild Mushroom Crostini 231
Wild Mushroom Demi-Glace 246
Wild Mushroom Salad 226
Wilted Spinach & Apple Salad 129

Y

Yellow Beet Purée 131
Yukon Gold Potato Soup 191
Yuzu Vinaigrette 42

Z

Zuppa di Farro 47
Zuppa di Porcini 162